Mayan Folktales
Cuentos folklóricos mayas

World Folklore Advisory Board

MAYAN FOLKTALES
CUENTOS FOLKLÓRICOS MAYAS

Retold and Edited by
Susan Conklin Thompson, Keith Steven Thompson,
and Lidia López de López

World Folklore Series

LIBRARIES
UNLIMITED
A Member of the Greenwood Publishing Group

Westport, Connecticut • London

Library of Congress Cataloging-in-Publication Data

Thompson, Susan Conklin.
  Mayan folktales = Cuentos folklóricos mayas / retold and edited by Susan Conklin
  Thompson, Keith Steven Thompson, and Lidia López de López.
    p. cm. — (World folklore series)
  Other title: Cuentos folklóricos mayas
  English and Spanish in parallel text.
  Includes bibliographical references and index.
  ISBN 978-1-59158-138-3 (alk. paper)
  1. Maya—Folklore. I. Thompson, Keith Steven. II. López de López, Lidia. III.
  Title. IV. Title: Cuentos folklóricos mayas.
  435.3.F6T56 2007
  398.208997'42—dc22   2007009267

British Library Cataloguing in Publication Data is available.

Library of Congress Catalog Card Number: 2007009267
ISBN-13: 978-1-59158-138-3

First published in 2007

Libraries Unlimited, 88 Post Road West, Westport, CT 06881
A Member of the Greenwood Publishing Group, Inc.
www.lu.com

Printed in the United States of America

The paper used in this book complies with the
Permanent Paper Standard issued by the National
Information Standards Organization (Z39.48–1984).

10 9 8 7 6 5 4 3 2 1

The publisher has done its best to make sure the instructions and/or recipes in this book are correct.
However, users should apply judgment and experience when preparing recipes, especially parents
and teachers working with young people. The publisher accepts no responsibility for the outcome of
any recipe included in this volume.

This book is dedicated to the Maya.

CONTENTS

Part 3: Stories About People

Part 4: Encountering the Supernatural

Part 5: Supernatural Animals

PREFACE

The first time my husband and I visited Cobá, Mexico, we were surprised to see a small town right beside the Cobá ruins. Although the ruins had been abandoned and reclaimed by the jungle growth until archeologists and local workers unearthed them over the last two decades, the local Maya had never really left the area. The descendants of the people who built the impressive stone temples, pyramids, and ball courts were still living right where their ancestors had for more than 2,000 years. Even though the residents are not isolated from outside influences (thousands of tourists travel through the jungle to visit the Cobá ruins each year), the town had maintained many of the Mayan traditions such as the stories and celebrations, as well as the lifestyle. For example, in a thatched-roof hut on the edge of town we met a man by the name of Víctor Rivas Palomo, who tells the stories of the ancient Mayan gods by batiking images of the gods on cotton fabric. One of his batiks showed the Mayan rain god Chac with Kukulcan, the snake who is the god of the wind. He had heard the stories of these and many other Mayan gods since he was a young boy, stories that were handed down through many generations.

The oral storytelling tradition of the Maya has remained strong, and the stories are related today, as they were in the past, to describe a local event; explain the origin of animals, people, customs, and beliefs; tell about gods or heroes; and teach a moral or lesson.

During our twelve years of traveling to Guatemala for educational and water projects, we became more and more aware of and familiar with Mayan traditions and beliefs. During this period we also adopted two children, a two-year-old and four-year-old from Guatemala. Their Mayan heritage is rich in history and beauty. Mayan tales are an important part of this heritage, and it is our hope that this book strengthens their and other children's connections to their ancestors.

Our close friend, Lidia López de López, and her family live in San Antonio Aguas Calientes, a small village at the base of a volcano in Guatemala. Her family still lives in a manner very similar to that of their Maya ancestors. They grow most of what they eat, follow the old traditions, weave on backstrap looms, and share Mayan tales with their families. We have been privileged to stay in San Antonio several times with Lidia and to experience daily life with her family. The rhythm of the daily traditions, such as making tortillas from corn, keeps the Mayan lifestyle strong today. Lidia's mother, Margarita, and her family taught us the importance of continuing traditions such as the spiritual cleansing of homes before a family moves in. We learned not only the common daily experiences, but the activities and beliefs that keep the Mayan way of life going strong.

One of the main activities exemplifying the history, stories, artistry, and traditions of the Maya is the weaving the women perform on backstrap looms. It is a pleasure to watch Lidia and other Mayan women weave; their hands moving deftly with colorful threads, the designs kept only in their heads and passed down from generation to generation. Watching Margarita cook has been another wonderful experience for us. Margarita cooks her tortillas on a *comal* (a flat, heavy pan) over an open fire, after grinding the corn into *masa* using a stone *mano* and *metate* (a shaped stone slab used as a base upon which grains, nuts, seeds, and mineral pigments are ground with a *mano,* a shaped, handheld stone; Ford, 2005), which she inherited from her mother-in-law, as in the common tradition. Having grown up in southwestern Colorado, I could picture the ancestral Puebloans (American Indians of the Southwestern United States) involved in a similar process a thousand years ago.

Several years ago we decided to work together with Lidia to compile a variety of Mayan tales, so they can be preserved and shared with present and future generations. When we began research for the book, we and Lidia collected tales and information from Maya in various parts of Guatemala. Storytellers were asked to tell a favorite tale and provide personal histories, which were recorded on a handheld tape or digital recorder. Along with the interviews, we and/or Lidia took photographs of the storytellers who felt they would be comfortable having their photographs in a book. Lidia continued collecting stories, using the same methods we developed together, over a period of two years. From this group of tales we selected the strongest to present in this book. Many of the stories were told in one of the many Mayan languages. Lidia and her sister-in-law transcribed the recordings and, for those not told in Spanish, translated the tales into Spanish.

To the group of tales we gathered in the field, we have added tales from a variety of collections to cover a broader range of geographical areas and other times. The Centro de Estudios Folklóricos of the Universidad de San Carlos de Guatemala allowed us access to their collection of Mayan stories, many of which have been published in the United States by the Yax Te' Foundation. We selected tales for reproduction in this book from the following sources: Victor Montejo's book *The Bird Who Cleans the World* and his Spanish-Mayan version *El pájaro que limpia el mundo;* José Juan's *Cuentos antiguos de animals y gente de San Miguel Acatán* (*Old Stories of Animals and People from San Miguel Acatán*), Ruperto Montejo's *Cuentos de San Pedro Soloma* (*Stories of San Pedro Soloma*), and Manuel Andrade's and Hilaria Máas Collí's *Cuentos mayas yucatecos* (*Yucatecan Maya Stories*). Translations from Spanish to English of the stories we collected and those taken from the above books, except Victor Montejo's *The Bird Who Cleans the World*, were done by Keith Thompson. The translations were reviewed by Miriam Carrasquel-Nagy of the University of Northern Colorado. Anthropologist and Mayan folklore expert James Sexton, of the University of Northern Arizona, reviewed the introductory material and tales we collected for accuracy and authenticity. Barbara Ittner, our editor, raised many thought-provoking questions and provided numerous insights that encouraged us to strengthen the manuscript.

Our intent is to represent a variety of types of Mayan stories, from old to new and from a variety of Maya ethnic groups. The tales are written in Spanish and English. The areas where Maya live are predominantly Spanish-speaking countries, and this makes the tales accessible to people from the region who speak Spanish.

In the back of the book you'll find information about the various storytellers with whom we worked, along with photographs of some of them. Some of the storytellers declined having their photographs reproduced in a book. Other photographs in the book are our own, taken between 1994 and 2005.

The stories we gathered with Lidia are recorded as the people tell them. We have kept the stories in the words of the storytellers, with only a few minor changes or additions to clarify the stories in places where print could not convey the same thing as an oral version. The reader will notice that each storyteller has a "voice" of his or her own. The oral tradition of storytelling is a fascinating process in itself, as the tales are reworked and left up to the creative nature of the storyteller. The tales vary from folklore to myths and legends. Some are trickster tales, in which one character tricks or deceives another; some are related to the spirit world; others explain an event; and yet others are used to instill moral values such as respect for elders and nature. As in oral traditions everywhere, it is difficult to determine the exact origins of any specific story, as the stories are passed from person to person and travel from town to town and country to country through the generations. Many of these stories exhibit features common to stories from other parts of the world. Obviously, Spanish people who came to inhabit the lands of the Maya have both contributed to and borrowed from many Mayan tales, so we see references to Christian customs. Other influences have undoubtedly made their marks as well. However, all of the tales included in this book have been passed down through many generations of Maya, the old way, through the telling and retelling of the stories.

The tales in this book are organized according to themes. Because of the overlapping themes in many Mayan tales, a tale might be presented here in one category but also be very appropriate in another. The majority of the tales can be enjoyed by children ages six and older. Younger children will need the tales read to them by an adult. Before you select a tale to read with children, be sure to read it first yourself, because some of the tales contain a mature theme and/or some violence.

Each tale is a story on its own, so feel free to browse through the book and find a good one to share. Children may enjoy a single story or may be encouraged to read several and discuss how they are similar and different. Discussing the stories with children will allow them to share their ideas, insights, and understandings with one another. Teaching the children some of the history of the Maya that is included in the introduction will make the reading of the tales a richer experience for children and young adults.

We have tried to provide enough detail in the introduction to support the desire of many Maya, stated eloquently by Victor Montejo (2005): "We want our culture to be seen, not just as a relic from the past (the classical Maya), but also in the present, as Maya who are creating and recreating our culture, even in the aftermath of war and violence. . . . Although modern Maya have not erected temples as our ancestors did, we, too, are Maya fighting for our space in this century and in the millennium just begun."

ACKNOWLEDGMENTS

This book was a fascinating and encompassing project from which we learned a lot. We thank the people who inspired us with their kindness, time, and talents, and we appreciate the time they have given us over the years, helping us learn about Mayan history and cultural traditions. Thanks to Lidia López de López, Wilfy López, Cesar López, Cesar Ludím López, and Margarita López for dedicating themselves to finishing this project and for sharing so much of their lives with us; to the storytellers who shared their stories; and to Kayenta Thompson, Rosalie Thompson, Flor de María Thompson, and Yoselin Thompson for helping us understand the importance of handing down cultural traditions. Thanks to Curbstone Press, the Yax Te' Foundation, Yax Te' Books, Editorial Piedra Santa, and the Universidad Autónoma de Yucatán for kindly granting permission to republish stories from their books and to the Centro de Estudios Folklóricos of the Universidad de San Carlos de Guatemala for leading us through their collections of Guatemalan Maya stories. Thanks to James Sexton for his input regarding the introductory materials and stories and for imparting his love of folklore to his students, and to David Romtvedt for reviewing our initial translations and providing valuable feedback. Many thanks to Miriam Carrasquel-Nagy, who proofread the Spanish-English translations of the stories and commented that she was happy to be reminded of the stories her grandmother used to tell. Thanks also to Sharon DeJohn for her careful work in preparing the manuscript for publication. And a special thank-you to our editor, Barbara Ittner, who believed we could write this book and supported us throughout the process.

INTRODUCTION

The Maya are a vibrant group of about nine million people still living in their ancient homelands in southern Mexico, Guatemala, Belize, western Honduras, and western El Salvador. The majority, about seven million, live in Guatemala, mostly in the mountainous southern highlands, and more than a million live in the adjacent state of Chiapas, Mexico.

Modern Maya in Antigua, Guatemala

Geography

The lands inhabited by the Maya form the heart of Mesoamerica, reaching from the dry tropical limestone plains of the northern Yucatán Peninsula to the mountainous highlands and coastal lowlands of southern Guatemala, Honduras, and El Salvador on the south. This area, with its numerous volcanoes, mountainous highlands, cloud forests, tropical limestone plain, and coastal lowlands, includes all of the geographic features typical of the entire Central American region. The great variety of flora and fauna and diverse habitat also represent most of the habitat types and species found in the area.

The Maya heartland comprises about 385,000 square kilometers (150,000 square miles), an area about the same as that of California, Iraq, or Paraguay. Three physiographic regions predominate: the limestone plain of northern Guatemala and Mexico's Yucatán Peninsula; the highlands of Chiapas, Mexico, central and southern Guatemala, and adjacent western Honduras and El Salvador; and the southern coastal lowlands of Mexico and Guatemala.

San Antonio Aguas Calientes, a village at the base of Volcán Fuego (Fire Volcano) in the southern Guatemala highlands

Limestone Plain

The original heartland of ancient Maya civilization is the great limestone plain that stretches from Guatemala's Petén region northward into Mexico's Yucatán Peninsula. This low-lying area is hot throughout most of the year and receives rain mostly between May and November. December through April is generally the dry season. Karst topography, with numerous caverns and sinkholes, is especially prominent in the Petén and Yucatán and results in a large number of lakes and swamps but no large, through-flowing rivers; most drainage is underground through fractures and caverns in the limestone. Water in the area is often obtained from water-filled sinkholes called *cenotes.*

Access to the area by road is difficult, and all but the northern part of this area is less populated and less developed than most other areas where the Maya currently live. However, this was not always so. The Petén and the southern Yucatán were once the center of the Maya civilization, and according to archeologists, the area was then one of the most densely populated regions on Earth.

The natural flora includes seasonal, wet subtropical forest in the south, transitioning to dry scrubland in the northern Yucatán. Although deforestation for agriculture (much of it subsistence farming) is a major concern today in the region and particularly in the Petén, much of the area remains in its natural state, and ecotourism is a growing part of the cultural landscape. The governments of Guatemala and Mexico have established the Maya Biosphere Reserve in Guatemala and the adjacent Calakmul Biosphere Reserve in Mexico. Together, they cover about five million hectares (ten million acres), including all of the northern Petén and much of southern Campeche, the heart of the Maya Forest, and are part of a plan to preserve the remaining forest while accommodating the needs of the area's growing population.

Highlands

The highlands form the backbone of the country and are home to the majority of the population of the Maya country. They include the *tierra fría*, the highest areas, which sometimes receive frost, and the *altiplano*, the remaining high areas. The mountainous, rugged terrain is the result of more than twenty volcanoes, four of which are currently active and eight of which are dormant but not extinct. Part of the "Rim of Fire" encircling the Pacific Ocean, they form a belt parallel to, and sixty to eighty kilometers (thirty-seven to fifty miles) inland from, the Pacific coast. Volcán Tajumulco in western Guatemala, at 4,222 meters (13,852 feet), is the highest point in Central America. The three other mountain ranges, two in the highlands north and east of the volcanic area and one on the Guatemala–Belize border, are not of volcanic origin. The Cuchumatanes and Maya Mountains are formed primarily of limestone and other sedimentary rocks, and the Sierra de las Minas are formed of igneous and metamorphic rocks.

Volcán Tolimán (Tolimán Volcano) and Lake Atitlan, in the southern Guatemala highlands

Guatemala and adjacent parts of its neighbors are one of the most seismically active areas in the world. The Chixoy-Polochic and Motagua faults divide the westward-moving North American tectonic plate north of the faults from the eastward-moving Caribbean plate south of the faults. Relatively infrequent but very large earthquakes occur along these faults; the disastrous earthquake of 1976 occurred along the Motagua fault. The Cocos plate off the Pacific coast of Central America is moving northeast and dives eastward beneath both of the other plates. The chain of volcanoes inland from the Pacific coast is fed by the melting of the Cocos plate as it moves downward beneath the continental plates, and its movement produces frequent though typically small earthquakes.

Even though the Maya region is in the tropics, the climate in the highlands is relatively cool and pleasant all year long because of the area's altitude. For example, temperatures in Guatemala City usually range between nighttime lows of 10° Celsius (50° Fahrenheit) and daytime highs of 25°C (77°F). Most of the highlands receive between 1,000 mm (millimeters) and 1,500 mm (40 to 60 inches) of precipitation during the rainy season from May through October, often in the form of torrential downpours during electrical storms, and some areas receive as much as 4,500 mm (177 inches) annually. The fertile volcanic soil of the highlands and ample rainfall make farming productive, and much of the region is cultivated by families engaged in subsistence farming. Natural areas are covered with mixed pine and oak forests and are home to a rich variety of other plants and animals.

Southern Coastal Lowlands

The slopes between the highlands and the Pacific Ocean form the southern coastal lowlands. The topography is much less rugged than in the highlands, and temperatures are warmer because of the lower elevations. Precipitation depends on elevation, with higher areas receiving more.

The lowest areas of the coastal plain, from sea level to about 500 meters (1,600 feet) elevation, are hot and humid all year but have a prominent dry season between December and April. This area is referred to as the *tierra cálida*. Temperatures typically range from nighttime lows of 22°C (72°F) to daytime highs of 35°C (95°F). Annual precipitation ranges from 800 mm (31 inches) on the coast to about 1,500 mm (59 inches) in the higher areas. This is a fertile area extensively developed for export agriculture, with sugar cane and bananas as the main crops and with much of the remaining land devoted to livestock grazing. The natural vegetation is dry, semideciduous forest, with deciduous trees forming a canopy over spiny trees and evergreen vines. Because of the extensive agriculture, very little of the area remains in its natural state.

The higher areas of the coastal plain, between 500 and 1,500 meters (1,600 and 4,900 feet) elevation, are some of the wettest in Guatemala. Known as the *boca costa* or *tierra templada*, they have a temperate climate without a well-defined dry season and are extensively developed for cultivation of coffee and other crops. Natural areas in this region sustain a richly varied, semitropical, moist, broadleaf forest, one of the largest intact fragments of montane forest left in southern Mexico and Central America. Howler monkeys, tapirs, peccaries, deer, and jaguars can be found in those areas, along with a great variety of birds such as scarlet macaws.

Maya History

The southern Yucatán peninsula and northern Guatemala are considered the birthplace of the Maya civilization. The Maya homeland extended throughout Guatemala, southern Mexico, Belize, and the western parts of Honduras and El Salvador starting nearly 3,000 years ago, and modern Maya continue to live in those areas to this day.

Corn (maize) was a staple food of the early Maya and still ranks as one of the most important food sources in most of the area. For the Maya, it was a sacred food and played a major role in their religion and rituals. Its domestication in Mesoamerica by about 5000 BC provided a food source more reliable and nourishing than hunting and gathering and is thought to have spurred a population increase in the area. By about 1800 BC, the Maya had developed stable, agriculture-based settlements from the Yucatán through Guatemala and into Honduras. The growth of larger and larger settlements and the development of the Maya culture with its large cities probably resulted, at least in part, from increasingly successful farming of corn.

Archeologists have divided Maya history into three main periods: the pre-classic, from about 1800 BC to AD 250; the classic, from AD 250 to 900; and the post-classic, from AD 900 to the arrival of the Spanish conquistadors in AD 1524 (Young, 2003). Maya history does not end with the arrival of the Spanish, though. The Maya living in Mexico, Guatemala, Belize, Honduras, and El Salvador today are, for the most part, the descendants of the pre-conquest Maya living in those same areas. Many town sites have been inhabited continuously for thousands of years.

Pre-Classic Maya Civilization

Pre-classic Maya civilization shows a continuous evolution from seminomadic hunting and gathering to permanently settled farming villages and towns. By the close of this period and the start of the classic period, well-developed farming methods suited to the various geographic areas were able to provide enough food to support larger and more densely populated towns and cities with significant populations of people not engaged in farming. The architecture at the transition from pre-classic to classic times included monumental pyramids constructed of stone, many elaborately decorated with hieroglyphic writing and murals, and other structures for which the classic-period Maya are so well known. Writing and the use of the round calendar had spread throughout the region.

Classic Maya Civilization

Classic Maya civilization is known throughout the world for its large city-states, which were highly developed culturally, were independent from one another, and warred with and traded among one another. The writings in what were then public places, like the present mall in Washington, D.C., with its many public buildings, chronicle life of those times: the births, marriages, and deaths of rulers; wars between the cities; trade relationships among the cities; stories of deities; and other cultural and religious topics. During the early classic period the Maya lands may have been more densely populated than they are today.

In late classic times, from the late eighth through ninth centuries AD, a tremendous depopulation of the great Maya cities took place. The cause is still debated, but possibilities include a combination of increased intercity warfare, invasions by outside groups, popular revolution, degradation of the land and its ability to support the large human population, and gradual change of the climate toward drier conditions (Coe, 1999). The destruction of principal cities by one or more large earthquakes along the Chixoy-Polochic and Motagua fault systems has also been suggested as a contributor.

Warfare between the city-states was widespread by the sixth century AD in the lowlands, as recorded on some of the last stelae (ornately carved columns) inscribed with historical dates. These wars had always included hostage-taking, usually only warriors and rulers, for ritual sacrifice. By late classic times, though, hostage-taking for slavery and ritual sacrifice had become much more extensive. In addition, outside invaders came from the west starting about that time.

Scientists studying pollen and oxygen isotopes in cores of sediments from lakes in the region have documented that the climate had been getting increasingly drier over a period of several centuries and that severe environmental degradation had occurred in the lowlands area by AD 800, possibly as a result of agricultural practices and overpopulation. These factors would have made it impossible to feed all the people and may have led to revolt against their leaders and the decay of the political structure. An extremely severe drought that began about AD 800 and lasted 250 years may have been the finishing blow to the classic Maya civilization.

By AD 900 the last of the great Maya cities had been abandoned. The strong city-state political structure had largely disintegrated, and the formerly grand cities were allowed to be overgrown by the jungle. This is how they were encountered 600 years later by the Spanish conquistadors and, except for the few sites that have been restored for tourism, how most remain today.

Post-Classic Maya Civilization

The post-classic Maya commoners continued to live much as they had during classic times, in thatched-roof houses and supporting themselves by farming and hunting. It is likely that the nobility were reduced to living similarly. The population of the area had greatly decreased, and the remaining people lived mainly in scattered, small villages. Despite this, and although nearly all the great city-states were deserted, the concept of the state as an area controlled by a king or chief remained, and a strong social structure and social history persisted. Maya history, customs, and legends written in books now called codices survived through the centuries leading up to the arrival of the Spanish conquistadors.

The Spanish Conquest and the Colonial Period

The Spanish Conquest and subsequent colonial times were very difficult for the Maya in all ways. The Spanish arrived to explore the coasts of Central America in the early 1500s and had established settlements on the coasts of Mexico and Panama by 1519. With the

Spanish came the epidemic diseases smallpox, influenza, and measles, which were previously unknown in the Americas. Because the Maya and other Native Americans had no resistance to these diseases, the diseases spread rapidly and sickened or killed many or most of the people even before the Spanish spread through the area. Eventually an estimated 90 percent of the native population fell victim to these diseases (Coe, 1999).

Hernán Cortés (Hernando Cortez in most English-language texts) and his conquistadors began the conquest by defeating the Aztecs in 1519–1521 in Tenochtitlan, which later would become Mexico City. Cortés sent Pedro de Alvarado south from Mexico in 1523 to conquer the Maya in Guatemala. By the time Alvarado and his army arrived in the Guatemala highlands in December 1523, smallpox, influenza, and measles had already devastated the Maya population. The conquest of the Maya was not like that of the Aztecs or Inca, who had a single ruler whose defeat meant that the entire empire fell under Spanish rule. Numerous groups comprised the Maya, and each group had to be defeated separately. Alvarado took advantage of the existing rivalries between the different Maya groups to create alliances that would help him in conquering the entire area. The two largest groups in the highlands were the K'iche' and Cakchiquel; the Pokomam and Tzutujil were their smaller and less powerful neighbors. Through force and treachery, Alvarado overcame the K'iche' and used them to defeat the Cakchiquel. Within three years the highlands and southern coastal areas were under Spanish control, and Alvarado established a capital city on the site of the Cakchiquel capital of Iximché in 1527.

The conquest of the northern part of the Maya lands took much longer. The Spanish conquistadors called the Petén lowlands "the land of war," and they were subjected to "jungle-style" warfare by the Maya living there. It took the Spanish until 1697 to defeat the last independent Maya kingdom, Tayasal, where the town of Flores now stands on an island in Lake Petén Itzá. Even afterward the Maya resisted dominance by the Spanish.

The surviving Maya, after being subjugated by the Spanish, were steadily deprived of their land, their customs, their religion, and even their Maya names. The Spanish crown established a system known as *encomienda*, which gave the most desirable lands to the conquistadors and their supporters. The Maya already living on the land were forced to work for the Spanish land "owners," often under brutal conditions, growing crops such as sugar cane, cotton, and indigo for export to Europe. The Maya social and religious customs were suppressed by the Catholic priests who came with the conquistadors; the Maya were required to convert to Catholicism, and most were given Spanish names. To make control and religious conversion of the inhabitants of the many hamlets and villages easier, the Maya were "consolidated" by being forced to move to and live in towns laid out and run by the Spanish, with all Maya inhabitants within earshot of the church bells. The Catholic priests systematically gathered the Maya codices and burned them as part of their effort to "civilize" the Maya and convert them from their "pagan" ways. Despite the fact that the Maya culture and history had been richly documented in the many codices, the thoroughness of the priests was such that only four codices are known to remain today.

The Maya suffered under the *encomienda* system until it was abolished in 1724. Afterward, conditions improved slightly, though not substantially, through the end of the colonial period in 1821, when most of the American colonies under Spanish rule declared their independence from Spain.

Post-Colonial Period

Independence for the countries that included the Maya homelands has not necessarily meant better conditions for the Maya. Scholars today agree that since the Spanish Conquest there has been a systematic, organized effort by the governing powers to eliminate the Maya and their way of life, either by assimilation of the Maya into Hispanic society or by directly banning Maya customs (Shea, 2001).

The Maya's strong ties to their families, communities, and land and their strong religious belief system have been both a strength holding the Maya culture together as well as a weakness that has been taken advantage of, allowing the Maya to be exploited by their oppressors. Although the conservative early governments of Mexico and Guatemala took an outwardly accommodating position toward the Maya population, the taking and transfer to Hispanic control of communal and individually held Maya lands continued. The outward appearance of accommodation, particularly in Guatemala, changed in the 1870s and 1880s during the presidency of Justino Rufino Barrios. Rufino Barrios undertook many reforms, including abolishing communal ownership of Maya lands, appropriating the Catholic church's land for the government, introducing coffee as an export crop, and imposing a system to force the Maya highlanders to work the coffee plantations. The forced seasonal migrations of laborers and the expropriation of their communal farm and pasture lands severely disrupted the subsistence farming that supported the Maya (Grandin, 2000). Similar events occurred in Maya areas of Mexico. In Guatemala and Chiapas the Maya revolted against these injustices, but the state governments violently put down the revolts. A long-lived, similar revolt in the Yucatán starting in the 1850s initially met with more success, but it, too, ultimately was suppressed by the Mexican army at about the same time as the revolts in Guatemala and Chiapas.

Between the 1870s and the early 1900s, formal title to the land in the most fertile areas became even more concentrated in the hands of a small, yet powerful, elite. In Guatemala this group used the land and the forced labor of the land-poor Maya to grow export crops such as coffee, cotton, and bananas. In the northern Yucatán large plantations growing henequen for making sisal rope used debt peonage to enslave the indigenous Maya for production of this export crop, a condition that continued until the 1920s, when alternative materials for rope making were developed and henequen production spread to other areas. Ownership of productive land gradually was obtained by foreign interests such as the U.S.-owned United Fruit Company, today known as Chiquita. Meanwhile, the small plots of land owned by Maya farmers became even smaller as the land was passed down through the generations and divided among the heirs in each generation (Grandin, 2000). Land ownership became so skewed that by 1950 less than 2 percent of the landowners held 75 percent of the best agricultural land in Guatemala.

Small farm in Guatemala highlands

The Mexican Revolution of 1910 resulted in a new constitution that was to redistribute land from the government and governmental businesses back to its original indigenous owners. However, the land reforms were left to be carried out mainly by the large businesses and landowners, who had little to gain from giving away their land. Consequently, the reforms went largely nowhere.

The Guatemalan government in the late 1940s and early 1950s began to institute similar land reforms, and with the support of the legislature and populace it was more successful, at least temporarily. In 1952 the Guatemalan congress passed a law that set land-holding limits and allowed for government expropriation of uncultivated agricultural land. Nearly all the land used for export crops, primarily coffee and bananas, was in the hands of a few landowners, and the vast majority of it was idle. Jacobo Arbenz Guzmán, the Guatemalan president, required large landowners, including a U.S. company, United Fruit Company, to sell excess idle land to the government at the price the companies had declared it to be worth for taxation. Between 1953 and 1954, more than one-third of rural households in Guatemala, mostly indigenous Maya, received some of the nearly 900,000 hectares (2.2 million acres) of expropriated land or state farms, in parcels ranging from 3.5 to 17.5 hectares (8.6 to 43.2 acres) (Shea, 2001). This ultimately led to the most well-known and harshest persecution of the Maya in recent times.

The U.S. government reacted to this land reform immediately and forcefully, in part because the United Fruit Company had powerful friends in the U.S. government and in part out of fear of communist influence. The Central Intelligence Agency secretly sponsored the overthrow of the Guatemalan president in 1954 and his replacement with an exiled Guatemalan army colonel friendly to the United States. The new government reversed the land reforms, and the expropriated lands were returned to the former landholders.

This instituted a series of military dictatorships in Guatemala and led to a civil war that lasted thirty-six years and resulted in the deaths of over 200,000 Maya and the uprooting of more than one million people. The underlying cause was the issue of land reform and the inequitable distribution of the land. Whole villages of mostly Maya population were forced to leave their homes. Virtually no one was safe from kidnapping or murder by the army, the government "death squads," or the revolutionaries, often for no more than simply being suspected of supporting one side or the other.

The bloody civil war ended in 1996 with the signing of peace accords between the government and the revolutionary groups. The peace accords included provisions for establishing a "truth commission" to investigate the real facts of human rights violations (mainly kidnappings, torture, and murder, but also offenses like forced relocation) during the war. The results of the investigation indicated that 93 percent of the violations were by the government and 3 percent by the revolutionaries (O'Kane, 2000). The peace accords also called for land reforms similar to those attempted by Arbenz Guzmán in the 1950s. The politically powerful landowners who control most of the prime farmland have strongly opposed implementing that provision of the accords, and little progress has been made toward its goals. Another of the peace accords commits the government to recognize, for the first time in Guatemala's history, the "multi-ethnic, pluri-cultural, and multi-lingual" nature of Guatemala. This accord requires the government to legally recognize the identity of the Maya; outlaw discrimination against them; and enact laws to protect the practice of the Maya's spirituality, the use of their traditional languages in education, the wearing of traditional clothing, and the use of Maya customary law in settling community disputes. Parts of this accord are being implemented, but full compliance with this and other accords most strongly affecting Maya life is still a continuing challenge.

Despite the discrimination the Maya have been subjected to since the Spanish Conquest, they have maintained their cultural identity, languages, ties to the land, and religious beliefs. Most Maya women still make and wear the colorful traditional clothing seen throughout Guatemala, Chiapas, and the Yucatán. Their beautiful blouses, called *huipiles*, and in a few areas men's clothing, are woven or embroidered with designs and colors customary for each village. Maya history and stories are passed down through the generations. Most Maya speak one of the twenty-six to thirty-one Mayan languages as their native language. The number of distinct Mayan languages is subject to continuing discussion (Dienhart, 1997; Shea, 2001; Gordon, 2005). Although Spanish is the national language of the Maya area except for Belize, where the official language is English, classrooms in Maya villages are often taught in the local Mayan language. In part because many Maya families rely on their *milpa*, their field planted with corn, beans, and other crops, for a large part of their diet, and in part because of their cultural heritage, they are strongly tied to the land, even though most of it is no longer controlled by them. They have incorporated many elements of the Catholic religion that was forced upon them by the Spanish, changing them to fit in with Maya religious beliefs and rites. Many still plant crops, celebrate holidays, and honor ancestors according to the Maya round or long-count calendar.

Maya Areas Today

The People

Most Maya (about 8 million of the total 9 million) today live in Guatemala (6–7 million Maya, about half the country's population) and Chiapas (1.5 million, about one-third of the state's population). Maya also comprise a substantial portion of the populations of the Yucatán Peninsula, western Belize, western Honduras, and western El Salvador. Of the many different Maya ethnic groups, the largest is the K'iche', with a population over 2 million. Yucatec, Cakchiquel, Mam, and Q'eqchi' are the next most populous groups, totaling another 2 million. Other large Maya groups include the Tzotzil, Tzeltal, Chol, Poqomchi', Jakaltek, Achi', Tzutujil, Q'anjob'al, Ixil, Chontal, Poqomam, Akatek, and Chuj, each with a population over 40,000. Smaller groups include the Chan Santa Cruz Maya, Sakapultek, Tojolabal, Ch'orti', Tacanec, Awakatek, Mopán Maya, Sipakapense, Uspantek, Tektitek, Lacandon, Mocho, and Itzá (Dienhart, 2005).

Most of population in the Maya area is rural, although many people today are migrating to the major cities in search of work. The highlands are the most densely populated area, with about half of the total population, while the Petén lowlands of northern Guatemala, with only a few percent of the population, are the least populated. In the highlands nearly all of the habitable areas are occupied, and most of the available farmland is cultivated. The majority of rural families live very simply, practicing subsistence farming, raising a few animals such as chickens, and with one or more family members working as wage laborers far from home during at least part of the year to provide enough income for survival. Although the average annual family income in Guatemala and the Mexican states with substantial Maya populations is small compared to more developed countries, the average does not give a very accurate picture of reality. This is because of the tremendous inequality in incomes between the few wealthy and the many less-fortunate families. Nearly two-thirds of all income goes to the top 20 percent of the population, while only 10 percent goes to the poorest 40 percent of the population (UNICEF, 2007a, 2007b). Much of this disparity has to do with the concentration of land in the hands of the wealthiest families. Recent estimates are that 75 percent of rural Guatemalans live in poverty and that one-third of Guatemalans live on less than $2 US per day. These numbers are typical of adjacent Maya areas as well.

Education

Education in Mexico, Guatemala, Belize, Honduras, and El Salvador varies widely between urban and rural areas and between groups with different levels of income. While children of wealthy families typically complete university educations, children of poorer families are lucky to complete more than a few years of primary education. Public schooling is widely available, but most public schools are under-funded and have very few supplies. There also are many private schools run by individuals and churches, mostly in the cities and large towns. These are relatively expensive and therefore not affordable to most residents, particularly those in rural areas.

Kindergarten classroom in Guatemala City

In rural areas, schooling typically is three years for boys and two years for girls, enough to learn to speak and write Spanish (one of the Mayan languages is typically spoken in the home) and do elementary mathematics. Although the overall literacy rate for Guatemala and adjacent Mexico and Honduras is about 70 percent, rural literacy rates are much lower. Nearly 20 percent of children never enroll in school, and more than 20 percent who do enroll leave school before third grade (UNICEF, 2007b). This is because so many children work to help their families survive. For a child to stay in school means that the family not only will have to do without the child's help at home or in the fields or the child's income from working outside the home, they also will have to provide clothes, shoes, books, and other materials for the child to attend school. For families with a very small income, providing these necessities and going without the child's help is extremely difficult.

Daily Life

Life in a Maya village often may be difficult physically, but there are also many rewards, such as celebrating the many cultural traditions; being with a close, extended family; and living in small communities that share the same pride in their history, ethnicity, art, language, and religious beliefs. Doing chores together provides companionship. For example, women and their children usually come together to community washbasins to wash their clothes and talk about their daily lives. This is the context for the version of the story "The Weeping Woman" ("*La Llorona*") presented here. There is also comfort and strength in the fact that families maintain their cultural identity through their art, food, language, ties to the land, and religious beliefs.

Maya children play just as children do in all parts of the world, by pulling each other around in boxes and crates, jumping over objects and around one another, and hiding and then jumping out to surprise others. Their play also revolves around real-world experiences such as helping to wash clothes, learning to weave, and making tortillas. Children are loved by their families and nurtured by the support of their extended families.

Art

Early Maya art cannot be viewed as simply pleasing to the eye. It includes their architectural creations and the accompanying decoration such as designs carved on and murals painted within the great pyramids, pottery with molded or painted designs, clothing, and jewelry or other body ornaments. Many of the art forms were based on religious use, and religion formed an integral part of daily life. Other items that we may consider art, such as inscribed stelae, were used to record or transmit information.

Modern Maya art is derived from this ancient art and takes many forms. Artists and craftspeople weave beautiful fabrics used for everyday clothing as well as for decoration in their homes and for sale for cash income. Weaving is an important cultural tradition and is still important as a social organizational system and as an expression of ethnic pride. In the past social status was reflected in clothing, with members of the royalty or elite classes wearing fancier clothing. Today, as in ancient times, clothing designs still identify people's villages: Clothing woven and worn in each village has a specific pattern and design (Asturias de Barrios, 1994). The designs are complicated and are not written down. A weaver remembers each intricate pattern, which carries meaning through its symbols. It takes great skill and talent to weave, and accomplished weavers develop and improve their skills over a lifetime. Weavings are sought after and purchased by many visitors to the Maya lands.

The early Maya used cotton fiber and natural dyes, with corn gruel worked into the fiber to make the cotton thread more resistant. Modern Maya have a wide range of materials available, from the native cotton fiber and natural dyes used by their ancestors, to wool obtained from sheep introduced by the Spanish, to pre-dyed or artificially colored synthetic fibers. The entire range can be seen in use. Because of synthetic dyes, women today use more colors in their weavings, and flowers are more prevalent in designs. Whatever materials and colors are used, though, the weaving process and techniques have remained essentially unchanged from ancient times, and the old motifs are still maintained (Asturias de Barrios, 1994).

The majority of Maya women still weave on backstrap looms, making the colorful traditional clothing seen throughout the area. Weaving on the backstrap loom is taught to young girls by their grandmothers, mothers, aunts, and other relatives. The women's beautiful *huipiles* (traditional blouses, pronounced wee-pea-lays) and, in a few areas, men's clothing, are woven or embroidered with designs and colors customary for each village and are worn proudly. Cloth takes a great deal of time to weave on a backstrap loom. After several months of weaving for several hours each day, there will be enough cloth to make garments such as a *huipil* and a long wraparound skirt (called a *corte*) tied with a sash (or *faja*). Societies in Mesoamerica traditionally used (and still do use) the fabrics as they were woven; the pieces were stitched together but not cut to fit the person. It was only when the Spaniards arrived that the concept of clothing cut and adapted to the shape of the body was introduced.

Margarita López weaving on a backstrap loom

A beautiful children's book about the weaving process is *Angela Weaves a Dream: The Story of a Young Maya Artist* (Solá, 1997).

Wedding shawl from San Antonio Aguas Calientes, Guatemala, woven on a backstrap loom; detail shows a quetzal

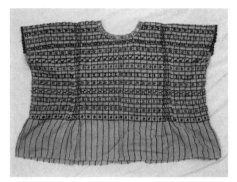

**Huipil from Cobán, Alta Verapaz, Guatemala, woven on a backstrap loom,
with embroidered collar**

Cooking and Food

Corn, we say, is sacred because it is the blessed food. Without corn
there are no tortillas, so corn is highly valued. The second of February,
we bring our corn seeds to the church so they can be blessed. Toward
the end of February and the first part of March, we plant the corn. The
yellow corn is best because it has the most vitamins. Because the corn is
valuable and sacred, we take good care of it—never a kernel is wasted
or lost.—Juana Acuchán, Santa María de Jesús, Sololá, Guatemala

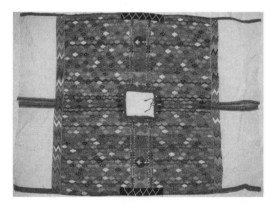
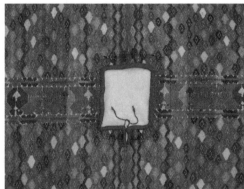

**Huipil from San Pedro Sacatepéquez, Guatemala, with stitched collar
and twisted closure**

The ancient Maya had a diet of maize, beans, chile peppers, and squash. Avocados, papayas, guavas, watermelons, maniocs, tomatoes, sweet potatoes, cantaloupes, plums, and cacao trees were also grown and contributed to the Mayas' diet. Protein sources included fish, deer, turkeys, ducks, peccaries, dogs, armadillo, quail, tapir, iguana, and monkeys. The Maya also ate oysters, turtles, sea birds, and eggs from turkeys. Honey from the bees that they raised was used as a sweetener. Their cooking methods were simple and rudimentary. For example, meat was normally cooked over a fire or in a pit, and ground corn was boiled in a clay pot.

These same foods have been eaten by the Maya for thousands of years, although cooking techniques have evolved and new ingredients have been added. The Spanish introduced the great variety of meats, nuts, and spices known and used in Europe, Africa, and the Middle East, as well as different methods of preparing foods with those ingredients. These have been incorporated into common Maya dishes. For example, iguana is still eaten today. Whereas before the Spanish arrived it would have been grilled on a fire, boiled, or cooked in a pit, after that time it may also have been sautéed in oil or animal fat with tomatoes as well as onion and chile.

Juana Acuchán, of Santa María de Jesús, Sololá, Guatemala

For centuries, corn has been grown and harvested by families, stored in bins until it is prepared for cooking. Each day fresh corn tortillas are still made by most Maya families. Traditionally the woman of the house started her day ahead of the rest of her family, rising early to start their morning meal of corn tortillas, beans, salsa, and eggs. She probably would have begun preparing the corn and beans the day before, since a lot of preparation goes into the tortillas and beans.

Corn Tortillas

Tortillas have been cooked this way since at least AD 500 (Peyton, 2000). To make corn tortillas, corn kernels are parboiled with an alkaline substance such as lime or wood ash, allowed to soak overnight, and then ground into *masa* (pronounced maw-suh), a thick corn dough. Traditionally the corn is ground using a stone *metate* (pronounced muh-taw-tee in English; in Spanish the final *e* sounds like a long *a*) and a *mano* (maw-no), although corn today is more often ground using a metal hand-cranked or electric grinder. The traditional metate and mano are passed down from the mother-in-law to her son's wife.

Harvesting corn

Children with the family's corn harvest

Taking corn to be ground into masa for tortillas

A small ball of masa is flattened and shaped by hand to make a flat, round tortilla. These handmade corn tortillas are smaller and thicker and have a richer flavor than pressed tortillas. The sight, smell, and taste of this Maya staple bring comfort to the entire family.

Newly shaped tortillas are grilled on a *comal* (a large, heavy, round, shallow, or flat pan) for a few minutes on each side. The women always flip the tortillas with their fingers, without burning themselves. This allows them to feel them for doneness, in addition to seeing and smelling the tortillas. When they are done, the outside is slightly crisp and the inside is soft and warm. In Maya communities, the fresh tortillas are often eaten with black beans or refried black bean paste, or served with tomato and chile salsa, and all this can be accompanied by eggs for a hearty and nutritious breakfast.

Grinding corn the traditional way with mano and metate

Eggs

The Maya gather fresh eggs from the chicken or turkey pen and fry them in oil or butter to accompany tortillas, beans, and salsa.

Meals Throughout the Day

In Maya households, tortillas left over from the morning meal are often wrapped in a cloth and sent off with the family members leaving the house for work. They provide a welcome lunch, combined with some avocado, mango, papaya, or other fruit later in the day!

Grinding corn the modern way

Cooking tortillas on a comal over an open fire

The evening meal will likely include one of the many other corn recipes that are still popular in the Maya culture. On a special occasion, it may include some type of meat. Turkey, venison, iguana, monkey, and various types of birds are traditional meats used to make the base for a soup or stew or the filling for tamales. Soups have always been made in the same way as they are today, with whatever appropriate ingredients were at hand or in season. Tamales in ancient times were made with fresh corn or corn hominy, with or without a filling of other vegetables or meat.

Recipes

Black Bean Paste (Refried Black Beans)

Ingredients:

2 cups dried black beans

4 cups water

1 tbsp oil

Directions:

1. Soak the dried black beans overnight in the 4 cups water.
2. In the morning, drain and rinse the beans, then cook them slowly in fresh water (covering the beans) until they are soft, adding more water if needed to keep the beans covered.
3. When the beans are soft, mash (puree) them.

4. Create a thick bean paste by heating the tbsp of oil in a skillet and adding 2 cups of the black bean puree.
5. Stir the mixture with a wooden spoon until the puree thickens and the liquid evaporates. The mixture will begin to come away from the skillet and can be shaken into a roll shape by moving the skillet back and forth.

Tomato and Chile Salsa

Salsa is made with ingredients native to Maya areas, as well as with ingredients introduced to the area since the arrival of the Spanish. Sour oranges are also called Seville oranges or, in Spanish, naranja amarga or naranja agria.

Ingredients:

9 or 10 tomatoes

2 onions

2 habanero chiles

juice of 2 sour (Seville) oranges (or orange and lime juice combined)

dash salt

Directions:

1. Chop the tomatoes, onions, and chiles into small chunks. (Use caution when handling hot chiles, as their oil can be extremely irritating to your skin. Wear plastic gloves or wash your hands well before touching your skin, eyes, etc.) Combine in a bowl.
2. Stir in the orange juice (or orange and lime juice). Add a dash of salt.

Corn and Bean Tamales

Ingredients:

1 cup dried beans, soaked overnight in 2 cups water

2 cups corn masa or corn meal

1 tsp salt

Directions:

1. Drain the presoaked beans. Cover them with fresh water in a pot and cook them until they begin to fall apart and about 4 cups of beans and liquid remain in the pot.

2. Let the beans cool and then mix them with the corn masa and salt. If you are using corn meal, pour the hot bean mixture onto the cornmeal, stir quickly, and add salt.

3. Form the corn-bean dough into 2-inch balls.

4. Flatten the balls into a roll or small loaf shape and wrap them in corn husks or foil.

5. Steam them for one hour.

Makes about 20 tamales.

Turkey Tamales

Turkey tamales are made during the festival of Hanal Pixán, the Day of the Dead. Burying the tamale in a cooking pit and resurrecting it is a symbolic representation of the ancient Maya practice of burying the dead before their transition into the other world.

Ingredients:

2 cups turkey broth

½ tsp achiote paste (can be purchased at Mexican grocery stores or online)

3½ cups corn masa harina

2 tsp solid turkey fat (when you prepare the turkey to use in this recipe, remove some of the fat before cooking and put it aside for use in this recipe)

corn husks (dry husks can be soaked in warm water for several hours to make them pliable)

3½ cups shredded, cooked turkey

1 small tomato, cut into small pieces

1 medium onion

1 sprig parsley

salt to taste

minced or diced habanero chile to taste

Directions:

1. Boil the broth with half of the achiote, a dash of salt, and a bit of masa harina for thickening. This will be part of the mixture that is inside the tamales.

2. Mix the corn masa with the turkey fat, salt, and remaining achiote to make a dough.

3. Place some of this corn dough on the top of each corn husk. Make a hollow in the dough and fill it by layering it with shredded turkey and broth, tomato, onion, parsley, and chile.

4. Cover the top layer with corn dough to completely encase the filling. Wrap each tamale in its corn husk and bake for 1½ hours at 375°F, or follow the traditional method of burying the tamales in a firewood and rock pit. If using the traditional method, let the tamales cook for 8 hours.

Corn Pepián

A side dish commonly served with dinner.

Ingredients:

10 ears corn

1½ cups cold water

3 tbsp olive oil

2 small onions, finely chopped

3 large cloves garlic, minced

1 tsp salt

2 tsp ground cumin

½ tsp ground black pepper

2 jalapeño peppers, finely chopped, with stems and seeds removed

4 oz. panela cheese, cut into small cubes

2 tbsp red wine vinegar

½ bunch fresh dill leaves, finely chopped

Directions:

1. Cut the kernels off 5 of the ears of corn and set them aside.

2. Cut the kernels off the other 5 ears of corn and combine in a blender with 1½ cups of cold water until smooth. Press the liquid through a fine sieve, pressing down to remove all the juice.

3. Heat the oil over medium heat, in a heavy saucepan. Add the onions and cook for approximately 5 minutes or until soft.

4. Add the garlic, salt, cumin, and black pepper. Cook for 2 minutes, then add the jalapeños and cook an additional 2 minutes.

5. Add the kernels from the first 5 ears of corn and cook for 5 minutes, stirring frequently.

6. Add the pureed corn and reduce the heat to low. Cook for 15 to 20 minutes, stirring occasionally and scraping the mixture off the bottom of the pan.

7. Stir in the cheese and vinegar, cooking the pepián for 5 more minutes. Then sprinkle on the dill leaves.

Fried Plantains

An excellent side dish.

Ingredients:

ripe plantains (about ½ plantain per person)
2 tbsp oil

Directions:

1. Peel the plantains and cut them diagonally into ½-inch thick slices.

2. Heat the oil and fry the plantain slices for several minutes on each side until golden brown.

3. Drain on a paper towel.

Honey-Vanilla with Fruit

A delicious dessert to serve with any main dish.

Ingredients:

1½ cups honey

3½ cups water

1 vanilla bean, split (1 tbsp pure vanilla extract can be substituted)

10–12 small, ripe, fresh guavas (or canned, if fresh are not available)

½ pound fresh, sweet black pitted cherries

1 ripe medium pineapple, peeled, cored, and diced

1 grapefruit, halved and thinly sliced

Directions:

1. Combine the honey and water in a saucepan. Bring to a simmer over medium heat and stir until the honey dissolves into a thin syrup. Place the vanilla bean in the syrup and continue cooking on low heat.

2. Place the guavas in a large saucepan of boiling water. After a few seconds, remove and peel them.

3. Add the guavas and cherries to the syrup and simmer for 15 minutes, occasionally stirring gently.

4. Add the pineapple and continue to cook and stir occasionally for another 5 minutes.

5. Turn off the heat and let the fruit cool in the syrup.

6. Remove the vanilla bean, rinse it, dry it, and store it for another time.

7. Garnish the fruit mixture with the grapefruit. Serve chilled or at room temperature.

Religion

The early Maya developed a complex system of beliefs about the origin and functioning of the world. As archeologists become better able to read classic Maya hieroglyphic writing, they are gradually learning more about the old religious beliefs and practices. According to this belief system, the world goes through a cycle of birth, growth, decay, and destruction, followed by rebirth at the beginning of a new cycle. The early Maya believed that we are living in the fifth creation of the world. In the earlier creations, the creators, called First Mother and First Father, made the sky and seas, then the animals, and finally the hero twins and their kin. They then destroyed all in a great flood, and the sky fell to the earth. The story of the hero twins, one twin associated with life and the sky and the other associated with death and the underworld, is told in the Popol Vuh, the Maya story of creation. The hero twins traveled to the underworld, where they were able to trick the gods of death. They returned to the world of life and later were reborn as the sun and Venus.

According to scholars of the ancient Maya, the religious beliefs of classic times involved many deities, including the corn god, Hun Hunahpu (one of the hero twins), and the rain god, Chak. They also taught that everything has an unseen power. The spirits who inhabit the mountains, valleys, and trees are examples of this unseen power, as illustrated in "The Goblin" ("*El duende*"), "Mirandía Hill" ("*El cerro Mirandía*"), and "The Master of the Canyons" ("*El dueño de los barrancos*"). The most important thing was to live in harmony with the earth, its cycles, and the spirits, as described in "The Song of the Owl and the Howl of the Coyote" ("*El canto del tecolote y el aullido del coyote*"). Some Maya also believed in a single supreme god, called First Father or Itzamná, who invented writing and was the patron of the arts and sciences. His wife, called First Mother or Ixchel, was the goddess of the moon and patron of weaving, childbirth, and medicine. The moon goddess has great power over the pregnant woman in the folk story "The Moon" ("*La luna*"). The many other deities were patrons of various aspects of the world or of everyday life. It is interesting to note how well this concept meshes with that of the many saints in the Catholic religion. Anthropologists also acknowledge the Maya concept of Hun-Hab-K'u (The-Only-One-God) of the Yukatek Maya, known as "The Heart of Heaven" among the K'iche' Maya of Guatemala (Montejo, 2005), and a prominent researcher has stated that "Inasmuch as all Mayan deities were aspects of the same power, the Mayan supernatural realm can be viewed as monotheistic" (Morley, 1983). These may be some of the reasons why the practice of Catholicism was not so very different from earlier Maya religious practice and why Catholicism was not rejected by the Maya.

The predominant religion of Guatemala, Mexico, Honduras, and El Salvador is Roman Catholicism, which was brought to the Americas with the Spanish Conquest. During the 1980s membership in evangelical Christian and Protestant religious groups began to rise as a result of the perceived aloofness and strongly hierarchical structure of the Catholic church.

Through the nearly five centuries that Catholicism has been in the area, many elements of Catholicism have been blended into the traditional Maya belief systems, and vice versa. In effect, the two religions have merged in daily religious practice. Many of the Catholic saints and their statues found in the Catholic churches have taken on the characteristics of Maya deities and, in fervent prayers, they are asked for help in every aspect of life, from success with planting and harvests to health, love, and money. The sacred mountains and caves of the Maya, which are believed to be the entrances to the heavens and the underworld, are often the places where statues of the Catholic saints and the Christian cross are placed for worship. For example, one anthropologist who has lived with the Maya for over thirty years says that it is common on Catholic feast days for a procession to begin at the church with a mass for Christ the Sun God and his mother the Moon Goddess, then proceed to a nearby hill for the veneration of ancestors and the Maya gods (O'Kane, 2000). Archeological excavations and investigations of religious sites in caves throughout the Maya region have found statues of Catholic saints with evidence of their veneration, in typical Maya fashion, dating to near the time of the introduction of Catholicism to the area.

Corn has been one of the most revered substances in the Maya religion and way of life, and the corn god is one of the most important ideas in Maya religious life. The Popol Vuh describes how, after several unsuccessful attempts to make men of other substances, the creators finally succeeded by using maize. One of the hero twins, as described in the Popol Vuh, is the corn god. The corn seed, mimicking the story of the hero twins, dies, goes to the underworld through being planted in a hole in the earth, and then is reborn as the corn plant emerges from the earth.

Many folk stories today reflect these religious beliefs, from ancient Maya beliefs to those colored by Catholicism today. The traditional ceremonies and celebrations are also a blend of the old beliefs mixed with the new. Masks, colorful clothing, candles, and incense bring beauty and an ancient feeling to the traditional celebrations. Two of the most well-known celebrations are the Lenten processions and the Day of the Dead practices. Lenten processions are a somber event, filled with reverence. Men and women from the congregation carry statues of Mary and Jesus through village streets, walking through and around carpets (*alfombras*) created by families from natural materials such as flowers, colored sawdust, beans, and rice. During Day of the Dead celebrations on November 1, families honor deceased relatives by going to their local cemeteries to have a feast and communicate with their loved ones. In preparation for this event, vaults, headstones, and tombs are painted bright colors and decorated with flowers, wreaths, and crepe paper. In some locations, giant kites are flown in remembrance of the dead.

In San Antonio Aguas Calientes, there is a village celebration during which people dance in the streets. Large puppets of giants dance with the people, and the story "The Giant Nimalej'mo's" ("*El gigante Nimalej'mo's*") is told. This is a good example of how traditions such as storytelling, celebrations, and cultural history all come together.

Storytelling

Storytelling for the Maya, as for most other indigenous groups, serves two purposes: to entertain and to teach. The sharing of history and stories is an important part of daily life and helps to preserve the culture of the Maya. Because of the primarily oral nature of relaying history and stories, the telling evolves through the years as people hear, remember, and interpret things differently and as the lessons taught by the stories are adapted to changing cultural conditions. The storytellers are usually older people, wise in the ways of people and the world, and therefore with knowledge and information to pass on to younger generations. The stories come from many sources, some as broad-based as the entire Maya culture and others regional, local, or familial. They range from far back in time to very recent times. The stories of the Popol Vuh, the ancient Maya story of creation, are passed on orally and in writing throughout the Maya areas. At the other end of the spectrum, a story told in one family may relate something that happened to one of its still-living members. Often several stories have a common theme or moral and a similar story line but have changed through generations of telling in different locations. The fact that Maya culture and stories today are affected by nearly 500 years of Spanish and other European influence cannot be ignored, as many of the stories being told today contain elements that are clearly products of that influence.

Victor Montejo succinctly describes Maya storytelling methods in *Maya Intellectual Renaissance* (2005):

> There are several techniques storytellers use to communicate with an audience. Among these discursive methods is the personalization of the stories as a way of inducing the listeners to be part of a direct experience of contact with their roots and heritage. For example, some storytellers start telling stories by insinuating that such an event occurred "here" in Xajla' (Jacaltenango), and it may occur again in the future since history follows a cyclical pattern. The storyteller makes the event more personal and timeless, and the listener becomes linked to the place and the people who performed such incredible deeds. In a sense, storytelling provides the young people with the elements that are basic or primordial in maintaining their underlying Maya ethnic identity or Mayaness. Communal values are preached by the elders and expressed in everyday life through the repetition of stories, fables, myths, and legends that enhance the values of respect, community solidarity, and the relation of humans with their environment. Thus, following the leaders' and principales' teachings, we Maya find it useful to tell our stories to the world, not because we are "exotic" people with "strange" stories, but because Maya traditions are the expression of our Maya-logical world, one that has been fading away for the past five hundred years.

References

Asturias de Barrios, Linda. 1994. *Mayan Clothing of Guatemala* (video). Guatemala City: Museo Ixchel del Traje Indígena.

Coe, Michael D. 1999. *The Maya*. 6th ed. New York: Thames & Hudson.

Coe, Michael D., and Mark Van Stone. 2001. *Reading the Maya Glyphs*. London: Thames & Hudson.

Dienhart, John M. 1997. *The Mayan Languages—A Comparative Vocabulary*. Odense University. Available at http://maya.hum.sdu.dk/mayainfo.html (accessed May 12, 2007).

Ford, Robert E. 2005. *Greater Salt Lake Ecoregion Virtual Tour and Learning Module*. Loma Linda University, Department of Earth and Biological Sciences. Available at http://resweb.llu.edu/rford/docs/VGD/GSLVT/index.html (accessed May 18, 2007).

Gordon, Raymond G., Jr., ed. 2005. *Ethnologue: Languages of the World*. 15th ed. Dallas, TX: SIL International. Available at http://www.ethnologue.com/ (accessed May 12, 2007).

Grandin, Greg. 2000. *The Blood of Guatemala: A History of Race and Nation*. London: Duke University Press.

Montejo, Victor D. 2005. *Maya Intellectual Renaissance: Identity, Representation, and Leadership*. Austin: University of Texas Press.

Morley, Sylvanus G. 1983. La Civilización Maya. [Mexico City]: Fondo de Cultura Económica.

O'Kane, Trish. 2000. *Guatemala in Focus: A Guide to the People, Politics and Culture*. Brooklyn, NY: Interlink Books.

Peyton, James W. 2000. *A (Relatively) Short History of Mexican Cooking*. Available at http://lomexicano.com/history_mexican_food_cooking.htm (accessed May 12, 2007).

Shea, Maureen E. 2001. *Culture and Customs of Guatemala*. Westport, CT: Greenwood Press.

Solá, Michéle. 1997. *Angela Weaves a Dream: The Story of a Young Maya Artist*. New York: Hyperion Press.

United Nations Children's Emergency Fund (UNICEF). 2007a. *At a glance: Guatemala— Statistics*. Available at http://www.unicef.org/infobycountry/guatemala_statistics.html (accessed May 12, 2007).

United Nations Children's Emergency Fund (UNICEF). 2007b. *Situación de la Niñez y la Mujer*. Available at http://www.unicef.org/guatemala/unicef_gt_situacion.htm (accessed May 12, 2007).

Young, Peter A. 2003. *Secrets of the Maya*. From the editors of *Archaeology Magazine*, with a preface by Peter A Young. Long Island City, NY: Hatherleigh Press.

MAP OF MAYA LANDS

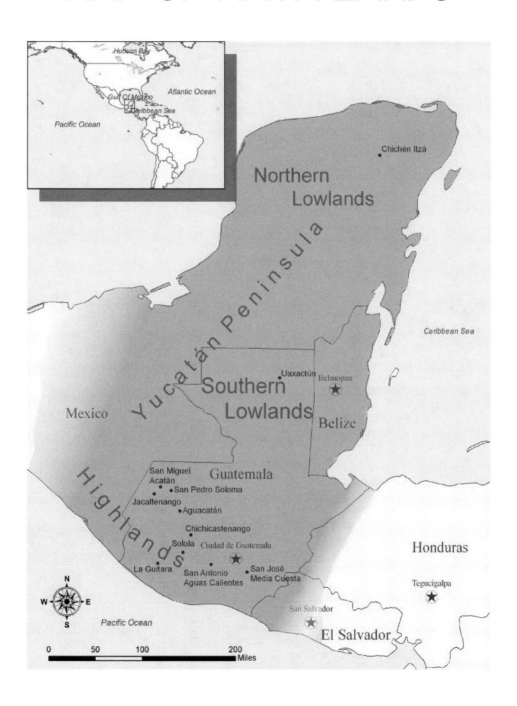

PART 1

ANIMAL TALES

UNCLE RABBIT, UNCLE COYOTE

There are innumerable stories about the rabbit and the coyote in Mayan culture. In some, like this one, the rabbit is the clever one and the coyote is trusting but not very smart. In others the roles are reversed. This story was told by Porfirio López of San Antonio Aguas Calientes, Sacatepequez, Guatemala.

*O*nce upon a time there were a rabbit and a coyote who lived in the forest. Naturally the rabbit was smarter, and the coyote let him be in charge. They were friends. Looking for food, the rabbit sat himself by the side of the road to get the attention of the people who passed by. The people going to or coming from the market always were carrying cheese, bread, fruits, or vegetables. They looked at the nice, pretty rabbit and threw him into their basket of things, but the rabbit knew what he was doing. Inside the basket, he would begin to eat whatever was there. When he was good and full and did not have room for anything else, he would look for a way to get out of the basket, and with a leap he would get away to the forest. That way he kept himself fat and pretty, while the coyote was thin and ugly, always looking and looking for something to eat; some days he ate and others not.

One day the coyote asked the rabbit, "Why are you so fat? You look like you eat well!"

The rabbit answered, "Yes, very well."

The coyote said, "And what do you do to get food?"

The rabbit said, "It is very easy. So you see that I am not jealous, I will tell you how I do it so that you can do it, too."

The coyote said, "Really?" "Yes," said the rabbit, and he told the coyote what he would need to do. Then the coyote went and sat himself by the side of the road like the rabbit had told him, waiting for someone to grab him. But when the people passed by and saw the coyote, they said, "What an ugly coyote, all skinny!" and they left him there. Then two young men came by. Thinking that the coyote wanted to take the food from the people, they hit him with sticks. Then the coyote, as best he could, ran to the forest, all beaten up and aching and hungry.

After the scare he had, the coyote decided to look for the rabbit to make him pay for it. You see, the coyote thought that the rabbit had lied to him, and he wanted to complain. When he found the rabbit, he told him, "It is your fault that I have been beaten and am now aching. What you told me to do did not work, and you are going to pay."

The rabbit replied, "No, I am not to blame!"

After this the rabbit found a swing and began to swing himself. The coyote said to him, "I want to swing, also." So the rabbit gave the coyote his place on the swing. The coyote was swinging when suddenly the vine that was holding the swing broke, and because the swing was at the edge of a cliff, the coyote fell to the bottom. The rabbit was frightened, so he followed to help the coyote.

But the coyote, all aching, just complained again, "You always do this to me. You hit me. You are bad!"

Later the two animals were walking; little by little, the night was falling. They sat down near a well when suddenly the moon reflected in the water and the rabbit said to the coyote, "It is a cheese, and if you drink the water from the well you can eat the cheese."

Because the coyote was very hungry, he agreed, but he said that they both would have to drink the water. The rabbit said he would, so they began to drink the water. But the rabbit did not really drink, he only acted like he was drinking, and the coyote drank so much water that he died. The rabbit tried and tried to revive him, but did not succeed. From then on, the rabbit felt sad, and he ended his days alone.

TÍO CONEJO, TÍO COYOTE

En la cultura maya, hay innumerables cuentos que tratan del conejo y el coyote. En algunos, como éste, el conejo es el listo y el coyote es él que confía, pero que no es muy inteligente. En otros, los papeles son al revés. Este cuento fue narrado por Porfirio López de San Antonio Aguas Calientes, Sacatepéquez, Guatemala.

Habíase una vez un conejo y un coyote que vivían en el bosque. Por naturaleza el conejo era más listo, y el coyote se dejaba dominar. Eran compañeros. Buscando que comer, un día el conejo se puso a la orilla del camino para llamar la atención de la gente que pasase por ahí. La gente caminaba hacia el mercado o venía del mercado, como siempre llevaban queso, pan, frutas o verduras. La gente miraba al conejo bonito, y lo metían en su tanate de cosas, pero el conejo sabía lo que . Al estar dentro del tanate, empezaba a comer lo que había ahí. Cuando estaba bien lleno y no le cabía nada más, buscaba la forma de salir del tañate. De un brinco se alejaba rumbo al bosque; así se mantenía gordito y bonito, mientras que el tío coyote estaba flacucho, siempre buscando y buscando que comer; unos días comía y otros no.

Un día el coyote le preguntó al conejo: «Y tú ¿por qué estás gordo? ¡Se ve que comes bien!» El conejo le respondió: «Sí, muy bien». El coyote le dijo: «Y ¿cómo haces para conseguir comida?» El conejo le dijo: «Muy fácil. Para que veas que no soy envidioso, te diré como lo hago para que tú lo hagas también». El coyote le dijo: «¡De verdad!" «Sí», dijo el conejo, y le explicó lo que tenía que hacer. Entonces el coyote fue, y se puso a la orilla del camino como el conejo le había dicho, esperando que alguien lo recogiera. Pero, cuando la gente pasaba y miraba al coyote, decían: «¡Qué coyote tan feo, todo flacucho!», y se alejaban de él. De repente, venían unos jóvenes, y se imaginaron que el coyote quería quitarle la comida a la gente, y con unos palos le pegaron al coyote. Entonces como pudo, el coyote corrió al bosque todo golpeado y adolorido y con hambre.

Luego del susto que llevó, decidió buscar al conejo para cobrársela. Él pensaba que lo había engañado, y le quería reclamar. De repente lo encontró y le dijo: «Por tu culpa he estado muy adolorido, y no resultó lo que me habías dicho así que me las vas a pagar». Y el conejo le respondió: «No, ¡yo no tuve la culpa!»

Luego de esto, el conejo encontró un columpio, y empezó a mecerse. El coyote le dijo: «Yo quiero mecerme también». Entonces el conejo le cedió su lugar. El coyote se estaba meciendo cuando de repente se rompió el bejuco que sostenía el columpio y, como éste

---

estaba en la orilla de un acantilado, fue a caer hasta el fondo. El conejo se asustó, y lo siguió para auxiliarlo, y el coyote todo adolorido le reclamó de nuevo: «Tú lo haces para que siempre me golpee. ¡Eres malo!»

Luego se fueron caminando y poco a poco fue cayendo la noche y se sentaron cerca de un pozo. De repente la luna se reflejó en el agua, y el conejo engañó al coyote, diciéndole: «Es un queso y que si beben el agua del pozo podrán comerse el queso». Como el coyote tenía mucha hambre, le dijo que sí, pero los dos tenían que beberse el agua. El conejo le dijo que sí, y empezaron a beber el agua. Pero el conejo no bebió; sólo fingió pero no tomó. Entonces el coyote tomó tanta agua que se murió. El conejo intentaba revivirlo, y no lo consiguió. El conejo se sintió tan triste, y terminó sus días muy solo.

THE RABBIT AND THE CRAB

This is one of the myriad of Mayan stories about the rabbit. In this one, he tries to trick the crab. This story comes from the book Cuentos antiguos de animales y gente de San Miguel Acatán (Old Stories of Animals and People from San Miguel Acatán) *by José Juan.*

*T*hey tell that a rabbit got together with a crab to plant some carrots. For several days they worked together and were in agreement. First they chose the seeds and sowed them. Later they cared for the shoots, the two always in agreement. They brought in the crop and separated the leaves from the carrots.

But arguments began when the time came to divide the harvest. The rabbit wanted to trick the crab with pleasant words:

"See? There we have two piles: one big and the other small. I'll let you have the big one and I'll keep the small one."

The crab, after seeing that the big pile was the one with the leaves and the small one was the one with the carrots, replied:

"I'm very grateful to you, friend, but I want to be fair. Let's divide both piles in half: I divide and you choose or you divide and I choose, however you prefer. How does that seem to you?"

"No, no! I don't agree," said the rabbit. "Better that we move away from here about thirty steps, and come back running. The one who gets here first will take the carrots and the other can keep the leaves. How does that seem to you?" asked the rabbit.

"Well, yes, it seems good to me," replied the crab.

"Finally we agree," said the rabbit, very happily, because he was sure to win.

"This makes me very happy. If you win, I'm inclined to give you all the carrots and the leaves. Okay?"

"Okay!" repeated the crab.

"There's still more," said the rabbit. "Because I know that you are slower than I, I am going to give you ten steps' head start."

"No, that is too much! I do not accept," said the crab, acting like he did not want to take an unfair advantage. "It is you who has to go out ten steps ahead, and don't tell me no."

"I accept, I accept!" the rabbit hurriedly answered, not wanting to contradict him, and with pleasure so the crab would not be angry and change his mind.

With this agreement they went together amicably to the place where the race would begin. The rabbit moved forward to take the ten steps' head start. But he had scarcely turned around when the crab, neither slow nor lazy, grabbed with his claws onto the little tail of the rabbit, without the rabbit realizing it.

On arriving where the carrots were, the rabbit believed that he had left the crab far behind.

Then the crab opened his claws and let himself fall very quietly atop of the carrots.

"Where are you, friend?" shouted the rabbit happily, when he didn't see the crab anywhere.

"Here I am!" responded the crab, behind him.

The rabbit jumped in surprise and was paralyzed by the impression; he could not believe it. There was the crab, walking happily atop the pile of carrots.

"Here I am! I got here before you!"

The rabbit could not beat the crab. That day was the first time he had lost. He was very sad because he could not manage to understand how it was that the crab got ahead of him. For that reason, the crab kept the carrots.

So ends the story of the rabbit and the crab.

EL CONEJO Y EL CANGREJO

Éste es uno de los miles de cuentos mayas sobre el conejo. En éste, intenta engañar al cangrejo. El cuento viene del libro Cuentos antiguos de animales y gente de San Miguel Acatán *por José Juan.*

*C*uentan que un conejo se asoció con un cangrejo para hacer una siembra de zanahoria. Varios días trabajaron juntos y estaban de acuerdo. Primero escogieron la semilla y la sembraron. Después cuidaron las matitas, siempre de acuerdo los dos. Recogieron la cosecha y separaron las hojas y las zanahorias.

Pero las discusiones empezaron cuando llego la hora de repartir la cosecha. El conejo quiso engañar al cangrejo con palabras agradables:

«¿Ves? Allí tenemos dos montones: uno grande y otro pequeño. Yo te dejo el grande, y me quedo con el pequeño».

El cangrejo, después de ver que el montón grande era el de las hojas, y el pequeño era el de las zanahorias, respondió:

«Te agradezco mucho querido amigo, pero me gusta ser justo. Dividamos por mitades los dos montones: yo divido y tú escoges, o tú divides y yo escojo, como prefieres. ¿Qué te parece?»

«¡No, no! No estoy de acuerdo», dijo el conejo. «Mejor nos alejemos de aquí unos treinta pasos, y volvamos corriendo. El que primero llegue se lleva las zanahorias, y el otro se queda con las hojas. ¿Qué te parece?», dijo el conejo.

«Pues sí, me parece bien», respondió el cangrejo.

«¡Por fin nos pusimos de acuerdo!», dijo el conejo, muy contento, pues estaba seguro de ganar.

«Me alegra mucho esto. Si tú ganas, estoy dispuesto a cederte todas las zanahorias y las hojas. ¿De acuerdo?»

«¡De acuerdo!», repitió el cangrejo.

«Todavía hay más», dijo el conejo. «Como sé que tú eres más lerdo que yo, te voy a dar diez pasos de ventaja».

«No, ¡eso es demasiado! No acepto», dijo el cangrejo, haciéndose que no quería abusar:

«Eres tú el que tiene que salir con diez pasos de ventaja, y no me digas que no».

«¡Acepto, acepto!», se apresuró a contestar el conejo, no queriendo contradecirlo, y con gusto para que así no se enojara, y se echara atrás el cangrejo.

Con este acuerdo se fueron juntos y amigablemente hasta el lugar en donde debía empezar la carrera. El conejo se adelantó para coger los diez pasos de ventaja. Pero, apenas dio la vuelta, el cangrejo, ni lerdo ni perezoso, se agarró con sus tenazas de la colita del conejo, sin que éste se diera cuenta.

Al llegar a donde estaban las zanahorias, el conejo se volvió creyendo haber dejado muy atrás al cangrejo.

Entonces, el cangrejo abrió las tenazas, y se dejó caer muy calladito sobre las zanahorias.

«¿Dónde estás amigo?» gritaba alegremente el conejo, al no verlo por ninguna parte.

«¡Aquí estoy!» respondió el cangrejo a su espalda.

El conejo dio un brinco de sorpresa, y quedó paralizado de la impresión; no podía creerlo. Allí estaba el cangrejo, caminando alegremente sobre el montón de zanahorias.

«¡Aquí estoy! ¡Y llegué antes que tú!»

El conejo no pudo ganarle al cangrejo. Ese día fue la primera vez que cayó. Estaba muy triste porque no lograba entender como fue que se le adelantó el cangrejo. Por eso el cangrejo se quedó con las zanahorias.

Así termina el cuento del conejo y el cangrejo.

SOMETIMES RIGHT IS REPAID WITH WRONG

From Victor Montejo's book The Bird Who Cleans the World, *this story provides an example of how life is not always fair.*

$\mathcal{T}$he rabbit kept borrowing money and things until he owed half the world. He had not repaid or returned anything. Now he was in a jam and tried to find a way to get out of it.

After some time he thought of a fantastic idea to escape his worries and his debts, though he would need the hunter to help him out. He went from house to house, visiting all the people from whom he had borrowed money and other things. He told them all that they should come to his house on the following day, and he would return and repay everything he had borrowed.

When the day arrived, the cockroach was the first to request her repayment. The shrewd rabbit put on a worried look and told her, "I know you have come to collect, friend cockroach, and today I will pay you back. But first, please scurry underneath the bed because here comes the hen!"

The cockroach quickly hid herself under the bed, just as the hen entered the room.

"I've come for my things," the hen said. And the rabbit told the hen what he had told the cockroach. "Of course I'll return your things, but first you must hide under the bed because here comes the coyote."

Fearfully, the hen hurried under the bed. But then she spotted the cockroach, snapped it up, and swallowed it in a flash.

"I want the money you owe me," the coyote announced.

The clever rabbit replied, "1 will certainly repay you, but quick, hide under the bed because here comes the jaguar."

The coyote, trembling at the mention of the jaguar, quickly leaped under the bed, where he found the hen and hungrily ate her.

"I've come to collect what you owe me," growled the jaguar menacingly.

The rabbit remained nonchalant and responded, "I'm going to repay you, I promise. But first please hide under my bed, because here comes the hunter!

The jaguar, fearing the hunter, squeezed under the bed in a flash. There he found himself next to the coyote and treated himself to a feast.

The hunter came running into the room with his rifle ready and called to the rabbit, "Here I am. Where is that troublesome jaguar you complained about?"

The rabbit pointed under the bed. In this way he repaid all his brothers who had once offered help in a time of need.

A VECES EL BIEN CON MAL SE PAGA

Del libro El pájaro que limpia el mundo *por Víctor Montejo, este cuento proporciona un ejemplo de cómo la vida no siempre es justa.*

$\mathcal{E}$l conejo había adquirido deudas con medio mundo, y no encontraba la forma de salir de sus apuros. Había fiado y había prestado, pero nada de todo esto había pagado o devuelto a sus prestamistas y bienhechores.

Entonces, el conejo ideó una fantástica forma de sacudirse de tanta preocupación y de tanto cobro. Para llevar a cabo sus planes, el conejo pidió la ayuda de un cazador. Pero antes, paso de casa en casa de sus bienhechores, anunciándoles que llegaran tal día a recibir lo que el conejo les debía.

Llegado el día señalado, se presentó primero la cucaracha exigiendo su parte; pero el astuto conejo le dijo con visible preocupación:

«Yo sé que vienes a cobrarme, amiga cucaracha, y hoy sí te pagaré. Pero antes, ¡métete debajo de la cama que ahí viene la gallina!»

La cucaracha, presurosa se fue a esconder debajo de la cama para no ser vista por la gallina.

«¡Quiero mi parte!», dijo la gallina, y el conejo volvió a exclamar, diciendo:

«¡Te pagaré, te pagaré, pero métete debajo de la cama que ahí viene el coyote!»

La gallina se escondió presurosa, y al ver ahí a la cucaracha, se la tragó en un santiamén.

El coyote llegó corriendo, pidiendo lo que le correspondía:

«Quiero mi parte ahorita mismo», dijo, pero el hábil conejo le respondió:

«¡Te pagaré, amigo coyote, pero preferible es que te escondas debajo de la cama que ahí viene el tigre!»

Por temor al tigre, el coyote se escondió debajo de la cama donde al encontrarse con la gallina, se la comió con apetito.

«¡Quiero mi parte!», gruñó amenazante el tigre, pero con toda naturalidad el conejo le dijo:

«Te pagaré, señor tigre, pero antes debes esconderte debajo de la cama que ahí viene el cazador».

El tigre, no queriendo ser visto por el cazador, se metió debajo de la cama donde sin querer, se dio un gran banquete comiéndose al coyote.

Llegada la hora que el conejo había fijado, llegó el cazador corriendo, y al instante le gritó así al conejo.

«¡Ya estoy aquí! ¿Dónde está ese tigre que ha hecho tanto perjuicio?»

El conejo señalo debajo de la cama y así les puso fin a sus hermanos que en un tiempo lo ayudaron cuando más lo necesitaba.

THE ANT, THE FLEA, THE PUMA, AND THE FOX

This story was told in 1930 by Mr. Ambrosio Dzib to Dr. Manuel J. Andrade in Chichén Itzá, Yucatán. It comes from the book Cuentos mayas yucatecos (Yucatecan Mayan Stories), *compiled by Dr. Andrade and Hilaria Máas Collí. It is about the value of work.*

*O*nce there were an ant, a flea, a puma, and a female fox who lived beneath a rocky overhang. Every day it was the job of one of them to look for food. First it was the ant's turn to go hunting, but she was very small and could not run to chase the animals. She began to look for a way to get close to a deer that was lying beneath a *subín* tree. Little by little she went climbing, until she was very close to the deer's ear, and there she stayed. The deer began to listen to a very pretty song, and so he said to her,

"Doña, if you get a little closer to my ears I would be able to hear your song better."

"Well, if that way you hear prettily, how would it be if I went into your eardrum? You would hear my pretty song better," answered the little ant.

So she started to slip into the inner ear of the deer, and the deer said,

"Little one, your song surely is beautiful."

When the ant had squeezed into the deer's eardrum and started to bite it, the deer began to run around, hitting its head on the sides and trunks of the trees, breaking its antlers. With very much work, the ant was able to kill the deer. Upon seeing that she had killed the deer, she climbed up the branch of a tree and began to yell for her friends to come and look for the deer. Soon the puma arrived and asked her,

"What did you do?"

"A little while ago I killed a deer, and how has it taken you so long to come?"

"Where is it?"

"There it is."

The puma saw the deer thrown on the ground with its antlers broken by the blows it received. Then he took the deer the ant had gotten, and afterward he said to the little ant,

"Now I see that you surely can hunt. Tomorrow the little flea will go hunting. The day after tomorrow it will be the little fox's turn."

Meanwhile, the little fox was sharpening her claws on the walls of the cave.

"I hope that the day after tomorrow comes soon so that I can go hunting, because I have the claws for it. Instead, the little flea that is going to hunt will not get any animal. If I were to go hunting, I would get many deer," said the little fox.

Well, then, at dawn the little flea left for the mountain. When she arrived at an edge of a little depression in the rock, she saw that it was full of water and she squeezed herself into a broken part of the rock and stayed there, because she knew that the deer were used to coming to the depression to drink water. Soon a deer arrived, and when it leaned down to drink water it saw the shadow of the little flea, who said to the deer,

"Drink me, drink me."

"Where is that thing that is talking?"

The deer saw that it was at the bottom of the depression, but it was not the little flea but only its shadow.

"I am going to drink all of the water, that animal is asking me to drink it all."

"Drink me, drink me," repeated the little flea. And the deer started to drink it.

"I will see where that little animal is singing, but for that I will have to drink all the water because it is at the bottom of the depression.

The deer continued drinking the water. When he got full he stopped drinking, but he heard that they were saying again,

"Drink me, drink me."

The deer opened its legs wide, got comfortable, and tried very hard to drink all the water so that he could see the little flea that was talking. When he wanted to turn around, his stomach split open. When the deer's stomach burst, the little flea climbed out of the depression, climbed up to the branch of a tree, and started to shout. Soon the old puma arrived and the little flea said to him,

"I've been waiting for a while for you to come for the deer that I killed."

The old puma went to where the deer was and saw the insides out because of the water that the deer had drank. He took the deer and carried it to the cave. When they arrived, they ate.

"Tomorrow the little fox will go," said the puma. At dawn the little fox said,

"I'm going now, father."

She went out running and left, and was running in the mountains: *ch'ij ki'in, ch'ij ki'in, so'on, so'on.* The noise that she was making was heard by the deer and they left. Then she realized that it was already night, she had not seen any deer, but she already had her nails well sharpened, so much that they would cut the trees.

"If I run into a deer I would kill it this way," said the little fox.

She ran through the mountains looking for deer but was not seeing any because all of them had fled. At dusk she looked for a cave entrance to sleep. The next day she again started to run in the mountains in search of any deer, but the day went by without her seeing any. Meanwhile, the old puma was waiting for her, and he went out of the cave every once in a while and shouted to the little fox.

"I think the little fox has been eaten, because she is not anywhere."

The third day, the little fox left running through the big path and suddenly saw many butterflies. She lay down in the path, opened her snout wide so that the butterflies would pile up. When her snout was full, they were trapped.

"Even though it is this I will show them when I arrive," thought the little fox.

When she arrived at the cave where the old puma was, she began to drag herself along. When they saw her show herself, the puma asked,

"What did you get?"

"Ju'u', ju'u'," said the little fox.

"Where is what you hunted?"

"Ju'u', ju'u'," she said. She could not talk because she had her snout full of butterflies.

"I'm going to teach you how to be a man, because you did not learn how to hunt. For three days I have not eaten; here are your little sisters hungry."

The puma chased after the little fox. They ran very much until the little fox got tired and was trapped by the puma, because he was very mad at the poor thing. When he trapped her, he tore her in two, and then he ate her.

When he finished eating, he took the rest to his friends who stayed in the cave.

That is how they stayed to live with the puma. It went well for them because they all were very hard workers.

LA HORMIGA, EL PIOJO, EL PUMA, Y LA ZORRA

Este cuento fue narrado en 1930 por el Sr. Ambrosio Dzib al Dr. Manuel J. Andrade en Chichén Itzá, Yucatán. Viene del libro Cuentos mayas yucatecos, *recopilado por el Dr. Andrade e Hilaria Máas Collí. Trata del valor del trabajo.*

*E*xistió una vez una hormiga, un piojo, un puma y una zorra que vivían debajo de una sascabera. Todos los días le correspondía a uno de ellos buscar la comida. Primero le tocó a la hormiguita ir de cacería, pero ella era muy pequeña y no podía correr para perseguir a los animales. Comenzó a buscar la forma de cómo acercarse a un venado que estaba acostado debajo de un árbol de subín. Poco a poco se le fue subiendo hasta que estuvo muy cerca de la oreja del venado, y allí se quedó. El venado comenzó a escuchar un canto muy bonito, entonces le dijo:

«Doña, si te acercaras un poquito más a mis oídos oiría mejor tu canto».

«Pues si así lo escuchas bonito ¿qué sería si yo entrara en tu tímpano? Oirías más bella mi canción», contestó la hormiguita.

Entonces se empezó a introducir en la oreja del venado, y éste dijo:

«Mamita, de veras que es hermosa tu canción».

Cuando la hormiga se metió en el tímpano del venado y comenzó a picarlo, el venado se echó a correr, golpeando su cabeza en las lajas y los troncos de los árboles, quebrando sus astas. Con mucho trabajo pudo matar la hormiguita al venado. Al ver que ya había matado al venado, se subió a la rama de un árbol y comenzó a llamar a gritos a sus compañeros para que vinieran a buscar al venado. Al poco rato llegó el viejo puma y le preguntó:

«¿Qué hiciste?»

«Hace rato que maté al venado y cómo han tardado en venir».

«¿Dónde esta?»

«Allí está».

El puma vio al venado tirado en el suelo con las astas quebradas por los golpes que se llevó. Entonces cargó al venado que había llevado, luego le dijo a la hormiguita:

«Ya veo que tú sí puedes cazar. Mañana irá el piojito de cacería. Pasado mañana le tocará a la zorrita».

Mientras tanto, la zorrita andaba afilando sus garras en las paredes de la cueva.

«Ojalá pronto sea pasado mañana para que yo vaya de cacería, porque yo sí tengo garras para ello, en cambio el pobre piojito qué va a cazar, no cazará ningún animal. Si yo llegara a ir de cacería, cazaría muchos venados», decía la zorrita.

Pues bien, al amanecer el piojito se fue al monte. Al llegar a la orilla de una sarteneja vio que estaba llena de agua, y se metió en una parte saltada de la piedra, ahí se quedó, pues sabía que en la sarteneja acudían venados a beber agua. Al rato llegó un venado, al inclinarse a tomar agua vio la sombra del piojito que le decía:

«Bébeme, bébeme».

«¿Dónde estará esa cosa que habla?»

Vio que estaba en el fondo de la sarteneja, pero no era el piojito sino sólo su sombra.

«Voy a beber toda el agua; este animal me está pidiendo que yo la beba toda».

«Bébeme, bébeme», repetía el piojito. Y el venado comenzó a beberla.

«Veré donde canta ese animalito, pero para ello tendré que tomarme toda el agua porque creo que está en el fondo de la sarteneja».

Siguió bebiendo el agua. Al llenarse la dejó de beber, pero oyó que le decían nuevamente.

«Bébeme, bébeme».

El venado abrió muy bien las piernas, se acomodó y se esforzó a beber toda el agua para que pudiera ver al piojito que hablaba. Cuando quiso dar la vuelta se le abrió el estómago. Al estallar el estómago del venado, salió el piojito de la sarteneja, se subió a la rama de un árbol y comenzó a gritar. Al rato llegó el viejo puma, y el piojito le dijo:

«Hace rato que los estoy esperando para que vengan por el venado que maté».

El viejo puma fue hasta donde estaba el venado, y lo vio con las tripas de fuera por el agua que había tomado. Lo cargó y lo llevó a la cueva. Al llegar, comieron.

«Mañana irá la zorrita», dijo el puma. Al amanecer dijo la zorrita:

«Ya me voy, papá».

Salió corriendo y se fue; andaba corriendo en el monte: *ch'ij ki'in, ch'ij ki'in, so'on, so'on.* El ruido que hacía era escuchado por los venados y se iban. Cuando se dio cuenta, ya era de noche y no había visto ningún venado, ya tenía bien afiladas las uñas que hasta los árboles quebraba.

«Si yo encontrara a un venado lo mataría de esta forma», dijo la zorrita.

Corría por el monte buscando venados pero no veía a ninguno porque todos huían. Al anochecer buscó la entrada de una cueva para dormir. Al día siguiente empezó nuevamente a correr en el monte en busca de algún venado, pero pasó el día sin que viera alguno.

Mientras tanto, el viejo puma la esperaba, éste salía por ratos de la cueva y gritaba a la zorrita.

«Creo que se comieron a la zorrita; no está por ningún lado».

Al tercer día, la zorrita salió corriendo por el camino grande, y de pronto vio muchas mariposas. Se acostó en medio del camino, abrió grande su hocico para que se amontonaran las mariposas. Cuando se llenó su hocico quedaron atrapadas.

«Aunque sea esto, les mostraré cuando llegue», pensó la zorrita.

Al llegar a la cueva donde estaba el viejo puma comenzó a arrastrarse; cuando la vieron asomarse, el puma preguntó:

«¿Qué cazaste?»

«*Ju'u', ju'u'*», decía la zorrita.

«¿Dónde está lo que cazaste?»

«*Ju'u', ju'u'*», decía. No podía hablar porque tenía el hocico lleno de mariposas.

«Te voy a enseñar a ser hombre, porque no aprendiste a cazar. Ya hace tres días que no he comido; ahí están todos tus hermanitos hambrientos».

El puma correteó a la zorrita. Corrieron mucho hasta que la zorrita se cansó y fue atrapada por el puma, pues estaba muy enojado con la pobre. Al atraparla, la partió en dos, y luego se la comió.

Cuando terminó de comer, llevó el resto a sus compañeros que permanecían en la cueva.

Así se quedaron a vivir con el puma. Les fue bien porque todos eran muy trabajadores.

THE BUZZARD AND THE DOVE

One of many stories about the wise but sometimes foolish buzzard, this tale tells the story of his enchantment with the beautiful dove. The story comes from The Bird Who Cleans the World, *by Victor Montejo.*

*T*here was once a wise old buzzard who found himself falling in love with a beautiful dove. The hand of heaven moved him. He thought long and hard about his wrinkled head, his heavy beak. Still, remembering that necessity sometimes wears a dog's face and "love has no boundaries," the lovesick buzzard fixed himself up as best he could and gallantly went out to find the dove.

When he saw the dove, she seemed even more beautiful than ever, and the buzzard stood back in awe. With all his heart he wanted to run to her, but his heavy feet refused to move. He began to doubt himself. Finally, he made up his mind and spoke out:

"Oh you divine princess, my lovely dove, I beg you, listen to what I ask. With great pain, with tears and pleas, I am your humble admirer and very proud to declare to you my tenderest love."

The dove, surprised by such sudden praise, answered:

"What are you saying? Are you crazy? None of your fellow hoarse-throats have ever been so brash! You are asking for my hand, you? Such worthless love from such trash."

The buzzard had already said too much to be silenced by her insulting behavior. With gentlemanly courtesy he responded: "Forgive me, precious one, if I offend you. But for a long time I have not lived in peace, thinking of nothing but you. And so my fair damsel, give me your compassion when I come to kneel at your feet and ask out of all love and submission that you join me in Christian marriage. That's all I'm asking."

But the dove, shocked by such impudence, answered in a harsh and merciless voice: "Without doubt you're drunk or crazy, you loathsome buzzard. Once and for all, before I lose my patience, I'm telling you a hundred times, I hate you. And don't ever bother me again!"

The lover wanted to continue his amorous arguments, but the dove did not want to hear any more drivel and gave him the cold shoulder.

She left the buzzard stunned and crestfallen, without spirit, without hope of winning her, muttering to heaven: "I was born humble and I'll die humble, the unluckiest creature on earth. I might as well die now and take along my fine feelings, for I live sad, poor and disgraced."

A long time passed, but the buzzard could not forget his love. Once more in his heart, a great passion blossomed for that princess who was the source of his misery.

Convinced that he could win his treasure by force of endurance and sacrifice, he scrubbed and scraped and combed and brushed. With a slow and tired step he set out to find the dove. He was sure that this time luck would not fail him and that his only duty was to fight to the death for his ideal, even if fighting for the impossible.

He caught the dove off guard when he returned to deliver his new inspiration. Like an eloquent courtier he addressed his love: "Señorita Paloma, forgive my awkwardness, but the impulses of my suffering and lovestruck heart bring me again to ask you at least for your friendship."

The dove, so proud of her beauty, interrupted his plea. With a vengeful fury she cut his fine sentiments to shreds with these words: "Oh it's you again, stupid beast. Chish, you pig. I'm telling you, I don't love you. Now get out of here before your smell offends me. Just seeing you brood scares me. What's more, the way you walk and sway is foolish and ugly."

The buzzard tried to defend himself as best he could. His eyes were filling with tears, his voice trembled. He summoned all his forces to explain to his loved one his peculiar, sad situation: "Beautiful little dove, don't judge me poorly. This smell I give off is valuable perfume. The suit I wear is my most serviceable finery. This distinct walk is how they taught me to march. So as you see, I'm not just anyone, as I appear to be, but someone ready to be received like a lieutenant or a colonel."

His explanation amused the dove. She laughed.

"Heee, heee. You call that smell from your beak perfume? And you call the disgusting color of your wings finery?"

The buzzard replied: "Señorita, instead of looking at my dress, look at the courage of my person. If you are descended from another line, don't make fun of my words or the color of my plumage."

The dove laughed again.

"Heee, heee, heee. You and your hoarse speeches. And what will you tell me about your dusty legs. That you spent a fortune to rent those stockings?"

The buzzard continued: "Fine little lady, I wouldn't have believed you were so cold as to discriminate against me like this. Be my condition what it may, my own dignity sustains me and I swear that if I was your suitor, it was because I did not know what a violent and prejudiced mind you have."

The haughty dove went on listing an infinity of faults in her suitor until she got tired. She took her leave, saying: "Enough. Leave me alone. Go back to your own kind, you insolent brute."

The buzzard stepped back, brooding, and made way for some "authorities" who approached just then on their routine rounds. He wiped his teary eyes and grew curious about what was going on.

First one official began a passionate speech, exalting things he had probably never seen: "And I, the leader of the campaign against pollution am proud to deliver this important award to our lovely dove in honor of her valuable participation in the animal plan for a clean world."

The buzzard, in a dark corner, watched the ceremony and wanted to speak out, but he knew that no one would listen. He looked at his claws and felt his beak. He had worked so hard against pollution and had never been recognized for his efforts. Instead, she who never stained her beak or her feathers was carrying away the honors. *Caramba,* what an injustice! So the buzzard started on his way home.

Meanwhile the decorated dove climbed the branches of a tall tree so that all could see her, so that everyone could applaud her. It was then that among the thick branches they heard a sudden noise. A hawk had plunged down and snatched the beautiful wild dove in its talons. This all happened so fast that the only thing those present saw were some feathers that fell as if waving goodbye to her grieving suitor.

Then, seeing that everything was over, the crestfallen buzzard beat his way upward on slow wings and went across the sky doubting, crying and thinking:

"What a fool I am to stay captive in this great valley of sorrows. Why not live like before, far from hatred and rancor and free of all these sorry tricks?"

A splendid reflection, that of the buzzard, to have left us his noteworthy thought in these lines: "This world will have a sad ending if corruption and deceit prevail like this, because where there is no love nor understanding, the only things that triumph, regrettably, are discrimination, hate and death."

LA PALOMA Y EL ZOPILOTE

Uno de los muchos cuentos del zopilote sabio pero a veces tonto, éste relaciona el cuento de su encanto con la paloma bella. Este cuento viene del libro El pájaro que limpia el mundo *por Víctor Montejo.*

*É*sta es la historia de un zopilote muy sagaz que a una hermosa paloma blanca su divino amor quiso declarar. Cierto es que lo tuvo que meditar mucho a causa de su poca favorecida condición, pero pensando que el amor no tiene fronteras y que la necesidad tiene cara de perro, el enamorado se arregló como pudo y esa misma tarde, muy gallardo a la paloma se fue a presentar.

La paloma aparece de pronto, muy bella; y el zopilote se queda extasiado al verla pasar. Quiere correr a hablarle pero se detiene y duda; y por fin se decide:

«¡Oh tú, divina princesa, oh tú, blanca luz del día, oh tú, paloma de Castilla! Dígnate escuchar, te lo pido, el dolor, el llanto, las querellas de este humilde vasallo tuyo que hoy viene con mucho orgullo a declararte su tierno amor».

La paloma, sorprendida por tan repentina alabanza, contestó:

«¿Que qué decías tú, loco atrevido? Nunca de tus chiflados compañeros semejantes cosa había oído. ¿Y se puede saber con que derecho me pretendes tú, a mi; vil amo del desecho?»

El zopilote, sin inmutarse ante el aire de superioridad de su interlocutora, con toda la reverencia de un tipo cortés respondió:

«Si la ofendo, perdóneme preciosa, pero hace mucho tiempo que no vivo en paz y sólo pensando en usted me mantengo; por eso mi doncella, téngame compasión que a sus divinos pies a postrarme vengo y a pedirle con mucho amor y sumisión, casarse conmigo, cristianamente, nada mas».

Pero la paloma, no tolerando tal imprudencia, con enérgica voz y sin clemencia, contestó:

«No cabe duda que estás demente o borracho tú, zope asqueroso, y para que sepas de una vez, antes de acabarme la paciencia, te digo cien mil veces que te odio y que ya no me molestes jamás».

El joven enamorado quiso continuar con su mensaje amoroso, pero la paloma de Castilla le había dado la espalda para no seguir escuchando sus necedades. Y así el zopilote, mudo y cabizbajo ya sin fuerzas, sin esperanzas de conseguir su objetivo; murmurando así, con quejas al cielo le decía:

«¡Que me lleve la que me trajo! Si en este mundo soy el más desgraciado; para eso, prefiero morir joven llevando conmigo mi claro pensamiento, que vivir triste, pobre y despreciado».

Poco tiempo pasó y el zopilote no lograba olvidar su gran romance. Nuevamente comenzó a florecer en su corazón de zope enamorado, el ferviente deseo de amar y amar a aquella princesa orgullosa y altiva que era el cruel motivo de su perdición.

Convencido pues, que lo más preciado se logra a fuerza de sacrificios y tenacidad; presuroso se arregló otra vez con mil galas, y con paso lento y ritmado se dirigió rumbo al palomar. Pensaba que esta vez no le fallaba la suerte, y que su obligación era luchar por su ideal hasta la muerte; aunque sea ridículo luchar contra lo imposible.

La paloma estaba descuidada cuando el pretendiente llegó a entregar su nueva inspiración. Y así, cual si fuera un elocuente orador, con muy fina cortesía se dirigió:

«Señorita paloma, perdone su merced, mi necedad; pues siguiendo los impulsos de mi sufrido corazón, enamorado acudo nuevamente a su suma bondad».

Pero la paloma, orgullosa de su celestial belleza, interrumpió el discurso y con ínfimo desprecio y gran vileza, furiosa pronunció estas groseras palabras de remate, que hirieron profundamente los sentimientos del zopilote.

«¡Ah, tú otra vez, estúpido animal! ¡Chish, puerco! Ya te dije que no te quiero; aléjate de mi presencia, que tu olor me ofende; pues verte de luto a mí me conmueve y espanta, y de ribete, tu andado mal equilibrado hacen de ti, un tipo abominable y feo».

¡Qué pena, qué tristeza! El zopilote, defendiéndose a capa y espada, ya con la voz temblorosa y los ojos llorosos; y sacando fuerzas de su conmovedora flaqueza; de ésta forma quiso explicar a su bien amada, la triste y lamentable situación en que se encontraba.

«Hermosa palomita no me justifique mal, este olor que despido es de un valioso perfume; esta ropa que yo visto, es mi uniforme de gala; el marcado paso que llevo me lo enseñaron en el cuartel; como ve, no soy tan cualquiera come aparento ser, sino alguien que muy pronto se recibe de teniente y coronel».

Le causó gracia a la paloma las explicaciones del enamorado, y se rió:

«¡Ji, ji, ji! ¿Perfume llamas tú al hedor insoportable de tu pico? ¿Y uniforme de gala al nauseabundo color de tus alas?»

«Señorita, no interesa tanto el traje como el valor mismo de la persona, y si usted es de otro linaje, sírvase no tomar en broma mis palabras ni el color de mi plumaje».

La paloma volvió a reírse:

«¡Ji, ji, ji! Me da risa tu discurso. ¿Y qué me dices de tus blancuzcas patas? ¿O acaso son también polainas que se han gastado tanto por el uso?»

Al escuchar esto, el zopilote respondió:

«Gentil señorita, no creí que fuera usted tan inconsciente al discriminarme de tal manera; pero sea mi condición cual fuera yo tengo mi dignidad que me alienta; y juro, que si fui su pretendiente, fue porque no la vi tan violenta».

Así se pasó la paloma, enumerándole infinidad de defectos al pretendiente; hasta que cansada le dijo, despidiéndole:

«¡Basta, te recomiendo meterte con los de tu clase y no conmigo, bruto, insolente!»

El zopilote se alejó pensativo para dar paso a las autoridades que se acercaban en esos momentos a realizar una de sus ya rutinarias actividades. Condecorar a uno de los suyos por su esforzado trabajo por el medio ambiente y en bien de la humanidad. El frustrado zopilote detuvo sus pasos y limpiándose sus ojos llorosos, dispuso curiosear lo que en esos momentos se iniciaba.

Uno de los funcionarios principales pido la presencia de la paloma y con un flamante discurso, exaltando cualidades que posiblemente sus ojos nunca habían visto, habló:

«Yo, el promotor de la campaña contra la contaminación, hago entrega de este significativo galardón a la señorita paloma de Castilla, por su valiosa participación en el plan regional de limpieza ambiental».

El zopilote, que en uno de los oscuros rincones observaba la ceremonia, quiso opinar, pero sabía de antemano que no sería escuchado. Se vio las uñas y se tocó el pico. ¡Cuánto había trabajo en limpiar el medio ambiente y contra la contaminación; y jamás le habían reconocido sus méritos! En cambio, quien jamás se manchó el pico y el plumaje, era quien se llevaba los galardones. ¡Qué injusticia, caray! Y así, el zopilote se alejó sin resentimientos. Mientras tanto, la condecorada ascendía una por una las ramas altas de aquel árbol, para que todos la vieran, para que todos le aplaudieran.

Fue entonces, que entre las peladas ramas se escuchó un ruido repentino. Un gavilán se había lanzando de pique y arrebatado entre sus garras a la hermosa paloma de Castilla.

Todo esto fue tan rápido, velozmente, que lo único que vieron los allí presentes, fueron varias plumas blancas que cayeron come diciéndole adiós al sentido pretendiente. Entonces, viendo que todo estaba concluido, el desdichado zopilote alzó lentamente el vuelo y se fue por los aires dudando, pensando y llorando:

«¡Tonto de mí, permanecer cautivo en este gran valle de dolores, lágrimas y discriminación! ¿Por qué no vivir come antaño, alejado de odios y rencores y libre de tristes desengaños?»

Hermosa reflexión la del zope, que nos ha dejado en estos renglones su preclaro pensamiento: «Triste fin tendrá el mundo presente si prevalece así la corrupción y el engaño, porque donde no hay amor ni comprensión lo único que triunfa y con pesar, es la discriminación, el odio y la muerte».

PART 2

STORIES OF MASTERS

MIRANDÍA HILL

The story of Mirandía Hill originated at the San Diego Escuintla plantation in southern Guatemala, where there is a well-known hill of that name. This story uses the voice of an unnamed spirit to teach a lesson about ambition and wanting more than one needs. The known geographical features and locations give the listener a feeling that it quite possibly could be true. It was told by Eulogio Shutuc, who is from Aquacatán, Huehuetenango.

*I*n Aguacatán, Huehuetenango, there once was a very poor family, with a father, mother, and four children, three boys and a girl. One morning the father, whose name was Eulogio, said to his wife Josefa, better known as Chepa, "I think it is about time to harvest coffee in the southwest. Considering our economic situation, I think we will have to go there to work for about six months, because here we don't have any way to get ahead, our children are growing, and the food costs are more." His wife said she agreed and said that he should make the decision he thought was best.

So early one day the family left Aguacatán for the southwest to look for coffee plantations. Luckily they found one where they were given jobs and a place to live. So they began to adjust to the area; although where they used to live was the country and the people were very different.

At first only don Eulogio worked harvesting coffee; but after two weeks he told Chepa that she also should come to harvest coffee, because the oldest of their children could take care of his brothers and sister. Chepa said that would be okay; but because she was a good mother, she left her children's lunch ready, and she and Eulogio carried theirs with them.

One Saturday Eulogio said to Chepa, "We have already been here two months and we don't know anything about this new area." So they decided to go for a walk. Embarking on the trip, Eulogio and his family went for two days, walking and walking. Suddenly they arrived at a very pretty place that looked like a vegetable garden. It was very strange to them to find a place like this on the side of a hill, called Mirandía, where it first had looked like there was nothing, only trees and more trees.

Eulogio was very excited to see the fruit and said to Chepa, "Look at all the fruit!" There were papayas, pineapples, bananas, plantains, peaches, jocotes, sapotes, cantaloupes, watermelons, and many more fruits that they had never seen on a tree. They were spectacular. Suddenly they heard a voice that told them they could eat anything they saw. Very happy and surprised, they began to cut and eat everything they could, until they grew very

---

full and tired. Night came and the family decided to spend it there and leave the next morning for the plantation.

The next morning Chepa and the children began to cut all kinds of fruits. They filled their sacks with the fruits, thinking they could sell them in the market. With the sacks full, they decided to leave that beautiful place. Suddenly they again heard the voice, which told them, "The fruits are only to eat here. You cannot take them from this place."

Then Eulogio put down his sack and emptied it, and so did the rest of his family. This was how he learned not to be so ambitious and to accept that he should have only what he needs to survive with his family.

EL CERRO MIRANDÍA

El cuento del cerro Mirandía originó en la finca San Diego Escuintla en el sur de Guatemala, donde hay un cerro bien conocido que se llama Mirandía. Por medio de la voz de un espíritu no nombrado, este cuento enseña una lección que trata de la ambición y de desear más de lo que es necesario. Incorpora lugares y rasgos geográficos conocidos para dar al oyente el sentido de que será un cuento verdadero. Fue contado por Eulogio Shutuc, de Aguacatán, Huehuetenango.

*E*n Aguacatán, Huehuetenango, había una vez una familia muy pobre, que se componía del padre, la madre y cuatro hijos, de los cuales tres eran varones y una niña. Una mañana el padre Eulogio le dijo a su esposa Josefa, más conocida como Chepa, «Creo que es tiempo de cosechar café al suroeste. Pensando bien en nuestra situación económica, creo que tenemos que hacer un viaje de seis meses, porque aquí, no tenemos la manera de avanzar, nuestros hijos están creciendo, y los gastos de comida son más». La esposa le dijo que estaba de acuerdo y que él tomara la decisión que creyera más conveniente.

Así fue como un día muy temprano salieron de Aguacatán hacia el suroeste en busca de las fincas de café. Con suerte, encontraron una donde le daban trabajo y donde vivir. Entonces comenzaron a ambientarse a esa área, porque en donde ellos vivían el campo, y la gente eran muy diferente.

De primero solo fue don Eulogio él que empezó a trabajar en el corte de café, pero pasadas dos semanas Eulogio le dijo a Chepa que ella también debería de ir a cortar café porque el mayor de sus hijos podía cuidar a sus hermanos. Chepa dijo que estaba bien, pero como buena madre, les dejaba el almuerzo listo a sus hijos y llevaban lo de ellos.

Pasados dos meses Eulogio le dice a Chepa: «Ya hemos estado aquí dos meses, y no conocemos nada del alrededor». Así que un sábado decidieron ir a caminar. Emprendieron el viaje Eulogio y toda su familia, y se fueron por dos días. Así que caminaron y caminaron y de repente llegaron a un lugar muy bonito parecido a una huerta. Para ellos fue muy extraño encontrar un lugar como ése en las faldas de un cerro llamado Mirandía donde parecía que no había nada, solo árboles y árboles.

Su emoción fue tan grande que Eulogio no pensó más en eso, y le dijo a Chepa: «¡Mira qué frutas!» Había papayas, piñas, naranjas, bananas, plátanos, duraznos, jocotes, sapotes, melón, sandia y muchos más que ellos nunca habían visto en un árbol. Eran espectaculares.

De repente escucharon una voz que les dijo que podían comer de todo lo que ellos veían. Muy contentos y asombrados, ellos empezaron a cortar y a comer de todo lo que había hasta cansarse. Llegó la noche, y ellos decidieron pasarla ahí y salir en la mañana siguiente para la finca.

La mañana siguiente, Chepa y los niños empezaron a cortar de toda clase de frutas. Llenaron sus sacos con las frutas, y pensaron que podían venderlos en el mercado. Llenos los sacos, decidieron irse de ese bello lugar. De repente escucharon la voz que les decía: «Los frutos sólo son para comerlos aquí. No pueden sacarlos de este lugar». Entonces Eulogio bajó su saco y lo vació, y así hicieron el resto de su familia también. Fue de este modo que él aprendió que no debía de ser tan ambicioso y que sólo debía de tener lo suficiente para sobrevivir con su familia.

THE DISOBEDIENT CHILD

This story is a beautiful example of teaching appropriate behavior to children and, at the same time, introducing one of the Maya's mythical characters who control nature. It comes from Victor Montejo's The Bird Who Cleans the World.

*I*n old times in *Xaqla'* Jacaltenango there was a very disobedient child who often disappointed his parents. No matter how hard they tried to teach him, he never changed.

One afternoon the boy ran away from home looking for someone who would tolerate his mischief. Walking through the woods, he discovered a lonely little house and ran up to it. On the porch of the straw-covered house sat an old man, smoking peacefully. The boy stood before him without saying hello or any other word of greeting.

When the old man noticed the boy's presence, he stopped smoking and asked him, "Where do you want to go, boy?"

"I am looking for someone who can give me something to eat," the boy answered.

The wise old man, who already knew the boy's story, said, "No one will love you if you continue being so bad."

The boy did not respond except to laugh.

Then the old man smiled and said, "You can stay with me. We will eat together."

The boy accepted his offer and stayed in the old man's house.

On the following day before going to work, the old man told the boy: "You should stay in the house, and the only duty you will have is to put the beans to cook during the afternoon. But listen well. You should only throw thirteen beans in the pot and no more. Do you understand?"

The boy nodded that he understood the directions very well. Later when the time arrived to cook the beans, the boy put the clay pot on the fire and threw in thirteen beans as he had been directed. But once he had done that he began to think that thirteen beans weren't very many for such a big pot. So, disobeying his orders, he threw in several more little fistfuls.

When the beans began to boil over the fire, the pot started to fill up, and it filled up until it overflowed. Very surprised, the boy quickly took an empty pot and divided the beans between the two pots. But the beans overflowed the new pot, too. Beans were pouring out of both pots.

When the old man returned home he found piles of beans, and the two clay pots lay broken on the floor.

"Why did you disobey my orders and cook more than I told you to?" the old man asked angrily.

The boy hung his head and said nothing. The old man then gave him instructions for the next day. "Tomorrow you will again cook the beans as I have told you. What's more I forbid you to open that little door over there. Do you understand?"

The boy indicated that he understood very well.

The next day the old man left the house after warning the boy to take care to do exactly what he had been told. During the afternoon the boy put the beans on the fire to cook. Then he was filled with curiosity. What was behind the little door he had been forbidden to open?

Without any fear, the boy opened the door and discovered in the room three enormous covered water jars. Then he found three capes inside a large trunk. There was one green cape, one yellow cape, and one red cape. Not satisfied with these discoveries, the boy took the top off the first water jar to see what it contained.

Immediately the water jar began to emit great clouds that quickly hid the sky. Frightened and shivering with cold, the boy opened the trunk and put on the red cape. At that instant a clap of thunder exploded in the house. The boy was turned into thunder and lifted to the sky, where he unleashed a great storm.

When the old man heard the thunder he guessed that something extraordinary had happened at home, and he hurried in that direction. There he discovered that the forbidden door was open and the top was off the jar of clouds, from which churning mists still rose toward the sky. The old man covered the jar and then approached the trunk with the capes. The red cape, the cape of storms, was missing. Quickly the old man put on the green cape and regained control over the sky, calming the great storm. Little by little the storm subsided, and soon the man returned to the house carrying the unconscious boy in his arms.

A little while later the old man uncapped the same jar and the clouds which had blackened the sky returned to their resting place, leaving the heavens bright and blue again. When he had done this the old man capped the jar again and put away the red and green capes.

Through all of this the boy remained stunned and soaked with the rains until the kind old man restored his spirit and brought him back to normal. When the boy was alert again and his fear had left, the old man said, "Your disobedience has almost killed you. You were lucky that I heard the storm and came to help. Otherwise you would have been lost forever among the clouds."

The boy was quiet and the old man continued.

"I am Qich Mam, the first father of all people and founder of *Xaqla'*, he who controls the rain and waters the community's fields when they are dry. Understand, then, that I wish you no harm and I forgive what you have done. Promise me that in the future you will not disobey your parents."

The boy smiled happily and answered, "I promise, Qich Mam, I promise." Qich Main patted him gently and said, "Then return to your home and be useful to your parents and to your people."

From that time on the boy behaved differently. He was very grateful for the kindness of the old man who held the secret of the clouds, the rains, the wind, and the storms in his hands. This happened here in our land of Xaqla'.

EL NIÑO DESOBEDIENTE

Este cuento presenta un buen ejemplo de la enseñanza de la educación a los niños y a la vez de la presentación de uno de los caracteres que controlan a la naturaleza. Viene del libro El pájaro que limpia el mundo *por Víctor Montejo.*

*E*n Xajla' antiguamente había un niño muy desobediente que les causaba muchos disgustos a sus padres, pues no había enseñanza alguna que podía rectificar su conducta.

Cierta tarde, el niño abandonó el hogar para salir en busca de alguna persona que pudiera tolerar sus travesuras y malcriadezas.

Andando por el bosque descubrió un rancho solitario al cual se dirigió a toda prisa. En el corredor de la casa de paja estaba sentado un anciano que fumaba tranquilamente. El niño se presentó ante el anciano sin hablar ni saludar.

Al notar la presencia del niño, el viejo dejó de fumar y le preguntó:

«¿A dónde quieres ir, niño?»

«Voy en busca de alguien que pueda darme de comer», respondió.

El sabio anciano, que de antemano sabía la historia del niño, le dijo como un recordatorio:

«Nadie te va a querer si sigues siendo desobediente».

El niño no respondió y sólo se puso a reír. Entonces, el viejo le propuso amablemente:

«Si quieres, puedes quedarte conmigo. Comeremos juntos».

El niño aceptó la propuesta y se quedó en casa del viejo.

Al día siguiente y antes de ausentarse de la casa, el viejo le recomendó al niño lo siguiente:

«Vas a quedarte en casa y el único oficio que debes hacer es poner los frijoles a cocer por la tarde. Pero escucha bien, sólo debes echar trece granos de frijol a esta olla y no más. ¿Entiendes?»

El niño manifestó que había entendido bien el mandado. Entonces, cuando llegó el tiempo de poner los frijoles a cocer, el niño puso la olla sobre el fuego y echó los trece granos de fríjol como se lo habían indicado. Hecho esto, el niño se puso a pensar que era muy poco fríjol para una olla grande y entonces desobedeció la orden, echando otros puñitos más a la olla.

Cuando los frijoles comenzaron a hervir sobre el fuego, la olla fue llenándose y llenándose hasta rebalsarse. Con mucho asombro, el niño fue a traer otra olla vacía para poner los sobrantes de la primera olla; pero esta también se llenó y por fin las dos ollas reventaron.

Cuando el viejo llegó a casa, descubrió montones de frijol junto al fuego y las ollas rotas sobre el suelo.

«¿Por qué has desobedecido mis órdenes al poner a cocer más de lo que te había indicado?» preguntó el viejo, enojado.

El niño bajó la frente y nada respondió. Entonces, el viejo volvió a dar sus instrucciones para el siguiente día:

«Mañana volverás a cocer los frijoles como te he dicho y además te prohíbo entrar por aquella puertecita cerrada. ¿Has entendido?»

El niño manifestó que había entendido bien el mandado.

Al siguiente día el viejo se ausentó de la casa, recordándole al niño sus obligaciones, y que debía cumplir con lo que se le había dicho al pie de la letra.

Por la tarde, el niño se puso a cocer los frijoles y después de esto se le entró la curiosidad de ver qué era lo que había detrás de la puerta por donde le habían prohibido entrar.

Sin ningún temor el niño abrió la puerta y descubrió dentro de aquel cuarto, tres enormes tinajeras tapadas. Luego descubrió otras tres capas guardadas dentro de un gran cofre. Los colores de las capas eran: una verde, una roja y la otra amarilla.

No satisfecho con lo que hacía, el niño destapó la primera tinajera para ver lo que contenía.

Y sucedió entonces, que de la enorme tinajera comenzaron a salir grandes nubarrones que pronto obscurecieron el cielo. Asustado por esto y tiritando de frío, el niño abrió el cofre y se puso encima la capa roja. En ése instante estalló un trueno en la casa y el niño convertido en trueno fue elevado al cielo donde se desató de inmediato una tempestad.

Al escuchar los truenos, el anciano supuso que algo fuera de orden sucedía en su casa y por eso regresó de inmediato a ver lo que pasaba. Allí descubrió que la puerta prohibida estaba abierta y la tinajera de las nubes destapada, de la cual seguían saliendo remolinos de nubes que se dirigían al cielo.

El anciano tapó la tinajera y luego se acercó al cofre de las capas. Hacía falta la capa roja, que era la capa de las tempestades.

Presuroso, el anciano se puso encima la capa verde y de inmediato tronó por el cielo, contrarrestando la furia de la repentina tempestad. Poco a poco la tormenta fue cesando y pronto el anciano regresó a la casa trayendo al niño desmayado en sus brazos. Luego, el anciano destapó la misma tinajera y fue así como las nubes que ennegrecían el cielo se fueron desenlazando y retornaron nuevamente a la gran tinajera; quedando otra vez el cielo despejado. Hecho esto, el anciano volvió a tapar la gran tinajera y guardó las dos capas, roja y verde.

Mientras tanto, el niño seguía atontado y empapado de lluvia; hasta que el amable anciano lo reanimó, volviéndolo a su estado normal.

Ya cuando estuvo consciente y curado del susto, el anciano le dijo esto:

«Tu desobediencia te ha llevado casi a la muerte, fue una suerte que yo haya acudido a tiempo en tu auxilio; porque de lo contrario te hubieras quedado perdido para siempre entre las nubes».

El niño seguía callado y el anciano siguió hablando:

«Yo soy Jichmam, el que controla la lluvia y riega los campos de los hijos del pueblo cuando es necesario. Entiende pues que yo no quiero hacerte daño y te perdono por lo que has hecho. ¿Me prometes que en el futuro ya no serás desobediente?»

El niño sonrió alegremente y respondió:

«¡Lo prometo, Jichmam, lo prometo!»

Jichmam lo acarició amablemente y por último le dijo:

«Regresa entonces a tu casa y se útil a tus padres y a tu pueblo».

Desde entonces el niño cambió de conducta, quedando muy agradecido de la bondad del anciano que tenía en sus manos el secreto de las nubes, las lluvias, el viento y las tempestades. Esto sucedió aquí en nuestra tierra de Xajla'.

THE MASTER OF THE CANYONS

This tale presents another account of beings that inhabit and watch over the earth. It originated in San José Media Cuesta, Santa Rosa, Guatemala, and was told by Santiago Morales.

One time a man named Santiago went with some friends to visit Lake Ayarsa near San José Media Cuesta in the department of Santa Rosa. They swam in the lake all afternoon, and that night they stayed at don José's house. They went out to the patio and sat around a fire; don José told them that there were many wild animals nearby because it was a mountainous area. So they arranged to go hunting around nine o'clock that night. They walked along streams, mountains, and narrow canyons but did not get any animals. Around 12:30 they got a raccoon, and then right away a possum, and some of the others got some other animals.

At about two in the morning, Santiago and his friends decided to go back to their shelter. They remembered only that when they started out they had gone down a rocky hill and at the bottom there was a little river; and when they found such a hill, they went down. When they arrived at the bottom there were bats hanging on the rocks. Santiago's friends began to bother the bats. A long time passed, and they wanted to get out. Carrying the animals, they did not find a way out. They looked around them. The place was full of rocks, and they all looked the same.

Suddenly, Santiago and his friends heard a great noise, as if pieces of trees were coming rolling toward the bottom of the hill; they also heard sounds like moans of people. The men did not panic, but they decided to build a bonfire so the spirit who made the noises would not approach them. When they tried to light torches of ocote pine, the torches would not light. They used all their matches but were not able to light any; the place where they were was possessed by the master of the canyons.

Then it occurred to one of them to throw a rope up into a tree, so they could use it to climb out of the narrow canyon. Each one had to pull himself up by the rope to get to the top. When they finally got out, they continued walking through the mountains. They managed to get out of the mountains without light, because while they were walking the day started to dawn.

Finally they arrived at the bank of Lake Ayarsa. On the bank they commented about what had happened during the hunt. Everyone who had gone on the hunt heard the noises when they were in the canyon, but no one said anything then, nor was anyone afraid. And that is the reason don José, a native of that place, said that if any of them had been afraid, they would not have gotten away from the cliff.

That is how they learned that the canyons have a master.

EL DUEÑO DE LOS BARRANCOS

Este cuento presenta otra cuenta de los seres que habitan y protegen la tierra. Originó en San José Media Cuesta, Santa Rosa, Guatemala, y fue contado por Santiago Morales.

*U*na vez un hombre que se llamaba Santiago fue con unos amigos a visitar la laguna de Ayarsa en San José Media Cuesta en el departamento de Santa Rosa.

Llegó y nadó en la laguna durante toda la tarde, y por la noche se les hospedó en la casa de don José. Salieron al patio y, sentados alrededor de una fogata, don José les contó que ahí había muchos animales silvestres porque es un lugar montañoso. Dispusieron cazar animales como a las nueve de la noche. Caminaron en riachuelos, montañas y barrancos, y no tuvieron éxito de cazar ningún animal. A eso de las doce y treinta cazaron un mapache y seguidamente un tacuazín, y otros compañeros cazaron otros tipos de animales.

Como a las dos de la mañana decidieron regresar a su albergue, cuando emprendieron el camino, solo recordaron que habían bajado un cerro con rocas, y al fondo de ahí había un pequeño río. Cuando llegaron al fondo había murciélagos colgando en las rocas. Sus compañeros empezaron a molestarlos. Pasó un largo rato, y quisieron salir. Cargando los animales, no encontraron la salida. Miraron a su alrededor. Estaba lleno de rocas y todo lo miraban igual.

De repente oyeron un gran ruido como si trozos de árboles vinieran rodando hacia el fondo y también como quejidos de personas. Decidieron encender una gran fogata para que a ellos no se acercara el espíritu que hacía los ruidos. Cuando trataron de encender rajas de ocote de pino, no encendían. Aun cuando se terminaron sus fósforos, no lograron encender alguno, porque el lugar en que estaban estaba poseído por el dueño de los barrancos.

De repente a un compañero se le ocurrió tirar una soga a un árbol, y cada uno tuvo que halarse de la soga para llegar a la orilla del barranco. Al llegar, siguieron caminando entre las montañas. Lograron salir de las montañas sin luz, porque mientras que caminaban iba amaneciendo. Por fin llegaron a la orilla de la laguna de Ayarsa. En la orilla comentaban de lo que había sucedido en el transcurso de la cacería. Todos los que habían ido a la cacería escucharon los ruidos cuando estaban en el barranco, pero nadie comentó nada en ese momento, ni tuvo miedo. Y es por eso que decía don José, oriundo de ese lugar, que si alguno de ellos hubiese tenido miedo, no hubieran salido del barranco.

De esa manera aprendieron que los barrancos tienen dueño.

THE TWO ORPHANS

This story teaches a lesson about respect and vengeance. It is from Cuentos de San Pedro Soloma (Stories of San Pedro Soloma), *compiled by Ruperto Montejo Esteban.*

They tell us that in past times, there were two orphan boys who suffered very much because of their father and their stepmother. When the parents would eat, the stepmother would always get mad at the boys' father. One day the stepmother said she no longer wanted to eat, because the boys were living in the house. She wanted to eat only in the company of the father; and besides, she said, the boys were taking her food. The stepmother then said to the father:

"Today I am going back to my village. I am going to go back to my house, because you haven't taken your sons from the house. But if you give them to someone or if you leave them on the mountain, then I will stay," she added.

The father became very sad when he heard that his wife had said that she was going to leave the house, and he immediately answered her like this:

"Tomorrow I will go with my sons to cut flowers and I will leave them there."

But it happened that the littlest of the two brothers was listening to what the parents were saying. When nightfall came, the two brothers went to go to bed. Their father arrived to tell them good night and said to them:

"Go to sleep, my sons; early tomorrow morning we will go to cut flowers on the mountain."

"Yes, father," answered the boys.

Then the little one started to tell his brother what he had heard about what their parents intended to do with them.

"My brother," said the little one, "according to what I heard, our parents have formulated a plan. Our father is going to leave us on the mountain tomorrow. Our stepmother doesn't want us," said the boy.

But at that moment a great idea occurred to the little brother and he told it to his brother:

"Tomorrow when we leave, each of us is going to carry a bag of ashes. That way we can leave signs in the path that we go on."

When dawn came their father arrived to get them up and he told them that they were going to the mountain, so they were not going to do it very late. The boys already knew their father's intentions.

"Eat well," their father said to them.

"Thank you, father," they answered.

When they finished breakfast, they all went to the mountain. Their father took them to a virgin mountain, where they would not be able to find another person. The little brother went along leaving signs of ashes on the rocks and on the trunks of the trees that they found on the way. They arrived at a beautiful place where there were many, many flowers of all colors: white, red, pink, and many other colors. It was a beautiful place!

"You can cut flowers on this side. Meanwhile, I will cut these flowers that are here," said the father.

After a little while of cutting flowers, the father left the place. The boys began to cry and shout, "Father, father!" Finally the boys understood that they had been left alone. So they decided to search for the way back to their house, guiding themselves by the ash signs. That day it had not rained, so the ashes had stayed in place where they had left them.

By following the ashes the brothers were able to go back to their house. When they arrived they found their father eating dinner with their stepmother. The two were eating an entire chicken. Seeing them, the stepmother said angrily to the boys' father:

"Then it was a lie when you told me that you had gone to leave your sons on the mountain. If you had done that, they would not have come back. Tomorrow I am leaving your house."

"No, don't go," the scared father replied, "Tomorrow early I am going with them again."

The boys knew that the next day their father was going to take them to the mountain again. That night the parents gave them a piece of chicken that was on the table, and later sent them to bed. Their father, when he told them good night, told them that that morning on the mountain he had been calling them but they had not responded to him.

"Maybe you did not hear me?" he asked the boys.

"No, father," they answered, "we were yelling but you did not respond to us. Why did you do that to us, father?" asked the boys sadly. "Why are you acting like that with us?"

"No, my little sons, go to sleep," said the father.

When dawn came they went again to the mountain in search of flowers. The boys still carried their bags of ashes and repeated what they had done the day before. When they were in the middle of the mountain, their father disappeared again. The boys noticed that their father left. That moment, it began to rain very hard.

"Now, my brother, now I know that we are going to die," the little one said to the big one, and they both began to cry.

"Where are we going to stay, since the ashes disappeared with the rain?" the brothers asked themselves.

They saw a tree and they said that if the tree would open perhaps they could stay inside of it. The tree heard what the boys said and then it opened up. The two boys were glad and they stayed inside the tree to wait for the rain to pass. In the early morning the brothers heard the songs of the birds and they said to the tree:

"Mister tree, if you were so kind, like when you let us in, would you not let us leave also?"

The tree opened up again and the boys went out into the light of the day.

"Now, where will we go? What are we going to eat?" the boys were thinking when they left the tree.

They looked for the way back to their house when suddenly they saw a man cutting hay.

"What happened to you, my boys?" the man asked them.

The boys started to tell the man what had happened to them and why they had arrived there.

"Our father brought us to leave here on the mountain, because our mother is not alive and our stepmother does not want us in the house. She says that we eat a lot and that it is her food," said the boys.

The man with whom they were talking was the Lord of All Things, Our Father, and he said to the boys:

"Don't worry, my sons, I will leave you a treasure, something that will help you. Today your father rejects you and your stepmother does not want you, but do not cry or be sad. Here I leave you my walking stick, and with this walking stick you can ask for anything you want. The walking stick will give you food, a house, animals, crops, and everything when you want it," added the Lord.

The Lord advised them to not be vengeful with their father, nor with their mother, because they would meet them at a party some day. The brothers paid close attention to what the Lord of All Things had said to them. They started going and, because they were very hungry, they thought they would ask the walking stick for food, "but a lot of food," they said. The brothers thought they would try their luck and they said to the walking stick:

"Mister walking stick, we want a good meal because we are very hungry."

The moment that they asked for the food, it was given to them in abundance. And that is how the time was going by, and they asked the walking stick for everything they wanted, they even asked it for a woman.

The village celebration began, the one that the Lord of All Things had talked to them about. They arrived at the party and had been there only a little while when they saw their parents. Their father and their stepmother were drunk and approached the boys.

"How are you?" said the brothers upon seeing that their parents were crying bitterly.

"What happened is that I went to leave my two sons on the mountain, because my wife said that she did not want them in the house," said the father to the boys, whom he had not recognized, because of how big and changed they were.

"That's right, what my husband says is true," said the stepmother, who had not recognized them either. "I am to blame for everything. I told him to lose them on the mountain."

The parents were dressed in clothes so old that they were almost falling off them in pieces. The boys responded to the parents:

"Sir and madam, forget about your sons, even though you rejected them. It is better that you do not remember them or cry for them still. We are your sons."

"Now, yes, you cry a lot," added the brothers, "but when we were little you did not pity us, you despised us greatly. But don't think that we are going to take revenge on you. We are going to buy you clothes.

The boys bought their parents clothes and they made them a house like the one they had. The boys did not take the parents to live with them, because they both already had families. Besides, they gave their parents everything that they wanted.

And that is how the little orphans met their parents. But the most important thing is that they did seek revenge on their parents. When someone acts badly with us, we do not look for vengeance, just as the two brothers did not. Because for everything good we do here on earth, in some way we will receive our reward.

This is the story of the two little orphans, which our grandparents, great-grandparents, and great-great-grandparents left us.

LOS DOS HUÉRFANOS

Este cuento nos enseña una lección sobre el respeto y la venganza. Es del libro Cuentos de San Pedro Soloma, *recopilado por Ruperto Montejo Esteban.*

*N*os cuentan que en tiempos pasados, había dos niños huérfanos que sufrían mucho por culpa de su padre y su madrastra. Cuando sus padres comían, la madrastra siempre se enojaba con el papá de los niños. Un día sucedió que la madrastra ya no quería comer porque los niños vivían en la casa. Ella quería comer únicamente en compañía del papá y además decía que los niños le quitaban su comida. La madrastra le dijo al papá:

«Hoy voy a regresar a mi pueblo. Voy a regresar a mi casa, ya que no has sacado a tus hijos de esta casa. Pero si los regalas a alguien o si vas a dejarlos en la montaña, entonces sí me quedo» agregó.

El señor se entristeció mucho cuando oyó que su mujer había dicho que se iba a ir de la casa, así que le contestó de inmediato:

«Mañana iré con mis hijos a cortar flores y los dejaré allí».

Pero sucedió que el más pequeño de los dos hermanos estaba escuchando lo que decían sus papás. Cuando anocheció los hermanos se fueron a acostar. Su padre llegó a darles las buenas noches y les dijo:

«Duérmanse mis hijos, mañana temprano saldremos a cortar flores en la montaña».

«Sí, papá», contestaron los niños.

Entonces el pequeño empezó a contarle a su hermano que había escuchado lo que sus papás intentaban hacer con ellos.

«Hermano mío», dijo el pequeño, «según lo que escuché, nuestros papás han formulado un plan. Nuestro papá nos va a dejar en la montaña mañana. Nuestra madrastra no nos quiere», dijo el niño.

Pero en ese momento se le ocurrió una gran idea al hermano pequeño y se la dijo a su hermano:

«Mañana cuando salgamos, vamos a llevar una bolsa de ceniza cada uno. Así vamos dejando señales en el camino por donde iremos».

Cuando amaneció llego su papá a levantarlos y les dijo que se fueran a la montaña, porque si no se les iba a hacer muy tarde. Los niños ya sabían las intenciones de su papá.

«Coman bien», les dijo su papá.

«Gracias, papá», contestaron.

Al terminar de desayunar salieron todos hacia la montaña. Su papá los llevó a una montaña virgen, en donde no pudieran encontrar a ninguna persona. El pequeño hermano iba dejando señales de ceniza sobre las piedras y los troncos de los árboles que encontraba en el camino. Llegaron a un precioso lugar en donde había muchísimas flores de todos colores: blancas, rojas, rosadas y de muchos otros colores. ¡Era un lugar muy bello!

«Ustedes pueden cortar flores por aquel lado. Mientras yo cortaré estas flores que están aquí», dijo el papá.

Al cabo de un rato de estar cortando flores el papá se retiró del lugar. Los niños empezaron a llorar y a gritar: «¡papá, papá!». Al final los niños comprendieron que se habían quedado solos. Así que decidieron buscar el camino de regreso para su casa, guiándose por las señales de ceniza. Ese día no había llovido y eso ayudó a que la ceniza permaneciera todavía en el lugar en donde la habían dejado.

Siguiendo la ceniza pudieron regresar a su casa. Cuando llegaron encontraron a su papá almorzando con su madrastra. Se estaban comiendo una gallina completa los dos. Al verlos la madrastra le dice muy enojada al padre de los niños:

«Entonces fue mentira cuando me dijiste que habías ido a dejar a tus hijos a la montaña. Si lo hubieras hecho, no habrían regresado. Mañana mismo me voy de tu casa».

«No, no te vayas», le respondió asustado el señor, «mañana temprano salgo con ellos de nuevo».

Los niños sabían que al día siguiente su padre iba a volver a llevarlos a la montaña. Esa noche les dieron de comer un pedazo de pollo que estaba sobre la mesa, y después los mandaron a dormir. Su papá al darles las buenas noches les dijo que esa mañana en la montaña, había estado llamándolos pero que ellos no le habían respondido.

«¿Acaso no me escucharon?» les preguntó a los niños.

«No, papá», contestaron. «Estuvimos gritándote pero tú no nos respondiste. ¿Por qué nos haces eso, papá?» preguntaron muy tristes los niños. «¿Por qué te portas así con nosotros?"

«No, m'hijitos, duérmanse», dijo el señor.

Cuando amaneció se fueron otra vez a la montaña en busca de flores. Los niños llevaban siempre sus bolsas de ceniza y repitieron lo mismo que el día anterior. Cuando estaban a media montaña su papá volvió a desaparecer. Los niños no se dieron cuenta cuando se fue su papá. En ese momento empezó a llover muy fuerte.

«Ahora, hermano mío, ahora sé que nos vamos a morir», dijo el pequeño al grande, y los dos se pusieron a llorar.

«¿Dónde nos vamos a quedar, pues la ceniza desapareció con la lluvia?», se preguntaban los hermanos.

En eso vieron un árbol y dijeron que si el árbol se abriera tal vez ellos podrían quedarse dentro de él. El árbol escuchó lo que los niños dijeron y entonces se abrió. Los dos muchachos se pusieron muy contentos y se quedaron dentro del árbol a esperar que pasara la lluvia. En la madrugada los hermanos escucharon el canto de los pájaros y le dijeron al árbol:

«Señor árbol, si fueras tan amable, así como nos dejaste entrar, ¿no nos podrías dejar salir también?»

El árbol se volvió a abrir y los muchachos salieron a la luz del día.

«Ahora, ¿adónde iremos? ¿Qué vamos a comer?», pensaban los niños cuando salieron del árbol.

Buscaron el camino de regreso a su casa y de repente vieron a un señor que estaba cortando pajones.

«¿Qué les pasó, hijos míos?», les preguntó el señor.

Los muchachos empezaron a contarle al señor lo que les había pasado y cómo habían llegado allí.

«Nuestro papá nos vino a dejar aquí en la montaña, ya que nuestra madre no vive y nuestra madrastra no nos quiere tener en la casa. Dice que comemos mucho y que es su comida», dijeron los niños.

El señor con quien estaban hablando era el Señor de todas las cosas, Nuestro Padre, y les dijo a los niños:

«No tengan pena, hijos míos; yo les dejaré un tesoro, algo que los ayudará. Hoy los desprecia su papá y su madrastra no los quiere, pero no lloren ni se pongan tristes. Aquí les dejo mi bastón y con este bastón pueden pedir todo lo que quieran. El bastón les dará comida, casa, animales, siembra, y todo cuanto quieran», agregó el Señor.

El Señor les advirtió a los muchachos que no fueran a ser vengativos con su papá, ni con su madrastra, porque los iban a encontrar en una fiesta algún día. Los hermanos pusieron mucha atención a lo que les había dicho el Señor de todas las cosas. Ellos emprendieron la marcha y como tenían mucha hambre, pensaron pedirle comida al bastón, «pero mucha comida», dijeron. Los hermanos pensaron en probar su suerte y le dijeron al bastón:

«Señor bastón, queremos una buena comida ya que tenemos mucha hambre».

En el momento en que ellos pidieron la comida les fue dada y en abundancia. Y así fueron pasando el tiempo, y le pedían al bastón todo lo que querían, hasta una mujer le pidieron.

Llegó la fiesta del pueblo, de la cual les había hablado el Señor de todas las cosas. Llegaron a la fiesta y tenían un rato de estar allí cuando vieron de lejos a sus papás. Su padre y su madrastra estaban borrachos y se acercaron a los muchachos.

Los dos huérfanos   **49**

«¿Qué les pasa, señores?», dijeron los hermanos al ver que sus padres estaban llorando amargamente.

«Lo que pasa es que fui a dejar a mis dos hijos a la montaña, porque mi señora decía que no los quería ver en la casa», dijo el padre a los muchachos, a quienes no había reconocido, debido a lo grandes y cambiados que estaban.

«Es verdad, es cierto lo que dice mi esposo», dijo la madrastra que tampoco los había reconocido. «Yo fui culpable de todo. Yo le dije que los fuera a perder a la montaña».

Los papás estaban vestidos con ropa bastante vieja, que casi se les caía en pedazos. Los muchachos les respondieron a los papás:

«Señores, olvídense de sus hijos, ya que los despreciaron. Es mejor que ya no los recuerden ni lloren más por ellos. Nosotros somos sus hijos. Ahora sí lloran mucho», añadieron los hermanos, «pero cuando éramos pequeños no nos tenían lástima, nos despreciaron muchísimo. Pero no vayan a pensar que vamos a vengarnos de ustedes. Les vamos a comprar ropa».

Los muchachos les compraron ropa a sus papás y les hicieron una casa como la que ellos tenían. No se los llevaron a vivir consigo, porque ya los dos tenían familia. Además les concedían todo lo que sus papás querían.

Y es así como los huerfanitos se encontraron con sus papás. Pero lo más importante es que ellos no buscaron vengarse de sus papás. Cuando alguien se porta muy mal con nosotros no busquemos la venganza, así como no lo hicieron los dos hermanos. Porque por todo lo bueno que hacemos aquí en la tierra de alguna manera vamos a recibir nuestra recompensa.

Éste es el cuento de los dos huerfanitos que nos dejaron nuestros abuelos, bisabuelos y tatarabuelos.

THE SPIRIT OF THE WATER

This story teaches a lesson about respectfulness, honesty, and greed. It comes from the book Cuentos de San Pedro Soloma (Stories of San Pedro Soloma), *compiled by Ruperto Montejo Esteban.*

*I*n very old times there was a man who lived very quietly. He was a man who was respectful with ladies and gentlemen, the old men and old women. But one day it happened that the man went out to a mountain that was near his house to bring firewood. Because he did not have an axe, he sent his wife to ask his friend to lend him his axe.

His friend lent him an axe, but this quiet man had a great weakness: he was very lazy. Just like that he tied his friend's axe with a knot so he could carry it tied on, only he did not tie it well, and just like that the axe, with every step, loosened up on him.

When the man arrived at the mountain he began to look for firewood. On the bank of a river there was a great tree, so he began to cut it. A little while after he was chopping the tree the axe came loose and fell to the bottom of the river. The poor man did not know what to do. The only thing he did was to cry and cry. He was crying when an old man, who was the Spirit of the Water, approached him to help.

"What happened to you, young man?" asked the old man.

"Sir, what happened is that the axe fell to the bottom of the river and it is not mine, but my friend's," answered the man.

"I am going to get out the axe for you," said the old man, "but with the condition that you do not move my walking stick because if you move it, I will not be able to find the axe."

"Thank you, sir."

"Is this your axe?" asked the old man, showing him an axe of silver.

"No, that one is not mine," answered the man.

The old man got back into the water, this time bringing out an axe of gold.

"This one surely is your axe," said the old man to the young man, showing him the axe of gold.

"No, that one is not mine."

For the third time, the old man got into the water, this time bringing out the man's axe. "Is this your axe?"

"Yes, that one is mine!" shouted the man, leaping about with joy and being very grateful to the old man.

"For being a young person and for being very sincere and honest, you can take these two axes as a gift. When you arrive at your house, put them away in a chest, because they are a treasure that will help you in your life from here forward," said the old man to the young man.

"Thank you, sir," answered the young man.

When he arrived at his house he said to his wife that she should return the axe that he had taken on loan from his friend. Meanwhile, the man stayed, putting away the other two. Thanks to these two axes, the man came to have great luck and he became a rich man.

When the friend found out what had happened, he decided to go to the river also to get firewood from the same place that the man had gone, and he also did everything in the same way as the man had done: he hauled his axe, but the axe did not come loose on him.

When he arrived at the mountain, the friend looked for a tree on the bank of the river. Then he set himself to cutting the tree, but because the axe did not come loose, he decided to throw it into the river himself. The old man came back and approached him and said to him:

"What happened to you, young man?"

"What happened is that my axe fell to the bottom of the river and the axe is not mine but my friend's," said the friend.

"I will help you get it out, but you have to hold my walking stick, and you must not move it while I go to look for the axe," said the old man.

The old man went down to the bottom of the river to look for the axe.

"Is this your axe?" the old man asked the friend, showing him an axe of silver.

"No, that one is not mine," answered the friend.

The old man went back down into the river and this time brought out an axe of gold.

"Is this your axe?" he asked again.

"Yes, that one is my axe," answered the friend very excitedly.

But the old man realized that the friend was tricking him, and so he gave him not the axe of gold, but gave him his old axe. Thus, the friend returned home with no reward.

EL ESPÍRITU DEL AGUA

Este cuento enseña una lección sobre el respeto, la honradez y la codicia. Viene del libro Cuentos de San Pedro Soloma *recopilado por Ruperto Montejo Esteban.*

*E*n tiempos muy antiguos había un hombre que vivía muy tranquilo. Era un hombre muy respetuoso con todos los señores, los ancianos y las ancianas. Pero sucedió un día, que el hombre salió para ir a traer leña hacia una montaña que quedaba cerca de su casa. Como no tenía hacha, mandó a su esposa a que fuera a pedir prestado el hacha de su compadre.

Su compadre le prestó un hacha, pero este hombre tenía una gran debilidad: era muy perezoso. Así que amarró el hacha de su compadre con un lazo para llevarla arrastrada, sólo que no la amarraba bien, así que el hacha a cada paso se le zafaba.

Cuando el hombre llegó a la montaña empezó a buscar leña. En la orilla de un río había un gran árbol, entonces empezó a cortar. Al rato de estar cortando el árbol el hacha se le zafó y cayó al fondo del río. El pobre hombre no sabía qué hacer. Lo único que hacía era llorar y llorar. Estaba llorando cuando se le acercó un anciano, que era el Espíritu del Agua, que llegó a auxiliarlo.

«¿Qué te pasa muchacho?», preguntó el anciano.

«Señor, lo que pasa es que se me cayó el hacha al fondo del río y no es mía sino de mi compadre», respondió el hombre.

«Te voy a sacar el hacha», dijo el anciano, «pero con la condición de que no me vayas a mover el bastón porque si lo mueves, no voy a poder encontrarla».

«Gracias, señor».

«¿Es ésta tu hacha?», preguntó el anciano, mostrando un hacha de plata.

«No, ésa no es mía», respondió el hombre.

El anciano volvió a meterse en el agua sacando esta vez un hacha de oro.

«Ésta sí es tu hacha», dijo el anciano al hombre, mostrándole el hacha de oro.

«No, ésa no es mía».

Por tercera vez, el anciano se metió dentro del agua, sacando esta vez el hacha del hombre. «¿Es ésta tu hacha?»

«Sí, ésta es mía», gritó el hombre, brincando de alegría y quedando muy agradecido con el anciano.

«Por ser una persona joven y por ser muy sincero y honrado te puedes llevar estas dos hachas como un regalo para ti. Cuando llegues a tu casa guárdalas en un cofre, ya que son un tesoro que te ayudarán en tu vida de aquí en adelante», le dijo el anciano al hombre.

«Gracias señor», contestó el hombre.

Cuando llegó a su casa le dijo a su mujer que fuera a devolver el hacha que le había tomado prestado a su compadre. Para mientras el hombre se quedó guardando las otras dos. Gracias a estas dos hachas, el hombre llegó a tener mucha fortuna y se convirtió en hombre rico. Cuando el compadre se dio cuenta de lo que había pasado, decidió ir también él a traer leña del mismo lugar a donde había ido el hombre, y también hizo todo igual a como lo había hecho él: jaló su hacha, pero el hacha no se zafaba.

Cuando llegó al lugar de la montaña, el compadre buscó un árbol a la orilla del río. Entonces se puso a cortar el árbol, pero como el hacha no se le zafaba decidió él mismo tirarla al río. El anciano volvió a llegar cerca de él y le dijo:

«¿Que te pasa, muchacho?»

«Lo que pasa es que se me fue mi hacha hacia el fondo del río y el hacha no es mía sino de mi compadre», dijo el compadre.

«Te ayudaré a sacarla, pero tienes que sostener mi bastón y no debes moverlo mientras yo voy a buscarla», dijo el anciano.

El anciano bajó al fondo del río a buscar el hacha.

«¿Es ésta tu hacha?», le preguntó el anciano, mostrándole una hacha de plata.

«No, ésa no es la mía», contestó el compadre.

El anciano volvió a bajar al río y sacó esta vez un hacha de oro.

«¿Es ésta tu hacha?», volvió a preguntarle.

«Sí, ésa es mi hacha», contestó el compadre muy emocionado.

Pero el anciano se dio cuenta de que el compadre estaba engañándolo, así que no le dio el hacha de oro sino que le dio la suya. El compadre regresó a su casa sin ningún premio.

THE SCREAMER OF THE NIGHT

This story originated in Nebaj, Quiché, in the Cuchumatanes Mountains of Guatemala. It was told by María Caley, from Chichicastenango, Quiché. She chose this story because it illustrates the need to respect nature even when it is not well understood. Stories such as "The Screamer of the Night," handicrafts, and uncommon celebrations have been passed down through generations of Ixil Maya living in Nebaj. Because Nebaj is in a very isolated area, the Ixils there have been able to preserve many very ancient cultural customs. Nebaj is one of only three Guatemalan villages that still retain much of the ancient Ixil culture.

A very adventurous young man named Anselmo, along with a group of friends, wanted to explore the countryside around Nebaj. They were not from that area, but had come from another place. Anselmo and his friends planned to go for a week, so they prepared for every type of inclemency. They set off on the trip excited and very happy. When they arrived at Nebaj, the closest town, they decided to spend the night there. Very soon a young man from Nebaj offered to accompany them on their trip; they gladly accepted his company. The next day they traveled deep into the mountains and at dusk looked for a place to camp. The third day they followed a path where they met country families from that area going up and down the trail, coming back from their fields with their harvests or going to work.

Nightfall came again and the boys looked for a place to spend the night. This time they camped at the summit of a hill with a very pretty view. Everyone got comfortable and chatted about the experiences of their first days. It was a dark, dark night, and by raising their eyes toward the heavens they could see a multitude of stars and hear the noise of the night birds and the coyotes. They were very happy. Tired, they went to bed and fell asleep. Anselmo, the one who was enjoying the trip the most, lay down but did not fall asleep right away like the others. He stayed awake for a long time looking at the sky and admiring the stars.

Suddenly he heard a scream that came from far away. He thought, "Who could be in this isolated place?" and again he heard the cry. Afterward, only the silence remained. Without so much as even thinking, he fell asleep. The next day the boys started their trip again. Anselmo refused to talk with the others about what he had heard the night before. He eagerly started the day, walking and walking until he was tired.

This time the boys camped in the mountains on the bank of a stream. As always, after eating dinner they all sat around the campfire and talked about their experiences and the beauty of the place. This time Anselmo and two others stayed awake for a while longer than the others, when suddenly they heard the scream, only this time it was a little stronger than it had been the night before. Anselmo knew because he had heard it before. The three stayed silent a few minutes, when again they heard the cry. Afterward everything remained in silence. They talked about it for a moment and then they slept.

The next morning the group started their hike again, only this time Anselmo's two friends mentioned the screaming to the rest of the group. Anselmo and the man from Nebaj did not join in the conversation; they only listened. They continued walking until nightfall and camped again in the mountains. They began to settle themselves in and had not even finished when suddenly everyone heard the scream. This time they all kept quiet. Again they heard the scream. One of the boys rushed to answer the scream, and instantly they heard the scream again. Each time it was stronger. It seemed to be getting closer to them. Then the man from Nebaj, very worried, said to Anselmo that every place has a special master and it was not good that he had been answered.

"This scream," he said, "comes from the master of the night. That is what we call him. When we hear it we never respond to him because it angers him and he comes closer. That is why we were hearing the cry closer and closer."

Then the man from Nebaj continued, "We cannot stop him from coming closer. The only thing we can do is pull our sheets over our heads and wait." The cry sounded very close and each time closer, until it finally arrived about them. They only thing they felt was something poking and yanking at their feet, and then the silence returned. They did not sleep.

Dawn came, and they all talked about what had happened. When the Nebaj man suggested they go back to town, they did just that. On the way back they talked and decided that it was not good to challenge the mysteries of the night. That was how they learned that the scream came from the screamer of the night.

EL GRITÓN DE LA NOCHE

Este cuento tiene su orígen en Nebaj, Quiché, situado en la cordillera de los Cuchumatanes. Fue contado por María Caley, de Chichicastenango, Quiché. Ella escogió este cuento porque demuestra la necesidad de respetar a la naturaleza aunque a veces no sea bien entendida. Cuentos como éste, artesanía, y fiestas pocos comunes se han pasado de generación en generación de los maya ixil que viven en Nebaj. Por estar Nebaj en un área tan aislada, los ixil allá han podido preservar muchas costumbres culturales muy antiguas. Nebaj es uno de los tres únicos pueblos guatemaltecos que quedan con mucho de la antigua cultura ixil.

Anselmo, un joven muy aventurero, junto con un grupo de amigos, quiso explorar alrededor de Nebaj. Ellos no eran oriundos de esa área sino que llegaron de otro lugar. Anselmo y sus amigos planearon hacer este viaje por una semana, así fue que se prepararon para todo tipo de inclemencias. Muy contentos emprendieron el viaje. Llegaron a Nebaj, el pueblo más próximo y allí pasaron la noche. Muy pronto un oriundo de Nebaj se ofreció a acompañarlos en su viaje, lo cual ellos con gusto aceptaron. Prosiguieron al siguiente día hasta internarse en las montañas. Al anochecer buscaron un lugar para acampar. Al día siguiente prosiguieron en una vereda donde encontraron a familias campesinas de alrededor de este lugar que bajaban y subían, regresando de sus tierras con cosechas o yendo al trabajo.

De nuevo anocheció y buscaron un lugar para pasar la noche. Esta vez lo hicieron en la cima de un cerro con vista muy bonita. Todos se pusieron cómodos y antes de dormir charlaron sobre sus primeros días y sus experiencias. Era una noche oscura, oscura, y al alzar la vista al cielo, podían ver la multitud de estrellas y escuchar el ruido de aves nocturnas y los coyotes. Ellos estaban muy felices. Cansados, se acostaron y se dispusieron a dormir. Anselmo, él que más disfrutaba del viaje, se acostó pero no se durmió al instante como los otros del grupo. Él se quedó por largo tiempo con la vista al cielo, admirando las estrellas.

De repente escuchó un grito que provenía de lejos. Él pensó: «¿Quien puede ser en este aislado lugar?», y nuevamente se escuchó el grito y después quedó el silencio. Sin tanto pensar quedó dormido. Al día siguiente emprendieron de nuevo el viaje. Anselmo no quiso comentarle a los demás de lo que había escuchado la noche anterior, sino que con mucha energía empezó el día, caminando y caminando hasta cansarse.

Esta vez acamparon entre montañas a la orilla de un riachuelo. Como siempre, después de cenar se sentaron todos al lado de la fogata y comentaron sus experiencias y la belleza del lugar. Esta vez Anselmo y otros dos se quedaron despiertos por un rato más que los otros, cuando de repente escucharon el grito, solo que esta vez fue un poco más fuerte, para Anselmo que ya lo había escuchado antes. Los tres se quedaron unos minutos en silencio, cuando de nuevo escucharon el grito; y después todo quedó en silencio. Lo comentaron por un momento y entonces se durmieron.

Al siguiente día emprendieron de nuevo la caminata, solo que esta vez los dos se lo comentaron al resto del grupo. Anselmo y el oriundo no mediaron palabras, solo se limitaron a escuchar. Siguieron caminando hasta el anochecer, y volvieron a acampar entre las montañas. Se acomodaron y ni bien se habían acomodado cuando de repente escucharon el grito. Esta vez, todos se quedaron callados. De nuevo se escuchó el grito. Esta vez uno del grupo se apresuró a contestar el grito, y al instante volvió a escucharse el grito. Cada vez era más y más fuerte. Parecía estar acercándose. Entonces el oriundo muy preocupado le dijo a Anselmo como cada lugar tiene en particular un dueño y que no era bueno que se le haya respondido. «Este grito», dijo él, «proviene del dueño de la noche. Así le llamamos nosotros. Cuando nosotros lo escuchamos, nunca le respondemos porque él se enfada y se acerca más y más. Así fue como el grito se fue escuchando más y más cerca».

Entonces el oriundo dijo: «No podemos pararlo hasta acercarse; lo único que podemos hacer es embrocarnos y pasarnos las sabanas en la cabeza y esperar». El grito se escuchaba muy cerca y cada vez más cerca hasta que al fin llegó hacia ellos. Lo único que sintieron fue un jalón en los pies, y luego volvió el silencio. Ellos no durmieron. Amaneció y todos comentaron lo sucedido. El oriundo de esa área les sugirió regresar al pueblo, y así lo hicieron. En el camino de regreso, comentaban y decían que no es bueno retar los misterios de la noche. Así fue como aprendieron que el grito provenía del gritón de la noche.

PART 3

STORIES ABOUT PEOPLE

Family making corn tortillas

Cooking chicken soup

Making punch from flower petals

Market

Drying chiles

Buying soap made from cow fat and ashes

Women washing clothes at the public washbasins

Men and boys at new water well

Transporting goods

Common way of carrying bundles

Mother and daughters selling baskets by roadside in Guatemala highlands

Girls playing jump rope with a rolled-up, handwoven skirt

Catholic church in Antigua, Guatemala

Modern wood carvings of saints (*santos*)

Cemetery on Day of the Dead

Altar to Maximón, whom many believe to be a reincarnation of a Maya god

Cleansing the procession route with incense before main float

**Families making carpets (*alfombras*) for
Lenten procession**

**Main float carrying image of Jesus in
Lenten procession**

DON JACINTO

This story comes from Cuentos antiguos de animales y gente de San Miguel Acatán (Old Stories of Animals and People from San Miguel Acatán), *by José Juan. It talks about the importance of not being greedy.*

When don Jacinto felt like the hour of his death was getting close, he called his three sons and asked them to divide his possessions into three parts, because there were three of them. That day, the youngest son stayed there taking care of him, and in the early morning don Jacinto died.

After the funeral, the boy sat down beneath a tree because of the bad night that he had gone through. In a little while, he fell deeply asleep. Then his two brothers arrived and seeing that the young man was sleeping, they decided to divide the father's possessions between themselves.

When the youngest brother awoke, he realized that the house was empty. Very surprised, he went out in search of his brothers, who[m] he found in the town square. Upon asking them what had happened, the oldest brother replied:

"We divided the inheritance into three parts, just like our father recommended: sleep, the animals, and the furniture. Upon doing the division, we saw that you had chosen sleep, because you were deeply asleep. So that left us with the furniture and the animals."

The young man could not believe what he was hearing, until some people who were nearby heard the conversation and were going to protest because of the injustice. But the young man said:

"It's all right. I accept the division, but let it be clear that none of us will be able to enjoy the part of the inheritance that belongs to the others."

The two brothers agreed that it would be done like that and each one left for his house.

During the night, the young man approached his oldest brother's house, which was dark and silent, and began to make a terrible uproar. Afterwards, he went to the other brother's house and did the same. For a week, he took it upon himself to come and make an uproar at midnight.

Tired of the bad nights that [they] had been passing, the two brothers decided to accuse him before the judge. The judge ordered that the young man be called, and he asked him what compelled him to not let his brothers sleep. Then the young man responded:

"When my brothers decided to divide the inheritance that our father left us, we agreed that none would be able to enjoy the part that belonged to the others. Sleep belonged to me, and so it is just that I try to prevent them from enjoying it."

On hearing that, there was nothing else the brothers could do but share the inheritance with the youngest, so that way they would have the right to sleep peacefully.

Such is the story of don Jacinto and his three sons.

DON JACINTO

Este cuento viene del libro Cuentos antiguos de animales y gente de San Miguel Acatán, *por José Juan. Habla de la importancia de no ser codicioso.*

*C*uando don Jacinto sintió que se le acercaba la hora de su muerte, llamó a sus tres hijos y les pidió que se repartieran sus bienes en tres partes, porque eran tres. Ese día, el hijo menor se quedó cuidándolo, y en la madrugada don Jacinto murió.

Después del funeral, el muchacho se sentó debajo de un árbol por la mala noche que había pasado. Al poco rato se quedó profundamente dormido. En eso llegaron sus dos hermanosy al ver que el joven dormía, decidieron repartir entre ellos dos los bienes del padre.

Cuando el hermano menor despertó, se encontró con que la casa estaba vacía. Muy sorprendido salió en busca de sus hermanos, a quienes encontró en la plaza del pueblo. Al preguntarles qué había pasado, el hermano mayor le respondió:

«Repartimos la herencia en tres partes, tal como recomendó nuestro padre: el sueño, los animales y los muebles. Al hacer el reparto vimos que tú habías escogido el sueño, pues estabas profundamente dormido. Así que nosotros nos quedamos con los muebles y los animales».

El joven no podía creer lo que estaba oyendo, hasta que algunas personas que estaban cerca oyeron la conversación e iban a protestar por la injusticia. Pero de pronto el joven dijo:

«Está bien, acepto el reparto, pero que quede claro que ninguno de nosotros podrá disfrutar la parte de la herencia que le tocó a los otros».

Los dos hermanos estuvieron de acuerdo en que se hiciera así y cada uno se fue para su casa.

Por la noche, el joven se acercó a la casa de su hermano mayor, que estaba oscura y silenciosa, y comenzó a hacer un escándalo terrible. Luego fue a hacer lo mismo a la casa del otro hermano. Y durante una semana se encargó de llegar a hacer escándalo a la media noche.

Cansados por las malas noches que estaban pasando, los dos hermanos decidieron acusarlo ante el juez. El juez mandó llamar al joven y le preguntó por qué se empeñaba en no dejar dormir a sus hermanos. Entonces el joven respondió:

«Cuando mis hermanos decidieron repartir la herencia que nos dejó nuestro padre, acordamos que ninguno podía disfrutar de la parte que le correspondía a los otros. A mi me tocó el sueño y justo es entonces que trate de impedir que ellos lo disfruten».

Al oír aquello, a los hermanos no les quedó mas remedio que compartir la herencia con el menor, para así tener derecho a dormir tranquilos.

Así es el cuento de don Jacinto y sus tres hijos.

THE SONG OF THE OWL AND THE HOWL OF THE COYOTE

This story points out the value of trusting in nature and being aware of unusual occurrences that may be signs directed to a person for his or her benefit. It was told by Victorino Canek, who has lived in Uaxactún, Petén, all his life. Victorino considers this story special because of the respect the tale shows for predictions and nature.

In the northern part of the Department of Petén, Guatemala, the only part of the country with incredible plants, animals, and natural beauty, is found Uaxactún. This town is where don Tranquilino, affectionately called Lino, was born. In Uaxactún he was taught by his family to be well mannered in the community. He had much experience and he respected the people's beliefs and the predictions that come from nature and animals. It was in this way that don Tranquilino told his story.

He lived in Uaxactún with his family—his wife and children—in a simple house with a roof of palm leaves and walls of bamboo that allowed ventilation, because it was a tropical area.

This is where don Tranquilino's story started. It was very early one day, about four in the morning, when the song of a bird arose from the roof of his little house. Don Tranquilino could not see the bird because it was not yet light and at that time there was no electricity, and no lanterns in the village. The villagers always lit their homes at night with campfires with firewood they gathered in the country. That morning don Tranquilino could not see what kind of bird was singing.

A few days passed and again the song of the bird arose from the same place. The only difference was that this time it was during the night. Again it was too dark to see what bird it had been. Don Tranquilino and his family talked it over and decided that they normally heard the birds, but this one was very special because it sang at a special hour. What distinguished that wooded area was that dusk, nightfall, and dawn were very special times for listening to nature in its totality.

Since childhood don Tranquilino had learned from his ancestors about nature. That is how he had an idea of what bird the song had come from, but he did not say anything to his children because he wanted to teach them how to decipher each thing in a natural way. He was also waiting for the third song of the bird.

Days and days went by, and suddenly one dawn the song of the bird was heard; this time don Tranquilino knew what it meant. But he wanted to guard the secret until the right time. The days and months went by, and the family continued their normal life in Uaxactún, except for don Tranquilino. He was aware that very soon something was going to change in his life and in that of his entire family. Of course he said that he was not afraid.

Don Tranquilino knew that to be sure of this prediction, there would have to be someone else to confirm it. The months went by and the year ended. Don Tranquilino was a good farmer and cultivated the earth with much care and respected nature. So it was that one day he was working in the fields when suddenly he turned to see a coyote gazing at him from some distance and walking slowly by. As soon as the coyote entered the forest he howled, and so Don Tranquilino now knew that the prediction was for good fortune.

Don Tranquilino understood that it would be better for his family to leave their hometown and look for another town in Guatemala so they could stay together. At dusk he returned to his house and told his family of the prediction. Everyone accepted it respectfully; they knew that the predictions that come from nature could be for good or for bad.

This time something touched don Tranquilino to improve his life and that of his family, since sometimes beings that inhabit the earth foretell the separation of a family member or a member of the community. So it was that don Tranquilino emigrated from Uaxactún to south-central Guatemala and lived for many years, until his death. He left his family established in that same place. The children continued the tradition of don Tranquilino, affectionately called don Lino, of being very mindful of the song of the owl and the howl of the coyote. No matter where they are found, nature's predictions should always be listened to.

EL CANTO DEL TECOLOTE Y
EL AULLIDO DEL COYOTE

Este cuento indica el valor de confiar en la naturaleza y dar cuenta de los hechos raros ya que estos pueden ser señales dirigidas a una persona para que se beneficie. Fue contado por Victorino Canek, de Uaxactún, Petén. Victorino considera especial este cuento por el respeto que el cuento da a las predicciones y a la naturaleza.

*E*n el departamento del Petén, Guatemala, el único que goza de flora, fauna y naturaleza increíbles, se encuentra Uaxactún situado al norte del Petén. En este pueblo fue donde nació don Tranquilino, a quien cariñosamente le decían Lino. Y como fue bien educado por su familia en la comunidad, tenía mucha experiencia y respetaba las creencias y predicciones que a través de la naturaleza y animales son predichos. Fue así como don Tranquilino contaba su historia.

Él vivía en este pueblo mencionado con su familia, esposa e hijos en una casa rústica, con techo de hojas de palma y paredes de bambú construidas de manera que pueda haber ventilación por ser un área tropical.

Fue aquí donde se originó la historia de don Tranquilino. Cuenta él que un día muy de madrugada, a eso de las cuatro de la mañana, cuando en el techo de su ranchito situado al frente del otro surgió el canto de un pájaro. Don Tranquilino no lo podía ver por falta de luz y como en este pueblo en ese tiempo no existía la energía eléctrica o linternas. Ellos que vivían allí siempre se alumbraban en las noches con fogatas con leña que recogían en los campos. Esa madrugada don Tranquilino no pudo ver que pájaro era.

Pasaron unos días, y de nuevo el canto del pájaro surgió del mismo lugar. Lo único diferente fue que esta vez fue por la noche. De igual forma él no pudo ver que pájaro había sido. Con su familia comentaban y decían que normalmente escuchaban a los pájaros, pero éste era muy especial porque cantaba a una hora especial. Por lo que se distinguía muy bien entre esa área boscosa donde el atardecer, anochecer y amanecer son especiales escuchando a la naturaleza en su totalidad.

Don Tranquilino era nativo de esa región y a través de sus antepasados había aprendido mucho sobre la naturaleza desde su niñez. Así es que él más o menos ya sabía de qué pájaro provenía el canto, pero no dijo nada a sus hijos porque solo quería educar a sus

---

hijos cómo descifrar cada cosa de manera natural, también él esperaba el tercer canto del pájaro.

Pasaron días y días y de repente una madrugada el canto del pájaro se escuchó. Esta vez don Tranquilino supo de qué se trataba. Pero quiso guardar el secreto hasta el final. Pasaron los días y los meses, y la familia siguió con su vida normal en Uaxactún, menos don Tranquilino. Él estaba consciente que muy pronto algo iba a cambiar en su vida y en la de toda su familia. Por supuesto él decía que no tenía nada de temor.

Él sabía que para estar seguro de esta predicción tendría que haber alguien más que se lo confirmara. Pasaron los meses y terminó el año, y don Tranquilino era un buen campesino, cultivaba la tierra con mucho cuidado y respetaba la naturaleza. Fue así como un día él trabajaba en el campo cuando de repente volteó a ver a una cierta distancia con la vista hacia él, y con pasos lentos iba pasando un coyote. Tan pronto como se internó al bosque aulló, y entonces don Tranquilino ahora sabía que la predicción estaba dicha.

Que para él y su familia era mejor salir de su pueblo natal y buscar otro pueblo en el país para mantener unida a su familia. Al atardecer regresó a su casa, y después de cenar les comunicó la predicción a su familia. Todos con mucho respeto lo aceptaron ya que a veces las predicciones que habitan en la naturaleza pueden ser para bien o para mal.

Esta vez a don Tranquilino le tocó algo para mejorar su vida con su familia ya que a veces los seres que habitan la tierra predicen la separación de algún familiar o miembro de la comunidad. Fue así como don Tranquilino desde Uaxactún emigró al centro sur de Guatemala y vivió muchos años hasta que dejó de existir. Dejó establecida a su familia en el mismo lugar. Los hijos siguieron la tradición de don Tranquilino, cariñosamente llamado don Lino, de estar muy atentos al canto del tecolote y al aullido del coyote. No importando el lugar donde se encuentren, las predicciones siempre serán las mismas a través de la naturaleza.

THE MOON

Each cultural group has its own beliefs and stories of its ancestors that hold sway in the present time. This story illustrates continuing beliefs about how natural phenomena affect or provide predictions related to people. In this example, Ik' *(pronounced "eek"), the Moon, predicts future events and influences those bathed in its light. This story was told by Felipa b'ix, of Sololá, Guatemala. She wanted to share this story because it demonstrates that many of her ancestors' beliefs were based on facts.*

*C*iriaca was born and raised in Sololá with her extended family of eight brothers and sisters, her parents, and the families of her mother and father. They all lived in the Pa'aj' area of Sololá. They lived on their land, where they grew vegetables and corn for their family to eat and also to sell at the market. So it was that the mother and grandmother of Cariaca educated the girl in the Mayan beliefs. Ciriaca grew and listened to her father and her mother talk around the start of winter. "Look at *Ik'* the moon! It is in the south seeing the ocean. That means we will have a winter with much rain. If *Ik'* the moon were in the north, that would mean we would have a winter with little rain." This is when *Ik'* the moon is in its first quarter.

Ciriaca grew older and fell in love with a young man in her community, and after some time he asked her to marry him. In a marriage engagement, the family of the groom brings presents to the family of the bride. The parents and witnesses of the bride establish the date of the wedding, which is a year or a year and a half from the start of the engagement. The engagement lasts long enough for the bride to prepare herself for the wedding, to weave clothing to wear with her future husband, and also to make presents that she will give to her mother-in-law and father-in-law.

When the time came, Ciriaca married. *Ik'* the moon forms part of a woman. Ciriaca became pregnant and, as she grew up in the Mayan culture, her grandmother and mother had told her how *Ik'* the moon would be one of her best confidants. Through *Ik'* the moon, she knew whether she was going to have a boy or girl. If the birth was during a full moon or close to a full moon, that would mean that it would be a boy. If the birth was during a new moon, the child would be a girl. Her grandmother also had said that if *Ik'* the moon was in eclipse, Ciriaca should not go out to the patio without covering her head with a cloth and a piece of red fabric so that her baby would not be affected in the womb.

Ciriaca was a woman respectful of her beliefs. She did everything her grandmother and mother had told her. She had four boys, every one born during the full moon, and two girls born, during the new moon. In the same way, Ciriaca learned how to plant and harvest the fruits and vegetables during different phases of the moon. Ciriaca continued living in the same Pa'aj' with her family in Sololá, Guatemala.

LA LUNA

Cada grupo cultural tiene sus propias creencias e historias de los antepasados, los cuales todavía en la actualidad se creen. Este cuento ilustra creencias actuales de cómo los fenómenos naturales afectan o proporcionan las predicciones relacionadas con la gente. En este ejemplo, Ik', la luna, predice los acontecimientos futuros e influencia a aquéllos que son bañados en su luz. Felipa b'ix, de Sololá, Guatemala, relató este cuento. Ella quería compartirlo porque el cuento manifiesta como tantos de las creencias de sus antepasados son fundadas en hechos.

Ciriaca nació y creció en Sololá al lado de su extensa familia de ocho hermanos, sus padres y parientes de su padre y madre. Todos vivían en el cantón Pa'aj' de Sololá. Ellos vivían en sus tierras donde sembraban verduras y maíz para el consumo de su familia y para vender en el mercado. Así fue como la madre y la abuela de Ciriaca la educaron en las creencias mayas. Ciriaca creció y escuchaba a su padre y su madre decir cuando empezaba el invierno. «Mira *Ik'* la luna. Está puesta al sur viendo el océano. Eso quiere decir que tendremos un invierno con mucha lluvia. O si *Ik'* la luna está puesta para el norte, eso quiere decir que tendremos un invierno con poca lluvia». Esto es cuando *Ik'* la luna esta en el cuarto creciente.

Ciriaca creció y se enamoró de un joven de su comunidad, y luego la entraron a pedir o lo que se le llama el compromiso de casamiento, lo cual consiste en que la familia del novio les lleva presentes a la familia de la novia. Los padres y testigos de la novia son los que establecen la fecha del matrimonio, lo cual es de un año o un año y medio, lo cual es suficiente para que la novia se prepare: para tejer su ropa para llevar con su futuro esposo y también elaborar regalos que le dará a su suegra y suegro.

Llegó el tiempo y Ciriaca se casó. Nuevamente *Ik'* la luna forma parte en la mujer. Ciriaca quedó embarazada y, como ella creció en la cultura maya, la abuela y la madre ya le habían dicho como *Ik'* la luna sería una de sus mejores confidentes; ella sabría si iba a tener niña o niño a través de *Ik'* la luna. Si el parto era en luna llena o cerca, eso quería decir que sería varón; si el parto fuera en luna nueva, seria niña. La abuela también le había dicho que si *Ik'* la luna estaba en eclipse que no saliera al patio sin cubrirse la cabeza con una tela y un pedazo de tela roja para que su hijo no fuera afectado en el vientre.

Ciriaca, como una mujer respetuosa de sus creencias, hizo todo lo que su abuela y madre le indicaban, procreó cuatro hijos, cada uno nacido en luna llena, y dos niñas nacidas en luna nueva. De igual manera, Ciriaca aprendió como sembrar y cosechar las frutas y verduras en las diferentes etapas de la luna. Ciriaca siguió viviendo en el mismo cantón Pa'aj, al lado de su familia en Sololá, Guatemala.

THE LYING KING

This story teaches that hard work, dedication, and honesty are worth a lot. It is from Cuentos antiguos de animales y gente de San Miguel Acatán (Old Stories of Animals and People from San Miguel Acatán), *by José Juan.*

*O*nce upon a time there was a king. He was very powerful and had a palace with many rooms and many servants. He also had a beautiful daughter and the two lived very happily in the great palace. In front of the palace was a cypress tree so big that not even seven men could put their arms around it. The curious thing was that the cypress was so hard that no one had been able to cut it down. One day the king ordered that it be told throughout his kingdom that he would give his daughter's hand to the man who was able to cut down the cypress, but there was no one who could cut it. A little shepherd who also heard the news decided to go to cut down the cypress. He readied his axe and his food to eat during the trip and headed toward the palace. On the way he encountered a great snake, who said to him:

"I am very hungry, little shepherd. Will you not give me a little food?"

"Why not?" said the shepherd, and he shared his food with the snake. The snake became very contented and said:

"If you need me you can call. I will come from wherever I am. You only have to say 'Snake, help me,' and I will go wherever you are."

"All right," said the shepherd to the snake.

The happy shepherd continued walking. He had gone very far when he encountered a great anthill. One of the ants said to him:

"We have not eaten in days and we are very hungry. Do you not have a little food that you can give us?"

When the shepherd heard this he took out the little food he had left, divided it in half, and gave it to the ants. The ants became very happy and said to him:

"If one day you need us, all you have to do is say 'Ants, help me,' and we will go at once."

The shepherd continued his walk. When a hawk who also was hungry approached him, he begged for a little bit of food. The shepherd, a good person, took out the little bread that he still had and gave it to the hawk. The hawk was very glad and said to the shepherd:

"If some day you need me, all you have to do is say 'Hawk, help me,' and immediately I will be at your side."

Finally the little shepherd walked a bit more and arrived at the king's palace and said to the king that he was going to cut down the cypress so that he could marry the king's daughter. But when the king's daughter met the little shepherd she did not grow fond of him. When the shepherd was cutting down the cypress, and already had made one pass around cutting it, the king's daughter appeared and began to spit on the cuttings.

This seemed very strange to the shepherd. When he finished the first pass around the tree, the shepherd realized that where he had cut, the tree had started to close. Then he realized that the saliva of the king's daughter was what had closed up the tree. He began to think what he might do, when he remembered the snake to whom he had given food and quickly called her. The snake came and scared the king's daughter, who began to run from fright and could not do anything any longer. This way the little shepherd could calmly chop the cypress.

When he had finished everything, the shepherd went to tell the king that he had finally cut it all, and that now he could marry the king's daughter. But because the king was not pleased that the shepherd should marry his daughter, he said to him:

"No, shepherd, you have not yet won my daughter's hand. If you want to marry her you have to separate two hundred *quintales* (about 10,000 pounds) of beans and rice in a day and a half."

The shepherd accepted, thinking "How am I going to do that?" when he remembered the ants to whom he had given food. He called them to help him; they came and commenced to help him. In a few hours they finished the work. The next day, the shepherd arrived very happily at the king's to tell him that he had already finished the work. Upon seeing the job, the king's jaw dropped, that he really had separated two hundred *quintales* of beans and rice. The king immediately thought of another job, and since he was such a liar he said to the shepherd:

"You still have not won my daughter's hand. You must do another job to have the right to marry my daughter."

"Here are twelve roosters. If you are able to take care of them for one month without losing any, you will be able to marry my daughter," said the king to the shepherd.

The big-hearted shepherd accepted, and he went to take care of the roosters. After a week, the king's maid, changed into other clothes, tested him. She arrived and said to him:

"Will you not sell me one of the roosters, little shepherd?"

"I will sell you a rooster if you hug and kiss me," the shepherd said to her.

The maid answered yes, and she hugged and kissed him. Afterwards, the shepherd gave her the rooster and she returned to the palace very pleased. They had gone quite far when the shepherd remembered the hawk to whom he had given food, he called him and told him to go to take the rooster from that woman. When the hawk learned that, he went quickly to bring the rooster and later was able to give it back to the shepherd. The maid became very sad because she could not do anything. Two weeks after the maid had come, the king's daughter herself went. She dressed as a villager and went to where the roosters were and said to the shepherd:

"Will you not sell me a few of your roosters?"

The shepherd then recognized her as the king's daughter and said to her:

"Yes, I will sell you a rooster, miss villager, but with one condition: that you hug me and kiss me."

When the king's daughter heard that, she began to hug him and kiss him, and they spent a long time like that. When they finished, she left very happily with the rooster, because she had manipulated the shepherd. She was going very hurriedly along the way. She had gone very far when the shepherd began to call the hawk once again. When the hawk arrived, the shepherd told him everything. When he learned this, the hawk left to snatch away the rooster from the king's daughter. Along the way he was able to grab it from her, and he went to give it to the shepherd.

When they took the rooster from the king's daughter, she became very sad and said like this: "I will have to marry that man, since I cannot even take a rooster from him." She was feeling very sad when she arrived at her father's house. When the day arrived, the shepherd was very pleased and he went to the king to leave the roosters. Not even one was missing; he returned them all to the king. The king still did not say anything, he did not see anything else that he could do, and he said to the shepherd:

"You, shepherd, still you have not failed. You did everything I told you. Now you are going to marry my daughter, already she is yours. The servants are going to bring her on horseback." The shepherd was very pleased and answered:

"Very well," and hugged the girl. They started to kiss; they were very happy.

That is how the shepherd got a wife and that is also how the lying king's daughter left. That's the end of this story.

EL REY MENTIROSO

Este cuento nos enseña que el trabajo, la dedicación y la honradez valen mucho. Es del libro Cuentos antiguos de animales y gente de San Miguel Acatán *por José Juan.*

*U*na vez había un rey. Era muy poderoso y tenía un palacio con muchos salones y muchos criados. Tenía también una hermosa hija y los dos vivían muy felices en el gran palacio. Al frente del palacio había un ciprés tan grande, que ni siete hombres juntos podían abrazarlo. Lo curioso era que el ciprés era tan duro, que nadie había logrado cortarlo. Un día el rey mandó decir por todo su reino, que daría la mano de su hija al hombre que lograra cortar el ciprés, pero no había quien lo cortara. Un pastorcillo que también oyó la noticia decidió ir a cortar el ciprés. Alistó su hacha y su comida, para comer en el camino y se dirigió hacia el palacio. En el camino encontró a una gran serpiente que le dijo:

«Tengo mucha hambre, pastorcillo. ¿No me das un poco de comida?»

«¿Por qué no?», dijo el pastor, y compartió su comida con la serpiente. La serpiente se puso muy contenta y dijo:

«Si me necesitas me puedes llamar. Vendré de dondequiera me encuentre. Solo tienes que decir: "Serpiente, ayúdame", y yo iré donde estés».

«Está bien», le dijo el pastor a la serpiente.

El pastor muy feliz siguió caminando. Había ido muy lejos cuando encontró un gran hormiguero. Una de las hormigas le dijo:

«Hace días que no comemos y tenemos mucha hambre. ¿No tienes un poco de comida que nos regales?»

Cuando el pastor escuchó esto sacó la poca comida que le quedaba, la partió a la mitad y se la dio a las hormigas. Las hormigas se pusieron contentas y le dijeron:

«Si algún día nos necesitas, solo tienes que decir: "Hormigas, ayúdenme", y nosotros iremos en seguida».

El pastor siguió su camino. Cuando se le acercó un gavilán que también tenía hambre, le pidió un poquito de comida. El pastor de buena gente, sacó el poquito de pan que le quedaba y se lo dio al gavilán. Estaba muy contento el gavilán y le dijo al pastor:

«Si algún día me necesitas, solo tienes que decir "Gavilán, ayúdame", e inmediatamente estaré a tu lado».

Al fin el pastorcillo caminó otro rato y llegó al palacio del rey y le dijo al rey que él iba a cortar el ciprés para casarse con su hija. Pero cuando la hija del rey conoció al pastorcillo no se encariñó de él. Cuando el pastor cortaba el ciprés, y ya le había dado una vuelta cortándolo, se le apareció la hija del rey y empezó a escupir sobre los cortes.

Esto le pareció muy extraño al pastor. Cuando terminó la primera vuelta, el pastor se dio cuenta que donde había cortado se había vuelto a cerrar. Entonces se dio cuenta de que la saliva de la hija del rey fue la que cerró el corte del árbol. Se puso a pensar qué podía hacer, cuando se acordó de la serpiente que le había dado de comer y de pronto la llamó. La serpiente vino y asustó a la hija del rey, que se echó a correr del susto y ya no pudo hacer nada. Así el pastorcillo pudo botar tranquilamente el ciprés. Cuando había terminado todo el pastor fue a decirle al rey que ya lo había cortado todo y que ya podía casarse con su hija. Pero como el rey no le gustó que el pastor se casara con su hija, le dijo:

«No, pastor, todavía no has ganado la mano de mi hija. Si quieres casarte con mi hija debes separar doscientos quintales de fríjol y arroz en un día y medio».

El pastor aceptó, pensando: «¿Cómo lo voy a hacer?», cuando se acordó de las hormigas que les había dado de comer. Las llamó para que lo ayudaran, vinieron y comenzaron a ayudarlo. En pocas horas terminaron el trabajo. Al día siguiente el pastor llegó muy contento con el rey a contarle que ya había terminado la tarea. El rey al ver el trabajo se quedó con la boca abierta, que en verdad había separado los doscientos quintales de fríjol y arroz. El rey inmediatamente pensó en otro trabajo y como era muy mentiroso le dijo al pastor:

«Todavía no te has ganado la mano de mi hija. Te falta otro trabajo para que así tengas derecho de casarte con mi hija».

«Aquí tienes doce gallos. Si logras cuidarlos durante un mes sin que se te pierda ninguno, podrás casarte con mi hija», le dijo el rey al pastor.

El pastor con dos corazones aceptó, y se fue a cuidar a los gallos. A la semana lo probó la sirvienta del rey, cambiada de otro traje. Llegó y le dijo:

«¿No me vendes unos gallos, pastorcillo?»

«Te vendo un gallo si me abrazas y me besas», le dijo el pastor.

La sirvienta le contestó que sí, lo abrazó y lo besó. Después de todo el pastor le dio el gallo y ella regresó muy contenta al palacio. Ya se había ido algo lejos cuando el pastor se acordó del gavilán a quien le había dado de comer, lo llamó y le dijo que le fuera a quitar el gallo a esa mujer. Cuando el gavilán lo supo, fue rápido a traer al gallo y luego llegó a entregárselo. La sirvienta se puso muy triste porque no pudo hacer nada. A las dos semanas de haber venido la sirvienta fue la hija misma del rey. Se vistió de aldeana y se fue hasta donde estaban los gallos y le dijo al pastor:

«¿No me vendes uno de tus gallos?»

El pastor luego la reconoció como la hija del rey, y le dijo:

«Sí, te vendo un gallo, señorita aldeana, pero con una condición, que me abraces y me beses».

Cuando oyó la hija del rey eso, empezaron a abrazarse y besarse; duraron mucho así. Cuando terminaron, se fue ella muy contenta con el gallo, porque había manipulado al pastor. Iba muy aprisa por el camino. Se había ido muy lejos cuando el pastor empezó a llamar al gavilán otra vez. Cuando llegó, le contó todo. Al saber esto el gavilán se fue a arrancarle el gallo a la hija del rey. Por el camino llegó a arrancárselo, y fue a dárselo al pastor.

Cuando le quitaron el gallo a la hija del rey, se puso muy triste, y dijo así:

«Me tendré que casar con ese hombre, ya que no puedo quitarle ni un gallo», dijo la hija del rey. Estaba sintiéndose muy triste cuando llegó a la casa de su padre. Cuando llegó el día, el pastor estaba muy contento y se fue al rey a dejar los gallos. No faltaba ni uno, los devolvió completos al rey. El rey ya no dijo nada, ya no más veía, y le dijo al pastor:

«Tú, pastor, ya estuvo que no fallaste. Hiciste todo lo que te dije. Ahora te vas a casar con mi hija, ya es tuya. Los mozos van a ir a dejarla a caballo». El pastor estaba muy contento y contestó:

«Está bien», y abrazó a la muchacha. Empezaron a besarse; estaban muy felices.

Así fue como consiguió esposa el pastor y así también fue como se marchó la hija del rey mentiroso. Se acabó este cuento.

PART 4

ENCOUNTERING THE SUPERNATURAL

THE WEEPING WOMAN

Stories by this name are very popular in many parts of the world where Spanish is spoken, and many variations of it exist. This Mayan version, told by Lidia López of San Antonio Aguas Calientes, Sacatepequez, Guatemala, incorporates the characteristics of the locale in which it is told and has a story line different from most other versions.

In east-central Guatemala there is a pretty town situated in a little valley surrounded by mountainous volcanoes. The little town is called San Antonio Aguas Calientes, so named for having hot water springs beneath the town. In that town lived a woman named Toribia, and she had one son. There are eleven washbasins in the town, each with its own name, used by the community to wash clothes. The largest is situated in front of the Catholic church and next to the town hall. This washbasin is carved. It was at that washbasin, called *pila de la plazuela* (plaza washbasin), that Toribia always washed her clothes very early in the morning. One day she took her son with her, and she washed and washed, not noticing where her son was. When she noticed he was not with her, she looked and looked for him around the washbasin, but she did not find him. Dawn came, and she still had not found her son, so she went back to her house crying because of her son's disappearance. She cried day and night. The days went by and she went back to the washbasin to wash, crying for her son. The years went by, Toribia got old and died, and in the town she was given the nickname *la Llorona* (the weeping woman).

It is to these washbasins that all of the women go daily to wash their clothes, very early in the morning as a daily chore. Washing was one of the first things they did then. Eulalia was one of the many women who went to wash at the *pila de la plazuela*. One morning very early, she went to wash, at about two in the morning. What a big surprise it was for her to see that there was already someone washing. Eulalia, as she usually did, started to wash about three basins away from the other person. It was the custom when other women were there to strike up a conversation with them. Eulalia was surprised that this woman did not raise her face, but kept it bent over. Eulalia did not place any great importance on it. After a little while, the other woman finished washing and left.

Two days later Eulalia went back to the washbasin as usual, again at the same hour, and again there was another person washing. This time Eulalia stationed herself two washbasins away from the woman and started to wash. But Eulalia noticed something strange about the basket of the other person: Every time she put the basket in the basin it gave off an extraordinary light. Eulalia continued washing, and the woman who was there before her finished and left.

Eulalia thought that the next time she had to wash she would go half an hour earlier and that way she would be the first to arrive at the washbasins. And that was what she did. The next day when she arrived she was surprised to see the other woman was already washing. This time Eulalia placed herself just one washbasin away from the other woman, and she tried to start a conversation with her. The other woman answered Eulalia's questions with only "yes" or "no." Again Eulalia noticed how the other woman's basket shone, and her curiosity was so great that she planned that she would return the next morning an hour earlier.

And that was what she did. To her surprise, again the woman was already washing. This time Eulalia placed herself right next to the woman and began to wash and wash. When Eulalia finished, she took leave of the woman.

But Eulalia had taken the other woman's basket, and the woman followed Eulalia trying to get back her basket. At dawn Eulalia heard someone crying. She thought it was one of her family, but the following night the voice cried and said, "Eulalia, give me my basket, please."

Two days later Eulalia returned to wash at the same time as always, but when she arrived she was surprised because the other woman was not at the laundry. That night she again heard the woman crying, saying that she was following Eulalia and begging for her basket. Eulalia decided to go out and see who it was, but when she went out no one was there.

Finally, Eulalia told a friend what was happening to her. Her friend knew of that person and said that it was the spirit of *la Llorona*. She told Eulalia the story of this poor woman and how she would not leave Eulalia in peace if Eulalia did not return the basket, because with the basket *la Llorona* could return to wash at the washbasins. She believed that at the washbasins she would be close to her son who had disappeared so long ago.

So it was that Eulalia returned to the washbasins and decided to leave the basket exactly where *la Llorona* always washed, and Eulalia never again went to wash so early. So it is that *la Llorona* appears at all the washbasins of the town when people wash very late or very early in the morning. Sometimes she can be heard crying in the streets as she walks to the washbasins. That is why the legend is called *la Llorona*, the Weeping Woman.

LA LLORONA

Este cuento viejo es muy popular en muchas partes del mundo donde se habla el español, y existen muchas variaciones. Esta versión maya, contada por Lidia López de San Antonio Aguas Calientes, Sacatepéquez, Guatemala, incorpora las características del lugar en donde se cuenta y tiene un argumento diferente de la mayor parte de las otras versiones.

*E*n un lugar muy bonito situado al este-central de Guatemala, en un valle pequeño rodeado de montañas y volcanes, se encuentra un pueblo llamado San Antonio Aguas Calientes, así llamado por tener agua caliente debajo de la tierra. En este pueblo había una mujer llamada Toribia que tenía un hijo. Y en el pueblo existen once pilas que son usadas por la comunidad para lavar la ropa, y cada una de estas esta tiene un nombre. La mayor está situada enfrente de la iglesia católica y a un costado de la municipalidad. Esta pila tiene labrados. Fue en esta pila, llamada la pila de la plazuela, donde Toribia iba siempre a lavar la ropa muy de madrugada. Un día llevó consigo a su hijo, y ella lavando y lavando no se percató donde estaba su hijo. Al darse cuenta de que él no estaba con ella, ella lo buscó y lo buscó alrededor de la pila, y nunca lo encontró. Amaneció y ya no había encontrado a su hijo, y regresó a su casa llorando por la desaparición de su hijo. Lloró día y noche y nunca lo encontró. Pasaban los días, y ella regresaba a la pila a lavar, llorando por su hijo. Pasaron los años, ella envejeció y murió, y en el pueblo le quedó el sobrenombre de la Llorona.

En estas pilas todas las mujeres salen a lavar muy temprano como el quehacer cotidiano. Lavar era una de las primeras cosas que hacían. Entonces Eulalia era una de tantas que asistía a lavar a esta pila llamada la pila de la plazuela. Una mañana muy temprano ella fue a lavar, a eso de las dos de la mañana. La sorpresa grande fue para ella ver que ya había alguien lavando. Eulalia, como lo hacía normalmente, empezó a lavar como a tres lavaderos de distancia de la otra persona. Como de costumbre cuando hay otras mujeres, se entablan conversaciones entre sí. Eulalia se sorprendió que esta mujer no levantaba la cara, siempre estaba agachada, pero no le puso mayor importancia. Al poco tiempo esta persona terminó de lavar y se fue.

Dos días después, Eulalia volvió a regresar a la pila como de costumbre a lavar, a la misma hora nuevamente, y había una persona lavando. Esta vez Eulalia se colocó a dos lavaderos separados de la mujer y empezó a lavar. Pero Eulalia notó algo extraño en el guacal de la otra persona, que cada vez que metía su guacal en la pileta, tenía un brillo extraordinario. Así Eulalia siguió lavando nuevamente, y la mujer que estaba antes terminó y se fue.

Eulalia pensó que la siguiente vez que tuviera que lavar se iría media hora antes, y así ella sería la primera en llegar al lavadero. Y así fue como lo hizo. Al siguiente día llegó y se sorprendió tanto porque la otra mujer ya estaba lavando. Esta vez ella se colocó a sólo un lavadero de distancia y trató de establecer conversación con la otra mujer. La otra mujer le contestaba a las preguntas de Eulalia solamente con un «sí» o «no». Nuevamente Eulalia notó como brillaba el guacal de la otra mujer, y su curiosidad era tan grande que planeó que regresaría al otro día una hora más temprano de lo acostumbrado. Y así fue como lo hizo. Pero su sorpresa era que la mujer ya estaba lavando. Esta vez Eulalia se colocó a la par de esta persona y empezó a lavar y lavar. Y cuando terminó, Eulalia se despidió de la mujer.

Pero Eulalia se fue con el guacal de la mujer, en dirección a su casa, y la mujer siguió a Eulalia tratando de recuperar su guacal. Al amanecer Eulalia escuchó que alguien lloraba. Ella pensó que era alguno de su familia, pero la siguiente noche lloraba y decía: «Eulalia, dame mi guacal, por favor».

A los dos días, Eulalia regresó a lavar a la misma hora de siempre, pero cuando llegó se sorprendió porque no estaba la mujer en el lavadero. Esa misma noche volvió a escuchar su llanto que le seguía pidiendo el guacal. Eulalia decidió salir a ver quien era, pero cuando salió no había nadie. Eulalia le contó a una amiga lo que le estaba pasando. Su amiga sabía de esa persona y que era el espíritu de la Llorona. Le contó la historia de esta pobre mujer y que no le iba a dejar en paz si no le devolvía el guacal, porque con el guacal la Llorona podía regresar a lavar a las pilas. Creía que al estar en la pila estaría cerca de su hijo que se le había desaparecido mucho tiempo atrás.

Así fue que Eulalia regresó a la pila y decidió dejar el guacal exactamente donde la Llorona siempre lavaba, y nunca más Eulalia salió a lavar muy temprano. Así es como la Llorona se aparecía en todas las pilas del pueblo cuando las personas lavaban muy tarde o muy temprano en la madrugada. A veces se le oía llorar a ella en las calles camino a las pilas. Es por eso que la leyenda se llama la Llorona.

THE STINGY OLD WOMAN

In this story from the book by José Juan, Cuentos antiguos de animales y gente de San Miguel Acatán (Old Stories of Animals and People from San Miguel Acatán), *the cleverness of a miserly old woman can be thoroughly enjoyed.*

*I*n a little town there lived a very poor old woman. Her only support was a great avocado tree that always gave lots of fruit. However, it was as if the tree gave none, because the boys from the village would climb the tree and steal her avocados.

While they joked about her, the poor, miserable old woman used to shout her head off, begging that they leave in peace her only means of livelihood, selling avocados.

One night, a traveler arrived at the miserable old woman's house and asked that she allow him to spend the night there. The old woman felt sorry for him and gave him lodging. The next morning, before leaving, the traveler said to her:

"Ask me for whatever you want, and I will give it to you."

"I have only one wish, that everyone who climbs the avocado tree not be able to come down without my permission," she answered.

"Granted," said the traveler, and he left.

Hours later, when one of the boys who was used to stealing her avocados climbed up the tree, he thought it strange that he didn't hear the old woman's screams. But when he tried to climb down from the tree, he could not. Then the old woman appeared and said to him:

"You will not be able to climb down without my permission. And I will not give it to you until you promise me that you will go through the whole village telling everyone that the old woman's tree has a spell on it and that whoever climbs it to steal avocados will not be able to climb down."

The boy promised the old woman that he would carry out the order, and she gave him permission to come down. From that day, the old woman lived happily and peacefully, eating her own avocados. Now she had more than enough, because now no one dared to climb the tree; until one night, someone called at the old woman's door.

"Who is it?" shouted the old woman.

"I am Death and I have come to take you," [a voice] answered.

"That's fine," said the old woman, "but before, I would like to eat a few avocados from my tree. Would you climb up and get them? I'm so old that I cannot reach them."

Death, neither slow nor lazy, did what the old woman had asked. He was surprised that he could not climb down from the tree. So, Death stayed up in the tree, furious to see that the old woman would not give him permission to come down.

Many days, months and years passed, and no one died in the village, since Death could not climb down. But finally, many people began to complain. The druggists and the doctors had no work. More than one person, tired of the world, called Death.

Then the old woman made a deal with Death. She would give him permission to come down from the tree if he would promise her to not take her.

Death agreed, and according to what they say around there, the old woman is still alive today.

So ends the story of the miserable old woman.

LA ANCIANA MISERABLE

Con este cuento del libro de José Juan, Cuentos antiguos de animales y gente de San Miguel Acatán, *se puede disfrutar la listeza de una anciana miserable.*

*E*n un pueblo vivía una anciana muy pobre. Su único sostén era un gran árbol de aguacate que siempre daba mucha fruta, pero era como si no diera nada, pues los muchachos del pueblo se subían al árbol para robarse los aguacates.

Como se burlaban de ella, la pobre anciana miserable se desgañitaba, pidiendo que dejaran en paz su único medio de ganarse la vida, la venta de aguacates.

Una noche un viajero llegó a la casa de la señora miserable y le pidió que le permitiera pasar allí la noche. La anciana se compadeció de él y le dio posada. A la mañana siguiente, antes de marcharse, el viajero le dijo:

«Pídeme lo que quieras, te lo daré».

«Tengo un solo deseo, que todos los que suban al árbol de aguacate no puedan bajarse sin mi permiso», contestó.

«Concedido», dijo el viajero, y se marchó.

Horas después, cuando uno de los muchachos que acostumbraba robarse los aguacates se subió al árbol, se extrañó de no oír los gritos de la anciana. Pero cuando trató de bajarse del árbol, no pudo. Entonces apareció la anciana y le dijo:

«No podrás bajar del árbol sin mi permiso. Y no te lo daré hasta que me prometas ir por todo el pueblo diciéndole a toda la gente que el árbol de la anciana tiene un hechizo y él que se suba a robar aguacates no podrá bajarse».

El muchacho le prometió a la anciana cumplir con el encargo y ella le dio permiso para bajarse. Desde ese día, la anciana vivía feliz y tranquila, comiendo sus propios aguacates. Ya le sobraban, pues ya nadie se atrevía a subirse al árbol; hasta que una noche, alguien llamó a la puerta de la anciana.

«¿Quién es?», grito la anciana.

«Soy la muerte y te vengo a llevar», le respondió.

«Está bien», dijo la anciana, «pero antes quisiera comer unos aguacates de mi árbol. ¿Podrías subir a cogerlos? Soy tan vieja que ya no puedo alcanzarlos».

La muerte, ni lenta ni perezosa, hizo lo que pedía la anciana. Se sorprendió de que no podía bajarse del árbol. Así, la muerte quedó encaramada en el árbol, furiosa al ver que la anciana no le daba permiso para bajar.

Pasaron muchos días, meses y años y nadie se moría en el pueblo, ya que la muerte no podía bajar. Pero al final, muchos empezaron a protestar. Los boticarios y los médicos ya estaban sin trabajo. Más de una persona, cansada ya del mundo, llamaba a la muerte.

Entonces la anciana hizo un trato con la muerte. Le daría permiso para que pudiera bajar del árbol si le prometía no llevársela.

La muerte estuvo de acuerdo y según dicen por ahí la anciana debe vivir todavía.

Así termina el cuento de la anciana miserable.

HOW THE SERPENT WAS BORN

This story deals with respect for one's parents. It comes from The Bird Who Cleans the World, *by Victor Montejo.*

*T*he care and devotion of a mother for her growing children is enormous. She denies herself and she pours forth the treasure of love from her heart in caring for her child. A mother is an angel. A mother is a treasure. A mother is a special being whom we ought to love every moment of our lives. But many of us do not have hearts big enough to repay her for all that we make her suffer.

There are some who insult and reject their mothers and make them suffer even when they are very old, even though the children ought to bless these women with love and care for all the great pleasures they have given.

So it was that once a certain mother wanted to visit her son's house and rest in the shade of his roof. Since he was her son, he might even give her some tortillas to quiet the great hunger raging in her stomach. But it was not to be so. When the son saw his mother approaching his house, he cursed her and ordered his wife to hide the bubbling pot full of chicken soup that she had cooked for dinner that day.

The old lady sat on the doorstep and the son said, "Old woman, why do you come to my house?"

His mother answered, "Son, I only come to rest in the shade of your roof."

"Well, *I* don't believe I have anything to give you, and besides these visits bore me."

The son and his wife had to work hard to fight the appetites that made them want to devour the succulent chicken soup right in front of the old woman who would then want a share. The old woman grew tired of sitting on the doorstep with not a kind word from her son. She turned back toward her little house, saddened by the ingratitude and indifference of that self-centered and ungrateful son.

"Now the old woman has gone away," the son said to his mate. "Let's eat the chicken soup."

The wife brought out the pot that had been hidden from the old woman's eyes. She put it on the table and lifted off the lid.

"Huuuuuuyyy, oh Jesus!" she exclaimed.

"What? What's happening?" her husband asked.

The moment she had lifted the lid, instead of the chicken soup she saw a poisonous serpent, coiled in the pot, its head poised, ready to strike. They wanted to kill it, but the snake, shaking its rattles, slithered out to hide.

It is said that the serpent was born this way, the beginning of the bad things that lie waiting for us. It was born of the heart of a son who did not want to know the courage of a mother's saintly love.

DE CÓMO NACIÓ LA VÍBORA

Este cuento trata del respeto para los padres. Viene del libro El pájaro que limpia el mundo, *por Víctor Montejo.*

*L*a preocupación y el desvelo de una madre por hacer crecer a sus hijos son de dimensiones incomprensibles. Su abnegación, entrega y el amor que ella atesora en su corazón para propiciar el cuido al hijo y a la hija es inmensamente grande.

La madre es un ángel. La madre es un tesoro. La madre es un ser especial a quien debemos amar en cada instante de nuestras vidas. Pero muchos de nosotros no tenemos un corazón hermoso como el de ella, para devolverle con bien todo el sufrimiento que ella ha padecido calladamente por sus hijos.

Algunos rechazan, desprecian y ofenden a sus madres y las hacen sufrir aún en su ancianidad; cuando estas benditas mujeres deben ser objeto del amor y del cuidado de los hijos, como un agradecimiento a la vida que ellas nos han dado con profundo amor.

He aquí pues, que una madre anciana quiso visitar la casa de su hijo y reposar a la sombra de aquel hogar, pensando que como hijo suyo que era el hombre, le daría siquiera unas tortillas para calmar el hambre que le hacía tronar el estómago. Pero no fue así, porque el hijo al ver que su desdichada madre se acercaba a su casa, con desprecio ordenó a su esposa que escondiera la olla rebosante del «gallo en caldo" que había cocinado para la cena esa tarde.

La anciana madre se sentó en el marco de la casa y el hijo con vivo desprecio le dijo:

«¡Vieja! ¿Qué vienes a hacer aquí a mi casa?»

La madre respondió:

«Hijo, únicamente quiero descansar a la sombra de tu casa».

«Pues, no creo que yo tenga algo que darte. Además, me aburre que me visites tanto».

El hombre y su esposa tuvieron que resistir el gusto de devorar el suculento caldo de pollo delante de la anciana por no compartir con ella la comida.

La anciana se cansó de estar sentada en el marco de la casa sin recibir la atención ni el aprecio de su hijo. Muy lentamente se puso de pie y retornó a su casita, triste y desconsolada por la ingratitud e indiferencia de aquel hijo mal agradecido.

«Ya se ha ido la vieja, comamos el gallo», dijo el hombre a su compañera de hogar.

La esposa trajo la olla que había permanecido oculta a la vista de la pobre madre y ya puesta sobre la mesa, la destapó.

«¡Huuuuyyyyyyy, Jesús!», exclamó asustada la mujer.

«¿Que pasa?», preguntó el hombre, asustado.

Lo que estaba pasando era que en vez del gallo cocido apareció enroscado dentro de la olla una víbora venenosa. Al momento de destapar la olla, la víbora sacó la horrible cabeza en actitud de ataque.

Quisieron matarla pero ésta se salió del recipiente y se deslizó sacudiendo sus cascabeles. La quisieron matar pero la víbora se ocultó rápidamente en el corral de piedra que circundaba la casa.

Se dice pues, que desde entonces nació la víbora, como el prototipo de la maldad asechante: nacida del corazón vil de aquel hijo que no quiso reconocer el sagrado amor de una madre.

THE GOBLIN

This story is another example of a lesson that teaches that it can be dangerous to consider oneself superior to other people and to confront the spirits who inhabit the earth. It was told by Santiago Morales, of San José Media Cuesta, Santa Rosa, Guatemala.

The goblin is known as a "man" of short stature who wears a big hat. He appears at night to proud or vain people who feel they are extraordinary. In this instance, the goblin appeared to a very important man of San Antonio Aguas Calientes, Sacatepéquez. Don Marcial Hernández was rich. He liked to ride his horse at any hour of the day or night. Many people were envious of him. He was well-educated, a teacher, with wealthy parents; everything that he asked for he was granted. One day his parents gave him a horse because they knew how much he liked horses.

Don Marcial had a girlfriend named Maria who lived in the village of Santiago Zamora. One day he decided to visit her. His father always used to tell him, "Do not to go out at night, because it is dangerous."

But don Marcial simply responded by saying, "I have no fear. Nothing makes me afraid. Giants and goblins exist. If they appear before me, I will confront them because I have no fear and I know what to do."

On one occasion Maria told don Marcial that her parents wanted to see him and formalize his engagement to their daughter. "They want to see you tomorrow night at eight o'clock."

Don Marcial was impatient. He did not wait for the time to go; he readied his horse at seven o'clock and left. He was on his way to Santiago when suddenly, behind the cemetery, he remembered what his father had said to him about goblins and giants. But he said to himself, "I am don Marcial and I have no fear."

Suddenly a goblin appeared before him. Don Marcial said to the goblin, "You are not going to defeat me, so get out of the way, because I want to pass." Don Marcial's horse resisted passing the goblin, and the goblin did not move from the middle of the road. Don Marcial spurred the horse, but the horse did not obey him. After trying again, he suddenly began to feel a strong headache and nausea, and he could not go on. He decided to return to his house.

When he arrived, three men helped him down from the horse. The men called a doctor to see don Marcial's condition. The doctor told them that he could do nothing to cure don Marcial because his illness had been caused by spirits. "I am going to give him a shot and see how he reacts," said the doctor. The doctor gave him some shots, but don Marcial did not come to.

Everyone went to visit don Marcial, asking what had happened to him. He refused to explain what had happened, saying he didn't want to bore them. After two days in bed, he had not recuperated. Don Marcial never recovered. His right hand and left leg remained shrunken forever, and he had to live like that for the rest of his life for having disobeyed his parents and for feeling like a superior man. A man cannot challenge bad spirits or spirits that are unreasoning. It is not a good thing to confront them as did don Marcial.

EL DUENDE

Este cuento es otro ejemplo de una lección que enseña que puede ser peligroso considerarse como superior a otra gente y también enfrentar a los espíritus que habitan la tierra. Fue contado por Santiago Morales, de San José Media Cuesta, Santa Rosa, Guatemala.

El duende se conoce como un hombre de poca estatura y un sombrero grande. Aparece en las noches a las personas orgullosas vanidosas y que se sienten únicas. En esta oportunidad se le apareció a un hombre muy importante de San Antonio Aguas Calientes, Sacatepéquez. Don Marcial Hernández era un hombre de buena condición económica. Le gustaba cabalgar a la hora que él quisiera de día o de noche. Muchas personas le tenían envidia. Era un hombre preparado, era maestro, y sus padres eran muy ricos, y todo lo que él pedía se lo otorgaban. Un día sus padres le obsequiaron un caballo porque ellos sabían cuánto le gustaban los caballos.

Tenía una novia llamada María que vivía en la aldea Santiago Zamora. Un día decidió visitarle. Su padre siempre le decía: «No salgas de noche, porque es peligroso», y él le respondió: «No tengo miedo. No me da miedo nada. Existen los gigantes y los duendes. Si se me aparecen, yo me les enfrento porque yo no tengo miedo y sé lo que hago».

En una oportunidad María le dijo a don Marcial que sus padres lo querían ver para hablar acerca de su noviazgo y formalizarlo. «Quieren verte mañana a las 8:00 de la tarde».

Don Marcial estaba impaciente. No hallaba la hora de irse; alistó su caballo a las 7:00 de la tarde y salió. Iba camino a Santiago cuando de repente atrás del cementerio se acordó de lo que su padre le había dicho acerca de los duendes y los gigantes. Pero dentro de si dijo: «Yo soy don Marcial, y no tengo miedo».

Al seguir su camino de repente se le apareció el duende. Y don Marcial le dijo: «Usted no me va a vencer, y quítese porque quiero pasar». El caballo se resistía a pasar, y el duende no se quitaba de en medio del camino. Don Marcial daba espejuelazos al caballo pero él no obedecía. Después de estar intentando, de repente empezó a sentir un fuerte dolor de cabeza y nausea, y ya no pudo seguir. Y decidió regresar a su casa.

Al llegar, tres hombres lo bajaron de su caballo, y luego llamaron al médico a ver la condición en que se encontraba don Marcial. El médico les dijo que lo que tenía no podía curarlo, porque era de espíritus. «Le voy a inyectar a ver como reaccione», dijo el médico. Y unas inyecciones le dio, pero don Marcial no volvía en sí.

Toda la gente iba a visitar a don Marcial y le preguntaba lo que le había sucedido. Se negó a explicarlo, diciendo que era para no cansarlos. Pasó dos días en cama y no pudo recuperarse. Don Marcial no tuvo cura. Su mano derecha y su pierna izquierda se quedaron encogidas para siempre, y así tuvo que vivir el resto de su vida por haber desobedecido a sus padres y por sentirse un hombre muy capaz. Contra los espíritus malos o los espíritus que no tienen facultad el hombre no puede hacerles frente. No es bueno enfrentarlos como lo hizo don Marcial.

THE SIMANAGUA

"The Simanagua" originated in the Patzité area of Chichicastenango and is about respecting customs and the consequences of not respecting them. This story was told by María Caley, of Chichicastenango, Guatemala.

*I*n the Patzité area of Chichicastenango, Quiché, there once was a young man named Tiófilo who was in love with a girl named Cástula, who lived in the Pa'ley area (which means "between *chichicastales*"). To meet with Cástula, Tiófilo had to walk an hour on a small trail through the mountains. The trail passed among small farms fenced with *chichicaste,* a bush with leaves and stems full of poisonous thorns that get into a person's skin when the bush is touched.

Tiófilo's relationship with Cástula went on for a year without the consent of their parents. In the Mayan custom a couple must go together three or four years before they can be married. Tiófilo still had not met Cástula's parents, because they had been meeting each other in the streets of Pa'ley three times a week at nightfall; he went to Pa'ley to meet with Cástula. The conversations between Tiófilo and Cástula were about the work they did every day. She was a housekeeper and also wove her own *huipiles.* He was a farmer who grew crops with his family. They planted corn, beans, and vegetables. Cástula and Tiófilo talked about some day getting married.

It happened one day that when they said goodbye to one another, Tiófilo did not go back to his village because he went to visit another family in Pa'ley. Since he was there, they invited him to eat with them. After eating he stayed to talk for a long time, and when he left to go back to his house it was much later than usual.

Tiófilo, seeing that night was coming, said farewell to his friends and left for Patzité. He had not walked thirty minutes when suddenly in the dark he saw a person coming toward him, covered with a cloak that hid the person's face. As the person got closer and closer, Tiófilo saw that the person was dressed in the same clothes as his girlfriend Cástula. He thought, "What is Cástula doing walking alone at this hour? Normally Cástula's parents don't let her go out after five in the evening." He was surprised when they got closer and passed one another and she didn't show her face or tell him goodbye. She had a cloak on her head and was going along bowed over.

Tiófilo was so surprised that he turned around and followed her. He called her by name and she did not answer. He called and called until he reached her and asked, "Why don't you answer me? What are you doing walking alone here?" She only laughed. She did not talk to him, did not face him, and only turned her back to him. Finally, Tiófilo became impatient and told her to please answer him. Then she told him that she had decided to go away with him. He was very surprised by this reply because he knew the customs of the families, and that what she was saying was against the customs.

Tiófilo told Cástula that he would take her back to her house. As she walked, he wanted to take her hand but she did not let him. She did not even show him her face. She kept hiding it, and when they were walking he asked her, "What is wrong that you will not show me your face?" She only smiled and did not show her face. He insisted on taking her hand, and all at once she lightly touched his hand. It made him shiver because her hands were very shaggy with fur, and he asked himself, "Who is this?" He kept walking, but he felt dizzy. Suddenly she disappeared.

Then Tiófilo decided to go back to his house. The next day he was still bothered about what had happened the night before and decided to go look for Cástula earlier than usual. He asked her if she had gone out in the night, and she responded that there was no way she could go out late at night. So Tiófilo told her what had happened to him the night before. Cástula told him that surely it had been the Simanagua and to go back and look exactly where she had disappeared, because he would see only a *chichicaste* bush.

Tiófilo returned from his visit with Cástula earlier than usual, and to his surprise where the woman had disappeared there was only a *chichicaste* bush, just as Cástula had said. Cástula told him that it was a lesson meant to teach him not to return to his house very late because the Simanagua likes to confuse young men in that way.

LA SIMANAGUA

El cuento «La Simanagua» se originó en el cantón de Patzité de Chichicastenango y trata del respeto a las costumbres y las consecuencias de no respetarlas. Este cuento nos contó María Caley, de Chichicastenango, Guatemala.

Había una vez en el cantón Patzité de Chichicastenango, Quiché, un joven llamado Tiófilo que estaba enamorado de una joven llamada Cástula, la cual vivía en el cantón Pa'ley, que significa «entre chichicastales». Para reunirse con Cástula, Tiófilo tenía que caminar una hora entre las montañas en una pequeña vereda, pasaba por pequeñas propiedades cercadas con chichicaste, el cual es un arbusto con hojas y tallos llenos de espinas que al tocarlo se introducen en la piel y son ponzoñosas.

Su relación llegó a un año sin el consentimiento de los padres, en las costumbres mayas las parejas tienen que tratarse tres a cuatro años. Tiófilo aún no era conocido por los padres de Cástula, ya que ellos se veían en las calles del cantón Pa'ley tres veces por semana al caer la tarde; él se encaminaba al cantón para reunirse con Cástula. Las conversaciones de ellos eran sobre los trabajos que ellos hacían diariamente. Ella era ama de casa y también tejía sus propios huipiles. Él era campesino que sembraba la tierra juntamente con su familia. Sembraban maíz, frijol, y verduras. De vez en cuando Cástula y Teófilo conversaban sobre si algún día contraerían matrimonio.

Sucedió que una vez cuando se despidieron, él no fue de regreso a su cantón, porque fue a visitar a otra familia en el cantón Pa'ley. Estando ahí lo invitaron a cenar y luego de cenar se quedó a conversar un largo rato, por lo cual se le hizo más tarde de lo normal que acostumbraba a regresar a su casa.

Tiófilo, viendo que entraba la noche, se despidió de ellos y se encaminó hacia el cantón Patzité. No había caminado treinta minutos cuando de repente vio en la oscuridad a una persona que venía cubierta con un manto, la cual no mostraba la cara. Cuando se fue acercando más y más, él vio que la persona vestía las mismas ropas de Cástula, su novia. Entonces él pensó: «Que hace Cástula caminando a esta hora sola, porque normalmente sus padres no la dejaban salir después de las cinco de la tarde». Pero cuál fue su sorpresa que cuando se fue acercando más y más, se cruzó con ella, no le mostró la cara ni le dijo adiós. Ella tenía un manto en la cabeza e iba agachada.

Entonces Tiófilo se sorprendió tanto que dio la media vuelta y la siguió. La llamó por su nombre, y ella no le contestó. Él insistía e insistía hasta que la alcanzó y le dijo: «¿Porqué no me contestas? ¿Qué estás haciendo caminando sola aquí?» Y ella solo se reía y no le hablaba; no le daba la cara, sólo la espalda. Al final Tiófilo se impacientó y le dijo que por favor le contestara. Entonces ella le dijo que había decidido irse con él. Él quedó muy sorprendido con esa respuesta, porque el sabía las costumbres de las familias y no era correcto lo que ella estaba diciendo.

Le dijo Tiófilo a Cástula que la encaminaría a su casa. Cuando iba caminando él quiso tomarla de la mano, pero ella no quiso, aun no le mostraba la cara. Seguía escondiéndosela, y cuando iban caminando le preguntó: «¿Qué te pasa que no me muestras la cara?» Solo sonreía y no le mostraba la cara. Él insistió de tomarla de la mano y de repente le rozó la mano. A él le dio un escalofrió debido a que sus manos eran muy velludas, y se preguntó a sí mismo: «¿Quién es ella?» Siguió caminando pero él ya se sentía mareado y de repente ella desapareció.

Entonces decidió regresar a su casa. Al día siguiente él no estaba conforme con lo que había sucedido la noche anterior y decidió ir a buscar a Cástula más temprano de lo acostumbrado. Le preguntó si ella había salido en la noche, y ella respondió que de ninguna manera ella podía salir a altas horas de la noche. Entonces Tiófilo le contó lo que le había pasado en la noche anterior. Cástula le dijo que seguramente había sido la Simanagua, y le dijo que regresara y que viera exactamente donde desapareció y que iba a ver sólo una mata de chichicaste.

Él regresó de su visita con Cástula más temprano de lo acostumbrado, y cuál fue su sorpresa que donde había desaparecido la mujer sólo había una mata de chichicaste, tal como se lo había dicho Cástula. Entonces Cástula le dijo que era una lección para que no regresara muy tarde a su casa porque a la Simanagua le gustaba confundir a los jóvenes de esa manera.

THE DWARF

"The Dwarf" is a tale about unseen inhabitants of an area, with whom the locals are familiar, but with whom newcomers may have problems. Macario Chigüil, who lives in La Guitarra, Retalhuleu, Guatemala, told this story.

*I*n the Department of Retalhuleu, in southwest Guatemala, there is a little hamlet called La Guitarra. On the plains around La Guitarra are cattle and horse ranches. It was to one of these ranches that many Mayan families emigrated from the cold highlands. Macario and his family were among those who moved there to work.

Macario's family consisted of two girls, two boys, and his wife. On the ranch they had a place to live, and the work Marcario was going to do was to care for the cattle and the horses. The family settled themselves and looked for a school where the children could study. The oldest daughter was named Eleodora, but was affectionately called Lolita. The children had lots of room to play and enjoy themselves and pick the fruits that were produced in the area. Time passed, and don Macario cared for the cows and the horses and planted crops.

One day don Macario put away his horse, Pajarero, whom he always rode when he worked, then went to his house to rest. The next morning he got out his horse Pajarero, like every day, to ride to work. When he went to mount, he was surprised to see that his horse's tail was finely braided. He tried to unbraid the horse's tail, but that took more time and patience than he had, and he was not successful.

After a while he took Pajarero back to the stable again. He left and told the workers about the braid, and one of them told don Macario that he had never heard of or seen anything like that happen to anyone on the farm.

Don Macario decided again to try to unbraid his horse Pajarero's tail. This time it was difficult, but he was patient enough to unbraid it. He told his friends and family that he was finally able to unbraid his horse's tail.

A week passed, and one morning upon arising very early, how surprised was don Macario when he saw that the very long hair of his little girl Lolita was braided in the same way that Pajarero's tail had been. Lolita did not even know. Her father asked her if she had braided her hair the night before, and she answered no, that she had not, and that she always left her hair loose. They tried to unbraid Lolita's hair but could not do it. Then don Macario, because he was very worried, went to look for the oldest man of La Guitarra hamlet to consult him about the situation that was occurring with his daughter's and his horse's hair.

The old man listened to him until the end and afterward broke into laughter. The old man said to him, "Ay, Macario, Macario, because you come from a faraway land you do not know the things that happen here. Those of us who work with the animals on the ranches know about the existence of the *nu'y* [pronounced new-ee] or dwarf, who loves to entertain himself by braiding the horses' tails during the night. And he does not like it at all if the braids are taken out like you did with the horse, so he braided Lolita's hair. Now what you must do is wait for the *nu'y*. As long as the *nu'y* returns to braid the tail of your horse he will be happy, and later you can unbraid the hair of your daughter Lolita."

Macario and his family did everything the old man had said to them. The *nu'y* came back and braided the tail of the horse Pajarero, and so they were able to unbraid Lolita's hair and everything returned to normal. They continued to live happily in La Guitarra, with the knowledge of secret things.

EL ENANITO

«El enanito" es un cuento sobre habitantes no vistos de un área, con quienes los oriundos son familiares, pero con quienes los recién llegados pueden tener problemas. Macario Chigüil, que vive en La Guitarra, Retalhuleu, Guatemala, relató este cuento.

En el departamento de Retalhuleu, situado en el suroeste de Guatemala, se encuentra un caserío llamado la Guitarra. Este pequeño caserío tiene una gran área de planicies con fincas de ganado y caballos. Fue a una de estas fincas hacia donde emigraron muchas familias mayas de tierras frías. Macario y su familia fueron una de ellas que se trasladaron ahí para trabajar.

Su familia la conformaban dos niñas, dos niños y su esposa. En esta finca a ellos les daban donde vivir; el trabajo que iba a realizar era cuidar el ganado y los caballos. Se establecieron y buscaron escuela para sus hijos para estudiar. La mayor de sus hijas se llamaba Eleodora a la cual por cariño le decían Lolita. Los niños tenían mucho campo para jugar y divertirse y cosechar las frutas que en ese lugar se producen. Pasó el tiempo, y don Macario cuidaba a las vacas y a los caballos y sembraba la tierra.

Un día don Macario fue a guardar a su caballo que se llamaba Pajarero que era él que siempre montaba para trabajar, y fue a su casa a descansar. A la mañana siguiente, don Macario sacó su caballo Pajarero como todos los días para ir a trabajar, y cuando lo iba a montar, cuál fue su sorpresa que la cola de su caballo estaba finamente trenzada. Y lo que él hizo fue tratar de destrenzar la cola del caballo, pero le llevó más tiempo y paciencia que la que él tenía y no tuvo éxito.

Después de un tiempo lo llevó de nuevo a su caballeriza. Fue y se lo comentó a los trabajadores, pero uno de ellos le dijo que él nunca había escuchado ni visto que a alguien le hubiera pasado algo igual.

Don Macario decidió de nuevo intentar de destrenzar la cola a su caballo Pajarero, y esta vez le costó pero lo pudo destrenzar. Les contó a sus compañeros y a su familia que al fin pudo destrenzar a su caballo Pajarero.

Pasó una semana y una mañana al levantarse muy temprano, cual fue su sorpresa que al ver a su hija Lolita, la cual tenía el pelo muy largo, trenzado de la misma forma que le habían hecho a su caballo Pajarero. Lolita ni se había dado cuenta. Su padre le preguntó si ella se había trenzado el pelo la noche anterior, y ella le contestó que no, que ella siempre se quedaba con el pelo suelto. Trataron de destrenzarle el pelo a Lolita y no lo pudieron hacer. Entonces don Macario, como estaba muy preocupado, fue a buscar al hombre más anciano del caserío la Guitarra para consultarle la situación por la que estaban pasando.

El anciano lo escuchó hasta el final y después soltó una risa y le dijo: «Ay, Macario, Macario, como vienes de tierras lejanas por eso no sabes las cosas que pasan aquí. Los que trabajamos con los animales en las fincas sabemos de la existencia del *nu'y,* o enanito, que le encanta entretenerse trenzando la cola de los caballos por la noche. Y no le gusta que de ninguna manera la destrencen. Como vos se la destrenzaste al caballo, entonces él ahora trenzó el pelo a tu hija Lolita. Ahora lo que debes de hacer es esperar al *nu'y*. Ya que él regresara a trenzarle la cola al caballo, así el enanito estará feliz, y luego tu podrás destrenzarle el pelo a tu hija Lolita».

Macario y su familia obedecieron todo lo que el anciano les había dicho. El *nu'y* volvió y trenzó la cola al caballo Pajarero, y así pudieron destrenzar a Lolita, y así todo volvió a la normalidad. Ellos siguieron viviendo felices en el caserío la Guitarra con conocimiento de cosas secretos.

THE GIANT NIMALEJ' MO'S

Each year there is a celebration in San Antonio Aguas Calientes during which giants dance in the streets. There are four giants in San Antonio, the hometown of Margarita López, the storyteller who told this tale: two with black faces and two with white faces, which may mean something about the indigenous and the ladino (nonindigenous) people. The people tell different stories about a giant who lived in a big cave in the mountains and who would go out at night looking for food. This is one of them.

The name Nimalej' mo's *(pronounced nee-ma-lay-h mo-s) is in the Cakchiquel language and is a combination of two words.* "Nimalej' " *means big, and* "mo's" *means a Spanish-speaking man who is not indigenous. The name* Nimalej' mo's *means "big man." The story does not name the giant, and there is no Cakchiquel word equivalent to the English word giant.."*

*T*he neighbors of the town tell about the giant, *Nimalej' mo's*, who lived in the mountains in a big cave and came out at night to look for food. One day, Pablo and his friends went to the mountains to look for firewood. Looking and looking, they worked their way far into the mountains and, seeing that the sun was about to set, they got ready to stay and sleep in the mountains. They looked for a comfortable place and, because of what they had been told about *Nimalej' mo's*, they arranged to tie themselves to one another in case something happened to them. However, they didn't know that this was the place where *Nimalej' mo's* met with other giants to dance.

At midnight one of the friends looked out and saw a great light far away, but coming toward them. Frightened, the boy woke the others and, as well as they could, they climbed up a tree to hide themselves. Waiting for what might come, all at once they saw *Nimalej' mo's* arriving with other giants, all to meet each other right beneath the tree where the boys were hiding. The giants had very long hands and very large clothing. They built a huge bonfire and began to dance. Some beat drums and others danced.

While Pablo and his friends watched, surprised by what the giants were doing and fearful that they would be discovered, one of Pablo's friends took out his machete, wanting to kill *Nimalej' mo's*. He threw himself on the giant but was only able to cut off one ear. Immediately the boy ran away and, seeing what had happened, the others followed him.

The giant *Nimalej' mo's*, injured and bleeding, ran toward his house, which was a great cave hidden among many trees, and went in. As dawn arrived, Pablo and his friends were frightened and running toward home. But Pablo, regretting what had happened to the giant, thought it would be good to take the giant's ear back to him. After convincing his friends, Pablo led them back to the place where everything had happened. But *Nimalej' mo's* was not there. Then Pablo and his friends discovered a trail of blood that had been left by the injured giant and followed it to the great cave. There, in the dark of the cave, the trail disappeared. None of them was courageous enough to go into the cave, so Pablo said to his friends that they should wait outside for him.

Lighting a torch, Pablo went in and, after walking a little way into the cave, he heard a noise. To his surprise, he saw a great, hungry lion. As luck would have it, the lion was chained to the rock wall and Pablo was able to go by slowly. Afterward he continued his march, when suddenly a hole filled with snakes appeared in his path. Being very alert, Pablo jumped over the hole and was able to pass. At the end of his hike, he came upon a giant keeping watch over the house of *Nimalej' mo's*. Pablo asked the giant if *Nimalej' mo's* was there, and the giant responded, "Yes, but he is in bed, sick." Pablo told the giant that he wanted to see *Nimalej' mo's* and had brought something for him. The giant agreed to let Pablo in to see *Nimalej' mo's*. Pablo entered the house and saw that *Nimalej' mo's* was sick in bed. Pablo went to him, gave him back his ear, and asked forgiveness for what had happened. *Nimalej' mo's* put his ear back on and in an instant he was healthy again. Pablo was surprised.

Nimalej' mo's, very grateful, gave Pablo a gift, a very heavy clay treasure chest. Pablo walked to the exit of the cave, thinking he would show his friends what he had been given. When he arrived there, his friends were not there; they had gone back to town. Anxious to see what the gift was, Pablo opened the chest and, to his great surprise, saw that it was filled with gold coins.

Pablo went back to town and shared his fortune with his friends. He had learned that not all persons who are different are bad.

EL GIGANTE NIMALEJ' MO'S

Cada año hay una fiesta en San Antonio Aguas Calientes en la cual bailan los gigantes en las calles. Hay cuatro gigantes en San Antonio, el pueblo natal de Margarita López, la cuentista que contó esta historia: dos con caras negras y dos con caras blancas, y esto tal vez significa algo sobre indígenas y ladinos. La gente cuenta varias historias de un gigante que vivía en la montaña en una gran cueva y que salía por las noches para buscar comida. Esta es una de ellas.

El nombre Nimalej' mo's es en el idioma cakchiquel y combina dos palabras. «Nimalej'» significa «grande», y «mo's» significa «hombre ladino, no indígena». Entonces la palabra dice «hombre grande». Este cuento no pone ningún nombre en el gigante y, en realidad, no existe una palabra específica para «gigante» en cakchiquel.

*C*uentan los vecinos del pueblo sobre el gigante *Nimalej' mo's* que vivía en la montaña, dentro de una gran cueva, y que por las noches salía a buscar comida. Un día Pablo y sus amigos salieron a la montaña a buscar leña. Buscando y buscando se metieron muy dentro de la montaña, y al ver que el sol se estaba alejando y estando lejos de casa, dispusieron quedarse a dormir en la montaña. Buscaron un lugar cómodo y, por lo que contaban del *Nimalej' mo's,* dispusieron atarse uno con otro por si les pasara algo. Pero ellos no sabían que ese era el lugar donde se reunía *Nimalej' mo's* a bailar junto a otros gigantes.

A media noche uno de ellos vio a lo lejos una gran luz que venía hacia ellos. Asustado, despertó a los otros y, como pudieron, se subieron a un árbol a esconderse. Esperando que era lo que venía, de repente vieron que llegó *Nimalej' mo's* con otros gigantes, todos a reunirse donde ellos estaban. Tenían largas manos y vestidos grandes. Hicieron una gran fogata y empezaron a bailar. Unos tocaban los tambores y otros bailaban.

En tanto que Pablo y sus amigos miraban sorprendidos lo que los gigantes hacían, y con temor a que los descubrieran, uno de los amigos de Pablo, con miedo, sacó su machete y queriendo matar a *Nimalej' mo's,* se le tiró encima pero solo pudo quitarle la oreja. En seguida huyó, al ver lo que pasaba, y los demás lo siguieron.

El gigante *Nimalej' mo's,* al verse herido y sangrando, corrió rumbo a su casa, que era una gran cueva escondida entre muchos árboles y se metió ahí. Empezaba a amanecer, Pablo y sus amigos corrían asustados rumbo al pueblo. Pero Pablo, arrepentido de lo que le habían hecho al gigante, pensó en que sería bueno en regresarle la oreja. Convenciendo a sus amigos, Pablo y ellos regresaron al lugar donde había pasado todo. Pero *Nimalej' mo's* ya no estaba ahí. Entonces descubrieron una huella de sangre que había dejado por la herida y la siguieron hasta la gran cueva. Ahí desaparecía la huella donde estaba muy oscura. Ninguno se animaba a entrar, entonces Pablo les dijo a sus amigos que lo esperaran ahí.

Prendiendo una antorcha, entró a la cueva, y caminando un poco escuchó un ruido. Cuál fue su sorpresa al encontrarse con un gran león, hambriento. Por suerte estaba encadenado, y así pudo pasar despacio. Luego siguió su marcha, cuando de pronto en el camino había un hoyo lleno de culebras. Muy atento saltó y logró pasar, y al final del camino, encontró a un gigante, custodiando la casa de *Nimalej' mo's*. Entonces Pablo le preguntó si se encontraba *Nimalej' mo's,* y el gigante le respondió: «Si, pero está en cama, enfermo». Pablo le dijo que lo quería ver porque le traía algo. El gigante le permitió entrar. Entró a la casa, y *Nimalej' mo's* estaba en la cama. Pablo entró, le dio la oreja y pidió disculpas por lo que había sucedido. *Nimalej' mo's* se la puso y en instantes se sanó. Pablo quedó sorprendido.

Nimalej' mo's, muy agradecido, le dio un regalo, una botija de barro muy pesada. Pablo caminó a la salida de la cueva, pensando en mostrarles a sus amigos lo que le habían regalado. Pero al llegar ahí, ellos ya no estaban; habían regresado al pueblo. Ansioso de ver qué le había regalado, abrió la botija y cuál fue su sorpresa al ver que estaba llena de monedas de oro.

Pablo regresó al pueblo y compartió su fortuna con sus amigos. Aprendió que no todas las personas que son diferentes son malas.

PART 5

SUPERNATURAL ANIMALS

THE MAN AND THE BUZZARD

This story appears in Victor Montejo's The Bird Who Cleans the World. *The buzzard, in spite of having been condemned to his role of cleaning up whatever might contaminate the environment, is often portrayed as a wise individual, as he is in this story.*

A man who had fine lands to plant didn't much like to work. His wife suffered deprivation until almost everything in the house disappeared. The man, instead of going to work, just sat around, passing the day producing nothing.

One of those days he saw a buzzard circling in the sky, lazily flapping his wings without a care in the world. "Oh, how I'd like to be that bird!" the man said, stretched out having a siesta as always.

The buzzard came down and sat near the man. The man came near and said with great interest, "I love to see you fly, good friend. I can see very well that you have the freedom to fly wherever you like. Ah, if only I too had wings. I would fly all over the world and no one would oblige me to work as they do now. What do you say we trade places? You stay here in my place and I take your wings and fly."

The buzzard answered, "Mister, at least you have land to work. And what would your wife say if we changed places?"

"I don't care. I prefer to enjoy myself and fly around without working rather than remain a bored prisoner here."

The buzzard said, "The life of a buzzard isn't very pleasant, either. Sometimes we find nothing to eat and we must bear the hunger. Now you, you can eat at whatever hour you want if only you work to grow what you need."

"It may be so, but I would still like to trade," insisted the man.

"What if you change your mind after the trade? I think you'd be better off cultivating your land and taking care of your wife."

The man insisted again, more strongly. "No, I want nothing more than to trade places. Do this favor right away. I want to be a buzzard."

It is said that the buzzard then gave in.

"What you ask for I will give you. Lie down on the ground and I will step over you three times." He did so.

The "buzzard" stretched his wings and went flying off.

The "man," identical to the one who had disappeared, went on his way home.

When the man reached the house the woman did not detect the change, but she did smell a certain bad odor.

"What have you been eating that makes you smell so putrid?" she shouted at him.

"It is because I was sweating and the smell of weeds clings to my body," the man said.

Because the woman insisted, the man bathed himself and little by little the odor began to disappear.

After a while the woman began to feel very happy about her companion's changed and repentant conduct. The man had begun to work very hard, and they always had enough to eat in the house. So she too got up at dawn to make the meal which he would take to work with him.

On the other hand the "buzzard" went flying aimlessly about. When he felt hungry he came to earth to try what the other buzzards were eating. The other buzzards sensed something strange about him and peeked at him mercilessly. Then he would withdraw and fly around, hungry, looking for another meal. The same thing always happened. He could never find a place among the other buzzards.

Some time later the buzzard arrived at the place where he had first made the trade. And when by chance he met the man who used to be a buzzard, he jumped up and presented himself, begging. "Forgive me if I bother you, but I want your help in changing my appearance. I want to return to my position as a man. As a buzzard I am almost dying of hunger. The other buzzards won t let me eat, and when I do get a bite, I throw up even those things that buzzards like so much."

"I am very sorry friend, but I can no longer oblige you. What is done is done. I begged you not to make the trade."

"I know that I was stubborn, but now I repent my foolishness. Let's change again. I beg you."

"I've already told you it is impossible. Besides I am tending very good crops, and your wife is very happy with me because I have treated her well."

The buzzard shook his wings, pleading. "Have pity on my misfortune. Wherever I go the other buzzards reject me. How can I live like this? Please, have compassion!"

The man answered, "I advised you earlier that the life of a buzzard is not as happy as some people think. We all have to work to get our daily meal."

"Yes, now I understand," the buzzard said. "Before I only wanted to fly and fly, looking around the world without worrying about my home, my land, and my people. But now I have returned. I want to stay in this little corner of the world."

Upon hearing the buzzard's sincerity, the man agreed. "Well, all right. We will trade again. But do you promise to work and to take care of your wife as I've taken care of her?"

"That is what I'll do. I promise."

"All right, we will trade, because in the end you are really made as a man and I as a buzzard. I do not want to keep what is yours. Lie down again and I will step over you just as I did when you first asked to trade places."

So it was that the man stepped over the buzzard three times, and in a wink the two had changed again. The buzzard became a man, and the real buzzard went flying away through the air, flapping his wings happily and looking for his own world where other buzzards fly and make circles in the air, far from the problems of men.

When the man arrived at home, the wife was surprised to see a different husband. He had gone off to work robust and chubby and after a few hours he had returned skinny and boney.

"What happened that you've come back so thin?" she asked.

"Oh, it's because I've had diarrhea and was very sick," he answered.

"How strange. When you left this morning you were healthy and strong and now you seem so feeble."

The man lied. "Yes, it was a very sudden illness."

"And there's that bad smell you used to have."

"Yes, it must be the smell of the mountain or maybe even the sickness itself."

The woman did not understand the problem, but went on tending to him as before. When he had recovered from his poor state, the man began to fulfill his promise to work diligently to support her. He even learned not to yearn for distant things, but to like what he had: his wife, his land, his people.

EL HOMBRE Y EL ZOPILOTE

Este cuento parece en el libro El pájaro que limpia el mundo *por Víctor Montejo. El zopilote, a pesar de que haber sido condenado a su papel de asear todo lo que pueda contaminar el ambiente, se representa como un individuo sabio, como en este cuento.*

*H*abía un hombre que tenía muy buenas tierras para sembrar pero que no le gustaba el trabajo. Su esposa sufría la carencia hasta de lo más indispensable en el hogar, ya que él, en vez de ir al trabajo, se quedaba sentado en alguna parte y así pasaba el día sin ningún provecho.

En uno de esos días, vio volar en círculo en el cielo a un zopilote que volaba y volaba, sacudiendo sus alas en el aire sin preocupaciones.

«¡Oh, qué diera yo por ser esa ave!», se decía el hombre, tendido en su siesta como de costumbre.

En cierta oportunidad el zopilote llegó a posarse cerca de donde él se encontraba; y entonces, acercándose al zope le dijo así con mucho interés:

«Me da gusto verte volar, querido amigo. Bien se ve que tienes la plena libertad de volar a donde tú quieras. ¡Ah, si tuviera yo también alas me iría a pasear por todo el mundo, y nadie me obligaría a trabajar así como me encuentro ahora! ¿Que dices si cambiamos de ser? Tú te quedas en mi lugar, y yo tomo tus alas para volar».

El zopilote le respondió:

«¡Hombre! ¿Acaso no tienes tierras para trabajar? ¿Y qué será de tu mujer si cambiáramos de ser?»

«No me importa eso; prefiero gozar y volar por todas partes sin trabajar que estar aquí aburrido y presionado».

El zopilote volvió a responderle:

«La vida de zope tampoco es muy dichosa. A veces no encontramos nada de que comer y aguantamos hambre. En cambio, tú puedes comer a cualquier hora que desees si trabajas para tener lo que necesitas».

«Así será, pero yo deseo que hagamos el cambio», insistió el hombre.

«Es que puedes arrepentirte después. Preferible es, a mi criterio, que trabajes tus tierras y que cuides a tu esposa».

Entonces el hombre insistió con más necedad:

«No, no quiero otra cosa más que cambiar. Hazme el favor pronto. ¡Quiero ser zope!»

Se cuenta entonces que el zope accedió:

«Ya que tú lo pides, te daré la oportunidad. Acuéstate sobre el suelo, y yo pasaré sobre ti tres veces».

El zopilote pasó sobre el hombre tres veces y al concluir la tercera vez, el hombre se convirtió en zopilote y el zopilote en hombre.

El nuevo zopilote desplegó sus alas y se fue volando. El «hombre», idéntico al anterior, se encaminó a su casa.

Cuando el hombre llego a casa, la mujer no reconoció el cambio, pero sí percibió un cierto mal olor.

«¿De qué te has embarrado que vienes tan hediondo? Báñate, que tu hedor es nauseabundo», le gritó la mujer.

«Es que sudé mucho y el olor del monte se me pegó al cuerpo», dijo el «hombre», ocultando la verdad.

Por insistencia de la mujer, el hombre se bañó y así poco a poco fue perdiendo el mal olor.

Mientras tanto la mujer se sentía feliz por el repentino cambio en la conducta de su compañero. El hombre se había vuelto muy trabajador, y siempre había en casa lo suficiente para comer; por eso, ella también se levantaba de madrugada y arreglaba con alegría la comida que llevaba su esposo al trabajo.

En cambio, el «zopilote» se fue volando sin rumbo determinado.

Cuando sentía hambre bajaba a querer probar bocados entre otros zopes, pero estas aves veían en el a un zope extraño y le picoteaban sin dejarle comer en paz.

Entonces se retiraba hambriento a buscar otro alimento, pero lo mismo le sucedía; no tenía cabida ni entre los mismos zopes.

Pasado algún tiempo, el zopilote llegó al lugar donde hicieron el cambio. Y cuando por casualidad los dos ahí se encontraron, el zopilote, dando saltos se acercó al hombre para presentarle la siguiente súplica:

«Disculpa que te moleste, pero quiero que me ayudes a cambiar de aspecto. Quiero volver a mi condición de hombre, porque como zope casi me muero de hambre. Los demás zopes no me dejan comer y además que si pruebo algún bocado, luego me causa vómitos eso que a los zopes les gusta tanto».

«Lo siento mucho amigo, pero ya no puedo complacerte. Lo que esta hecho, hecho está. ¿Acaso yo te exigí hacer el cambio?»

«Comprendo que yo fui el terco, pero ahora estoy arrepentido por mi necedad. Cambiemos otra vez, te lo suplico».

«Ya te he dicho que ya no se puede; además que ya tengo muy buenas siembras y tu mujer está muy contenta conmigo porque la he tratado muy bien».

El zopilote sacudió sus alas suplicantes:

«Compadécete de mí que soy un desgraciado. A donde yo voy, los demás zopes me repelan. ¿Cómo podré vivir así entonces? Por favor, tenme compasión».

El hombre respondió:

«Te advertí antes que la vida de zope no es tan dichosa como muchos lo piensan. Todos debemos trabajar para conseguir el alimento de cada día».

«Ahora lo comprendo», dijo el zope. «Antes, sólo deseé volar y volar, conociendo el mundo sin importarme mi hogar, mi tierra y mi pueblo; pero ahora he vuelto con deseos de quedarme en este pequeño rincón del mundo y trabajar».

Al escuchar la sinceridad del zope, el hombre accedió:

«Está bien, volveremos a cambiar. ¿Pero te comprometes a trabajar y a cuidar a tu esposa como yo la he cuidado?»

«Eso es lo que haré, lo prometo; perdona pues mi mal proceder».

«Si, cambiaremos, porque al fin y al cabo a ti te han hecho hombre y a mí zopilote, y yo no puedo quedarme con lo que es tuyo. Acuéstate nuevamente y pasaré sobre ti como aquella vez que me suplicaste cambiar».

Fue así entonces que el hombre pasó tres veces sobre el zope y al momento los dos cambiaron de aspecto. El zope se fue volando por los aires, sacudiendo alegremente sus alas y buscando su propio mundo donde los otros zopes volaban y hacían círculos en el cielo, ajenos al problema de los hombres.

Cuando el hombre llegó a su casa, la esposa se extrañó al verlo llegar diferente. Había salido al trabajo gordo y rechoncho y en pocas horas regresaba flaco y cadavérico.

«¿Qué te paso, que vienes tan enflaquecido?», preguntó ella sorprendida.

«Es que tuve diarrea y deposiciones y por eso me he enflaquecido tanto», respondió el hombre.

«Qué raro, cuando saliste al trabajo estabas muy sano y fuerte, en cambio ahora vienes muy debilucho y otra vez hediondo».

El hombre volvió a mentir:

«Sí, fue una enfermedad tan de repente».

«¿Y ese mal olor que otra vez se te siente?»

«Ha de ser el olor del monte o quizá de la misma enfermedad».

La mujer no entendió el problema y siguió atendiendo al marido como de costumbre.

Recuperado de sus malestares, el hombre comenzó a cumplir con su promesa de trabajar decentemente para sostenerla y también de esta forma aprendió a valorar lo que tenia: su esposa, su hogar, su tierra, su pueblo; y a no despreciar lo propio por lo extraño.

THE LITTLE BOY WHO TALKED WITH BIRDS

This story appears in Victor Montejo's The Bird Who Cleans the World. *It is about communication between animals and people and about family relations.*

*T*he song of the birds is a salute to life, and in each song is a message of love. Happy are they who can understand the notes trilled so clearly by the beautiful birds.

Some say that birds speak with each other in their own language and that this language is universal and full of harmonies that have no equal in the world. Among the Mayans who lived long ago there were people who could understand clearly those messages of the birds and who enjoyed immensely those beautiful dialogues and all the words they sang. Sometimes they were quick to heed the prophecies they heard. Sometimes the birds only sang, but other times their notes were messages for passers-by.

So it was with the young worker who went with his father to work in the fields every day. He never complained, even when his father treated him badly. On the contrary, he loved and respected his parents like any decent boy. When lunchtime came, the father and his son would sit in the shade of a tree beside the fields and drink the grain soup and eat their *tortillas* with beans and the wild *chipilín* greens. At this hour a beautiful bird also arrived and perched in the tree above them. Each day he sang in the same way.

After listening intently to the bird's song, the boy would laugh, or sometimes only smile so his father would not notice his odd behavior. This happened every day he went to work in the cornfield. Whenever the bird began to sing, the boy would laugh, trying not to annoy his father.

One day, however, the father asked gruffly, "What is it saying, this bird that comes to sing to us?"

"It just feels like singing," the boy answered.

"And why do you laugh when it sings if it is only singing?"

"Only because I enjoy hearing it sing, nothing more," the boy said.

"If it pleases you, then it is because it is saying something. Tell me!" the angry father ordered.

"It doesn't say anything," the boy replied casually.

"Don't try to hide it from me. Tell me quickly or I'll give you a beating!" the father warned.

The father's threats grew more severe. Because the boy did not want to anger his father anymore, he said, "Since you insist, I will tell you. It says you will have to salute me one day."

The father felt insulted. "Salute you! Are you crazy?"

"No. It is not I who says it, but the bird."

The father became even angrier and exclaimed, "All right, how is it going to happen that a father salutes a son?"

"I don't know. You insisted and I have only told you what the bird was singing."

The father was very upset by all of this because he thought his son was losing respect for him and that a day would come when the boy would humiliate him. The rigid man began to treat the boy even more unjustly, finally throwing him out of the house.

The boy bore this injustice patiently and wandered aimlessly about the world, like an orphan or a lost child. When he had traveled for a long time, the boy came to the domain of a great chief where by chance he heard the following proclamation:

"He who can interpret the squawks of the crows who come every afternoon fluttering about the chief's window, can marry the chief's daughter and inherit the kingdom."

Many had tried to pass the test, but their interpretations had not satisfied the chief. The proof of this was that the crows kept coming to the window every afternoon to disturb the chief, never heeding any reply to their squawking. Then someone told the chief that a strange boy had arrived in the community, and the chief immediately ordered that he be brought before him.

The boy came before the great chief and asked why he had been called. The chief replied, "Two crows come here every afternoon to flutter about and squawk through my window. Now I am fed up with them. How should I know what they want? Many have tried to understand what these birds say, but they have all failed. Stay here until they come and let's see if you can resolve this problem."

That afternoon the two birds arrived at the usual hour and began to squawk loudly. The boy approached the window and then smiled as he listened to the excited squawking. When they finished, the boy told the chief what he had understood.

"The male crow says that the female crow abandoned her eggs and that he had to keep them warm until the little boy crow and little girl crow hatched. And the female crow says the male crow didn't carry any food to the nest and that's why she disappeared. But now she has reappeared to claim her legitimate children, the two baby crows."

"*Ay, caramba,* and now, now what do we do?" the chief asked.

The boy answered quickly. "Well, the male crow should take the little girl crow and female should take the little boy crow."

So the boy told this to the crows that very afternoon and they were immediately satisfied with the solution, and flew off happily.

After that, the chief was satisfied, and he soon fulfilled his vow by marrying his daughter to the boy, who soon inherited all that he owned. All the people from the neighboring villages attended the wedding feast. Among them came two old people whom the boy soon recognized.

Everyone came forward to salute the new chief, including the old couple. They greeted him respectfully, "Good health to you, great lord!" the trembling old man said.

The young chief rushed forward to greet the old man and said, "Don't bow before me and don't salute me, because I am your son. Don't you remember me and that bird and how you made me tell you what he said in his song?"

"Oh, my son! Forgive me for what I have done to you," the old man sobbed.

The boy embraced his parents and announced, "Don't worry, father. I'm not angry. From today on, you and mother will live near me so our family can be reborn in peace and happiness."

And so, when the prophecy of the bird who sang by the cornfield came to pass, thus ended the story of the boy who understood the language of the birds.

EL NIÑO QUE HABLABA CON LOS PÁJAROS

Este cuento aparece en el libro El pájaro que limpia el mundo *por Víctor Montejo. Trata de las comunicaciones entre los animales y la gente y de las relaciones familiares.*

*E*l canto de las aves es un saludo a la vida, y en cada canto hay un mensaje de amor. Dichosos los que pueden descifrar los mensajes que estas hermosas aves trinan con candor.

Se sabe que las aves se comunican en su propio idioma y que este idioma es universal y tan lleno de armonías como no hay otro igual en el mundo. Se sabe también que antiguamente (entre los mayas) había personas que podían entender claramente el mensaje de los pájaros y deleitarse sobradamente de sus hermosos diálogos y dichos cantados, o tomar precaución por el anuncio de sus augurios.

La mayoría de las veces los pájaros cantan por gusto, pero otras veces sus cantos son mensajes a los transeúntes.

Éste es el caso de un joven labriego que todos los días acompañaba a su padre en las labores del campo y sin quejarse tampoco del mal trato que su padre a veces le daba. A pesar del mal trato, el joven amaba y respetaba a sus padres como todo joven decente y respetuoso.

Cuando llegaba la hora del almuerzo, padre e hijo se sentaban bajo la sombra de un árbol a orillas de las siembras y allí bebían su posol y comían sus tortillas con fríjol y chipilín.

A esa misma hora llegaba también a posarse en el árbol bajo cuya sombra descansaban, un hermoso pájaro que llegaba a cantar todos los días y de la misma manera.

Después de escuchar detenidamente el canto del pájaro, el muchacho a veces se reía o solamente se sonreía, ocultando ante su padre el motivo de su extraña actitud. Esto sucedía todos los días cuando iban al campo a trabajar la milpa.

Siempre que el pájaro comenzaba a cantar, el joven se reía, haciendo que su padre se enojara. Hasta que un día, el padre preguntó malhumorado:

«¿Qué dirá ese pájaro que todos los días viene a cantar junto a nosotros en este árbol?»

«Solamente tendrá ganas de cantar», le respondió el hijo.

«¿Y por qué te ríes cuando canta, si sólo está cantando?»

«Nada más porque me causa gracia oírlo cantar», dijo el hijo.

«Si te causa gracia, es porque algo dirá. ¡Dímelo!» ordenó el padre, enojado.

«Pues nada dice», respondió el hijo con indiferencia.

«No trates de ocultármelo. ¡Dímelo rápido, o te daré una paliza!», amenazó el padre.

Las amenazas del padre aumentaron en tono severo, y no queriendo enojar más a su padre, el hijo le respondió:

«Ya que usted insiste, se lo diré: el pájaro dice que usted me tendrá que saludar algún día».

El padre se sintió ofendido y reclamó:

«¿Ah? ¿Saludarte a ti? ¿Estás loco?»

«No soy yo quien lo dice, sino el pájaro», se defendió el hijo.

Entonces, el padre, más enojado, reclamó:

«¿Ah sí? ¿Pero como va a ser eso que el padre salude al hijo?»

«No lo sé, usted ha insistido; por eso le he dicho únicamente lo que el pájaro ha cantado».

El padre tomó muy en serio el asunto, pensando que el hijo le estaba faltando al respeto o que algún día llegaría a humillarlo; por eso el inflexible señor comenzó a actuar con injusticia contra su hijo, hasta despedirlo de su casa.

El joven se resignó pacientemente y se fue sin rumbo fijo, aventurándose por el mundo como un huérfano o como un muchacho perdido.

Después de haber caminado mucho tiempo, el joven llegó a los dominios de un gran cacique donde por casualidad se pregonaba el siguiente aviso:

«Aquel que pueda interpretar los graznidos de dos cuervos que cada tarde llegan a revolotear en la ventana del gran cacique, ése se casará con la hija del cacique y será el heredero de las riquezas del Señor».

Muchos habían intentado aquella prueba, sin satisfacer al cacique con sus interpretaciones. Prueba de eso era que los dos cuervos seguían llegando cada tarde a molestarlo en su ventana, sin poder responder a sus graznidos.

Entonces, alguien dio el aviso al cacique que un joven forastero había llegado al poblado; y por eso lo mandaron a llamar de inmediato.

El joven se presentó ante el gran cacique y preguntó para que se le había mandado a llamar. El cacique le respondió así:

«Dos cuervos vienen aquí todas las tardes a revoletear y a graznar en mi ventana y ya estoy muy aburrido de ellos sin poder entender cual es su deseo. Muchos han intentado entender qué es lo que quieren decir esos pájaros, pero han fracasado. Quédate aquí, mientras vienen; a ver si tú puedes resolver este problema».

Aquella tarde, los dos pájaros llegaron a la misma hora y como siempre comenzaron a graznar fuertemente. El joven se acercó a la ventana y luego se sonrió al oír graznar acaloradamente las dos aves.

Cuando los dos cuervos dejaron de graznar, el joven comunicó así al cacique, lo que había entendido:

«El cuervo dice que la cuerva abandonó sus huevos y que él tuvo que calentarlos hasta que nacieron los cuervitos (un cuervito y una cuervita). Y la cuerva dice que el cuervo no llevaba alimentos al nido y que por eso ella había desaparecido; pero que ahora regresaba a reconocer como sus legítimos hijos a los dos cuervitos».

«¡A la caramba! ¿Y hora, qué hacemos?», dijo el cacique.

El joven le respondió prontamente:

«Pues que el cuervo se lleve a la cuervita y que la cuerva se lleve al cuervito».

Así les fue dicho a los dos cuervos aquella tarde y prontamente se mostraron satisfechos por la resolución, alejándose a revolotear por los aires muy agradecidos.

Después de aquel acontecimiento, el cacique había quedado muy satisfecho y poco después cumplió con su palabra casando a su hija con el joven, quien poco después fue el heredero del Señor.

A la fiesta de su boda acudieron todos los habitantes de los pueblos vecinos y entre toda la multitud iban dos viejecitos que el joven heredero reconoció rápidamente. Todos pasaron a saludar al nuevo cacique y llegando el turno a los dos viejecitos, se acercaron con respeto saludando:

«¡Salud, gran señor!», dijo el viejo con voz temblorosa.

El joven cacique corrió al encuentro del viejo y le dijo:

«No te inclines ante mí, ni me saludes porque yo soy tu hijo. ¿Te acuerdas de mí y de aquel pájaro que me obligaste a decir lo que decía en su canto?»

«¡Oh hijo mío, perdón por lo que te hice!», exclamó entre sollozos el viejo.

Luego, abrazando a su padre, el joven be anunció:

«No te preocupes, padre mío, que yo no guardo rencor contra ti. Desde hoy, tú y mi madre vivirán muy cerca de mí, para que en nuestra familia vuelva a renacer la paz y la alegría».

Así termina la historia del niño que entendía el idioma de los pájaros y así se cumplió el augurio del pájaro que les cantó mientras descansaban después de limpiar la milpa, hace mucho, pero muchísimo tiempo.

THE CADEJO

There are many stories about the cadejo *(pronounced cah-day-ho), a spirit who takes the form of an animal, throughout the Mayan areas. Some people say the* cadejo *protects men who are out walking late at night. Others say there are two types of* cadejos: *white ones who protect men and black ones who can do bad things to people. Here is a story about a white* cadejo, *as told by Porfirio López of San Antonio Aguas Calientes, Sacatepéquez, Guatemala.*

*I*t is said that the *cadejo* looks like a dog, but the old folks said that some of them were bad and others were good; it depended on how a person treated them. The good ones protect a man, especially when he is drunk.

Late one night don Porfirio was walking through the streets. His father had told him about the *cadejos,* but he was not really thinking about them that night. About 12:30 he was walking by Nimaya school when he turned and saw that a white dog was following him. He asked himself why the dog was following him, but still he was not afraid. He continued walking, when suddenly he shivered and said to himself, "This is a *cadejo*!" He remembered that his father had told him not to do anything to a *cadejo.* He turned to see that it was still following him. The walk from the school to the second corner felt very long and he felt very scared, but he said to himself, "This must be the friendly *cadejo,* because he is not doing anything to me." When he turned to look back again, the *cadejo* was gone, and he was only a few steps from his house.

When his sister Margarita opened the door for him and he entered his house, he told her what had happened and she told him that the *cadejo* had accompanied him to the house to protect him. After this conversation they decided to go to sleep. For a long time Porfirio could not sleep because of what had happened, but finally after much thinking he fell asleep and slept soundly until the next day.

After this experience don Porfirio didn't usually walk on the streets so late at night.

EL CADEJO

Hay muchos cuentos del cadejo, un espíritu que toma forma de un animal, por todas partes del mundo maya. Algunas personas dicen que el cadejo protege a los hombres que andan por las altas horas de la noche, otras dicen que hay dos tipos de cadejo: el blanco que protege a los hombres y el negro que los molesta. Aquí hay un cuento de un cadejo blanco, contado por Porfirio López de San Antonio Aguas Calientes, Sacatepéquez, Guatemala.

Se dice que el cadejo se parece a los perros, pero los antiguos decían que de éstos algunos eran malos y otros eran buenos. Todo dependía de que uno no les hiciera daño. Era un animal que protegía a los hombres, más a los que beben bebidas alcohólicas.

Pero en una ocasión iba don Porfirio, caminando por las calles a altas horas de la noche. Su padre le había contado sobre los cadejos, pero esta noche él no estaba pensando en eso. Venía caminando a eso de las 12:30 de la noche por el colegio Nimaya cuando volteó a ver que un perro blanco lo seguía. Él se preguntaba por qué el perro lo seguía, pero ya no tenía miedo. Siguió caminado cuando de repente sintió muchos escalofríos y se le dijo: «¡Este es un cadejo!» Entonces se acordó de lo que le había dicho su padre de no hacerle nada. Volteaba a ver que el perro lo seguía de tal manera que del colegio al cantón segundo sintió el camino muy largo. Don Porfirio se sentía muy asustado, pero se dijo: «Este ha de ser el cadejo amigo ya que no me hace nada». Cuando volteó a ver el perro ya no estaba, y él estaba a pocos pasos de su casa.

Cuando su hermana Margarita le abrió la puerta y él entró a su casa, le contó lo que sucedió, y ella le dijo que el cadejo le había acompañado a la casa, pero para cuidarlo. Luego de la conversación con su hermana, decidieron ir a dormir. Él no lograba conciliar el sueño por lo que le había sucedido, pero de tanto pensar se quedó bien dormido hasta el otro día.

Y después de esta experiencia ya no acostumbraba a caminar por las calles a tan altas horas de la noche.

THE MAN WHO BECAME RICH

This story from Ruperto Montejo Estaban's Cuentos de San Pedro soloma (Stories of San Pedro Soloma) *gives a lesson on treating people and animals well.*

*I*n times long ago there was a man who had a very poor mother. They had their little hut. Their clothes were full of patches.

When her son grew, he began to help her. One day he decided to go out to earn money far away, because he realized how miserable it was at home.

He thought to himself, "I am going to say to my mom, 'Perhaps you'd like me to go out to work a little in other towns'."

"Mother, why don't you go ask the king to borrow some money? That way I can purchase some things to sell far away," he said to his mother.

"You poor thing, son. Do you think he is going to lend money to just anyone? Look, we are very poor," she said.

"No, mother, in any case, go ask him if he will take pity on us."

"I am going to try now, then; in any case it's only a question," said the man's mother.

When the mother arrived at the king's, she began to tell him about their misery. "Sir, I come to you on an errand."

"What is your errand, madam?" said the king.

"I come to ask you if you can help up by lending us money, to me and my son, because he wants to go in search of money. He intends to buy some things to sell, going to distant villages," she said.

"And if he cannot find money, do you promise to repay me?" asked the king.

"Yes, sir, but he is going to find money."

"Very well, I am going to lend you the money," said the king.

When she arrived at the house, she was very happy in her heart, and later she knelt to pray. Her son was at work.

"Hello, mother. Did he lend us the money?" he said.

"I brought the money, but it will have to go for the sales you talk about," she said.

"Yes, mother, I must go to get the money," he said.

He took the money and left on the trip. He took clothes to sell.

When he arrived at a village where they were killing a dog, there were many people around the animal.

The man saw this and went to see what was happening. He had been standing there only a little while; he felt sorry for the dog.

"What wicked thing has this dog done, that you are killing it?" he said.

"Look, brother, this dog has done a lot of bad things, he bites people. He goes into the houses," said a gentleman.

"That cannot be, you are lying. What bad has this dog done? Let him go. I am going to leave my merchandise in exchange for him," he said.

"Very well, brother, if you feel sorry for the animal, leave your goods," said the people.

He left his goods in exchange for the dog. When he returned to his mother he was not carrying anything.

"Hello, son. How are you? Did you come back all right?" said his mother.

"I came back fine, mother, only they did not pay me for the clothing. When I go again they are going to pay me," he said.

"Now, why don't you go to the king again? To see if he will lend us a little more capital, and when I return we are going to go give him his money," he said to his mother.

"He is not going to give us money, son, look how we are not paying him now," she said.

"No, he can give me a little more capital. Anyway, go and try," he said.

And the mother went to ask the king. She went fearfully, because she was not bringing the money that she had borrowed the first time.

"King, sir, I come to tell you about another of my needs, because we are not going to be able to give you now the money that you lent to us. That is why my son sent me to see if you can lend us more, because he left the merchandise on credit, and when he goes again they will pay him," she said.

"Very well, I am going to help you, but he should be concerned about bringing me the money," said the king.

The mother took the money again.

"Here is the money. Make an effort to get the money together so that we are not left with a lot of debt," she said to her son.

"Don't worry, mother, I am going to bring the money," said the boy.

He took the money and went to sell again. This time he had more capital. He went to buy merchandise where he had the first time, and he went to sell again. When he arrived at another village they were killing a cat.

"What wicked thing has this animal done? Why are you killing it?" he said to the people standing around the cat.

"No, brother, this cat only lives like this. It does nothing, keeping itself alive eating chicks. At that it is very good," said the people.

"Then let it go now, the poor little thing. Why is it to blame? That is its nature," he said.

"Very well, brother, leave us what you bring. It is not bad what you are going to do, if you feel very sorry for him," said the people.

He left his merchandise again and returned home. When he got to his mother, he did not have any money with him.

"You have already come, son. How are you? Did you sell the merchandise well?"

"I was fine, mother, except that I did not bring the money this time either. It is because I did not go through the village where I left the clothing the first time. I did not manage to make my sale, and so I did not go through there. Tomorrow I am going to go again to where I went to sell the first time. Only I have to take a little more clothing to sell. That way I can leave a little more with the people where I left the things on credit the first time. If I don't go there, they are not going to pay me. If you go to the king again to ask for another loan, I will be able to take more merchandise to sell. This is the last time you have to go, and if I do not bring the money, I will start to work for him to pay him for the loan," he said.

"He's not going to give us the money, son. Look, it's already been two times. We're not even paying back the money from the second time. The gentleman is not going to give it to us," said the mother.

"In any case, you have to go try; maybe he will help us," he said to his mother.

The woman went another time to the king. She felt very ashamed because of what she was doing. It was the third time that she was going to borrow money from the king.

When she got to the king, he was sitting and resting at the entrance to his house.

"King, sir, I beg your pardon because I am coming to you again with respect to the money that you have lent to me. Notice that my son is learning to sell to the villages. Another thing, he scarcely has started to sell, and so that is why I cannot pay you the money now. Do not think that I am not going to pay you. Yes, I am going to pay you the money. May you will take pity on us again and lend us more money," said the woman. The king was worried because it was the third time she was asking.

"Very well, I am going to lend it to you, but tell your son to be careful, to not invest his money in something that is not worthwhile. He should be careful on the road, because he does not know the situation where he is going to sell," said the gentleman.

"Thank you, sir. I am going to advise my son a little, so that he will be interested in looking for the money for you," she said.

She returned with the money but she had doubts about her son. She did not know whether he really had left the merchandise on credit. She arrived again with the money, and she gave it to her son.

"Hello, mother. Did the king give you the money?" said her son, although he knew that he had not given anything on credit.

"Here is the money, son. Only I recommend that you take an interest in earning money, and that you don't leave us in debt," she said.

"No, mom, don't worry about the money. I am going to return with the money this time."

Having said that, he left. This time, he took more merchandise than the other times. He took the merchandise and he left.

When he arrived at a village he saw that many people were meeting downtown in the square. He approached to observe what it was that those people were doing.

"What are these people doing?" he asked himself.

When he arrived among them, he saw that they were killing a big snake.

"Why are you killing this snake? What bad has it done to you?" he asked the people. "This snake is our sister."

"It has done not just one crime, rather it has done many bad things. It has bitten the people and some of our animals," said the people.

"If you would like, brothers, I will leave my merchandise in exchange for you letting her go. Surely you have bothered her," he said.

"If you leave your merchandise, we will let her go," they said.

He left them his merchandise, and afterwards they began to divide it among everyone.

The man started back to his house. When he was on the road, he began to think about how he was going to repay the borrowed money. He did not come across anything that he could do, and he sat down. He began to get worried because of all the money he owed, and he began to cry bitterly.

A moment later he became aware of a movement of plants close to where he was seated. He only thing he heard was a snake crawling that was coming close to him. When he noticed, the snake was already close to him. Then he got up in fright, forgetting about his worries. When the snake heard, she began to talk to him:

"You, brother, don't be afraid of me, because I have come to help you in your need. One day, you saved me from death, and now I am going to return your kindness," said the snake.

On the snake's head there was a little ball that was shining. The man felt very afraid of the animal.

"This ball that I have on my head is what I come to leave with you. You can ask it for whatever you want, money, a house, fields, everything you want. If you are very afraid of me, look for a stick and push it off of my head," said the snake.

The man looked for a little stick and took the little ball off her by pushing it.

"When you get home, do not say anything about how you got the little ball. Besides, when you arrive, put it away in a safe place. As you are going to see the next day, already you will have the money from the little ball," so said the snake.

The man became very contented and returned to his house. Everything happened just as the snake had said. When he arrived at his house, his mother was waiting for him.

Afterward, he went to put away the little ball.

When he went to see the little ball the next day, the place where he had left the ball was full of money. Only he saw it, and he said nothing to his mother.

At daybreak he gave the money to his mother. When his mother received that money, she became very glad.

"I am going to pay back the money. The king will be expecting us to arrive with the money," she said.

She went to leave the borrowed money with the king. The king became very pleased because they returned his money, just as she had promised.

"If you need money, don't worry, come here," said the king.

They spent some days together and one day the boy said to his mother:

"You know something, mom, maybe I'll get married. See, I'm already a young man," he said.

"Think about it, son, and if you think so, we will look for a wife for you," she said.

"Why don't you go to the king? To see if he would agree to let me marry his oldest daughter," said the boy.

"You poor thing, son. Maybe the king will give us his daughter? Look at how poor we are," she said.

"No, mother, in any case go and ask him, to see what the king says."

Upon listening to all of this and paying attention, she went to the king. So she arrived to the king and went into his house.

"What errand do you have?" asked the king.

"Sir, you can see that my son is already a young man and he sent me to you to see if you would agree to give us your oldest daughter so that she can marry my son, because he has been thinking of her," said the man's mother.

"I will give you my daughter, if you put money like a carpet on her way when she goes to get married. The money has to reach from the entrance of my house to the door of the church," the gentleman said.

The Man Who Became Rich

When the woman got back to her son, she was very sad.

"Hello, mother. What did the king say?" asked the man.

"Remember what I have told you, son. Maybe you think that the king is going to give his daughter to just any person? Only if you have money to carpet the path when she goes to get married. If the money starts from the door of her house and reaches the door of the church, then she will marry you."

"The gentleman demands a lot," he answered.

When morning came the next day, the woman awoke. She saw with surprise a new house, where she had slept. You see, during the night her son had asked the little ball for a house.

And when the king arose, he went out to the patio of his house. And he could not see because of the reflection of the money that was shining in the road. The gentleman just saw that and he went into his house and began to cry bitterly.

"Notice, wife, that my daughter is already gone. Look how the man already carpeted the road with money, and likewise his house, so that the only thing that can be seen is the gleam," he said to his wife.

And that was how the man married the king's daughter. When they married, there was a great party.

His mother was very happy. When the wedding of her son and the king's daughter was over, she lived very happily.

A few months went by, but he had not told his wife anything about how he had gotten the money, or where he asked for it. Well, a day came and he said to the wife how he had gotten the money.

"Listen, wife, I am going to tell you something. When we married I didn't tell you anything; well, now I am going to tell you this. When we were not yet married, I sent out to sell when my mother went to our father to borrow money. Since that time I obtained a fortune," he said to his wife.

"This is the fortune that I have acquired, it is this," he said, and he showed her the little ball.

When she saw the little ball, she found it very strange.

"The one who gave me this little ball was a snake," the man said.

"This snake gave me the little ball because one time the people were killing the snake in a village when I arrived with my merchandise. When I saw that, I defended her, and I gave up my merchandise to save her. When I was returning home, I had no money in my bag, and I became sad," he said.

"I was crying in the road, so the snake came close to me and later began to talk with me."

"'Now, brother,' she said, 'I am grateful to you for you having saved me from death in a time now past. Now, then, I am going to return your kindness. The little ball that is on my

Part 5: Supernatural Animals

head is yours, but if you are afraid of me, look for a little stick and with that you can push the little ball and so take it off of me,' so said the snake to me," said the man.

"That is how I got this gift. Now, then, look how we are together. You are going to take care of it. Since I am always going out, you are going to have to take care of it."

"We can ask this little ball for any goodness that we want," said the man to his wife.

Only this man's wife, maybe she did not love him. Maybe she had only married him for the money.

At first, the couple got along very well. But then this happened. Another man became involved with her. Her husband was not home, because he was out doing errands, so they say. And when he got back to the house she was not there. When the man noticed this, he immediately went to inform his father-in-law.

"Now, dad, I come to inform you that your daughter has disappeared from my house. I don't know where she has gone. I had left her taking care of our house, and when I returned she was no longer there," the man said to his father-in-law.

"I don't know, brother, my daughter was fine when I gave her to you. I don't know what happened; but I want my daughter back," the father-in-law said to the man.

The father-in-law became angry and locked the man in prison.

He had not even entered the prison when the king started a great fire.

"If my daughter is not back by dawn, you will have to pay for your offense," said the king. "When I gave her to you, she was alive and well. But now who knows where you have left her."

Now the man began to feel afraid. Later, when he was alone, he started to feel sad, so they say. One time when he was feeling very sad, he heard a cat and a dog howling. He was glad when he heard the noise from the animals.

"Brothers, open up so my animals can enter, because they are very dear to me. That is why they have come to look for me," he said to the guards.

The men let the dog and cat enter. When they got to him, the animals were happy.

"Brother, we have come to visit you, because we found out that something bad had happened to you," the animals said.

"Thank you, brothers, for coming to see me," said the man.

"What we want to say to you now is that we have come to repay you because you saved us from death one time in the past. Just as you saved us, that is how we are going to save you now," the cat and dog said to the man. "But tell us how we can help you in your need," said the animals.

"Thank you, brothers, for helping me because you feel sorry for me. My wife and another man stole my gift. That gift is a little ball that our sister, the snake, gave to me. Please, go and look for it and bring it back to me. I am going to use it to bring back my wife and the man who took it," he said.

"We surely will bring it to you, don't worry," said the animals.

The animals left. That village was on the shores of the sea. The dog knew how to swim in the water, and the cat held fast to the dog's back. When they arrived at the other side of the sea, there was another village that was close to the man's village. The cat went to meet all the mice that were in all the houses of that village.

"If you do not go with me to look for a little ball, you are going to die," the cat said to the mice.

"Yes, brother, we are going to help you look for it. We are going to tell our other partners and they are going to look for the little ball with us," the mice said to the cat.

All of the mice got together, and they went to look for the little ball in all of the houses. When they arrived to look for the little ball, it was already midnight. All of the people were sleeping when the mice arrived. The mice tickled the people's noses, until they found the man's wife. They hardly tickled the woman's nose, and she sneezed. When they noticed, the little ball fell. The mice picked up the little ball and they took it to show it to the cat.

"Is this the little ball, brother?" they said.

"Yes, this is it, brothers; now you can go and be glad, because you brought the little ball," said the cat.

All of the mice were happy, so they say. The dog went back with the cat.

"Now, you will have to carry the little ball, because I will have to guide our way. Carry the little ball in your mouth," said the dog to the cat.

"Very well, we must hurry though; he is waiting for us and the little ball," said the cat.

When they were going through the water, the cat almost fell. He opened his mouth and the little ball dropped. But the cat did not tell the dog right away that he had lost the little ball. Only when they arrived at the other side, did he tell the dog that he had let go of the little ball in the middle of the water.

"Now, brother," he said, "what are we going to do? The little ball just dropped out of my mouth. We were going over the water, and I was about to fall, so I opened my mouth and it dropped," said the cat.

"We must look for a way to get it out, of course. Don't you see that we want to help our brother? Oh, why did you let the little ball fall?" the dog replied.

The dog began to drink all of the water. As he drank, he noticed that many fish were coming to him.

"Why are you drinking all of our water? Maybe you don't see that we live here?" they asked.

"Now, brothers, we will leave you alive, if you find a little ball that was left in the middle of the water," said the dog.

After a while, one of the fish arrived with something.

"Isn't this the little ball?" he said.

"It is the little ball, brother," exclaimed the cat and the dog.

"Thank you, now we will leave you in peace," they said.

Now dawn was already breaking. So the dog and cat hurried to the man, so they say.

By the time they arrived at where the man was imprisoned, he was trembling with fear. When he heard that the dog and cat had come back, it gave him strength. He had thought maybe the two animals were going to disappoint him.

"Open up, so my animals can enter, brothers," he said to the prison guards.

The guards heard and let the cat and dog enter.

"Hello, brother, are you all right?" the animals said to the man.

"I am fine, brothers, thanks to you. Were you successful? Nothing bad happened to you?" he asked them.

"We were lucky, brother; here is the little ball," they said.

"Thank you, brothers," said the man.

"Don't worry, brother, because we are many. We help ourselves with anything bad that comes up," so said the cat and dog.

The man was happy that they found the little ball. You see, it was because he had first defended the cat and dog. For that good deed, the animals now saved him from his punishment.

At dawn, the king went to the prison. On the way, he saw his daughter in bed with the other man, and he was ashamed. So he set his son-in-law free.

Then the man said to his father-in-law, "Sir, here is your daughter. I wonder what you are going to do with her. Don't go and say that I abused her. You can see for yourself which road she has taken."

"Yes, my son-in-law, I now see that you are a good man. I said you had abused her; but it was my daughter who deceived you," said the king.

Now the man's wife was crying about what she had done, since her father had found her out.

"My father, my husband, forgive me for what I have done to you. I did not obey you, although you were very good to me; but now you have discovered me," said the wife.

The king turned to his son-in-law, saying, "Now you are going to marry another one of my daughters, because you are not to blame. I am going to pay for the entire party that we will have when you get married."

Thus ended the suffering of the poor man and his mother.

EL HOMBRE QUE SE HIZO RICO

Este cuento del libro de Ruperto Montejo Esteban Cuentos de San Pedro Soloma *da una lección en el buen tratamiento de la gente y los animales.*

*E*n tiempos muy pasados había un hombre que tenía su madre muy pobre. Tenían su ranchito. Su ropa que usaban estaba llena de remiendos.

Cuando creció su hijo, éste empezó a ayudarle. Un día decidió salir a ganar dinero muy lejos, porque se dio cuenta de la miseria de la casa.

«Voy a decirle a mi mamá, "Tal vez quiere que yo salga a trabajar un poquito en otros pueblos"», dijo pensando por sí solo.

«Madre, ¿por qué no vas a pedirle prestado dinero al rey? Así puedo ir a vender un poco muy lejos», le dijo a su madre.

«Pobre de ti, hijo, ¿crees que él va a prestar dinero a cualquiera? Mira, somos muy pobres» dijo.

«No, madre, en todo caso ve a preguntarle si se puede compadecer de nosotros».

«Voy a probar ahora pues; en todo caso es sólo una pregunta», dijo la madre del hombre.

Cuando llegó su madre con el rey, empezó a contarle su miseria.

«Señor, vengo a decirte un mandado», dijo la señora.

«¿Cuál es tu mandado, señora?», dijo el rey.

«Vengo a pedirte si puedes ayudarnos prestándonos dinero, a mí y a mi hijo, porque quiere ir a buscar algo de dinero. Intenta ir a vender yendo por los pueblos lejanos», dijo.

«Y si él no puede encontrar el dinero, ¿tú te comprometes a pagármelo?», preguntó el rey.

«Sí, señor, pero él va a encontrar el dinero».

«Está bien, les voy a prestar el dinero», dijo el rey.

Cuando llegó a la casa estaba muy contenta en su corazón, y luego se hincó a rezar. Su hijo estaba en el trabajo.

«Hola, madre, ¿nos dio el dinero prestado?», dijo.

«Traje el dinero, nada más que tiene que salir el dinero de la venta que dices», dijo.

«Sí, madre, siempre voy a sacar el dinero», dijo.

Tomó el dinero y salió de viaje. Llevó ropa a vender.

Cuando él llegó a un pueblo en donde estaban matando a un perro, había mucha gente alrededor del animal.

Vio el hombre eso y fue a ver lo que estaba pasando. Llevaba ratos de pararse allí, y se compadeció del perro.

«¿Qué maldad ha hecho este perro, que lo están matando?» dijo.

«Mira, hermano, este perro ha hecho mucho mal, muerde a la gente. Se mete en las casas», dijo un señor.

«No puede ser; ustedes mienten. ¿Qué mal ha hecho este perro? Suéltenlo. Voy a dejar mi mercancía a cambio de él», dijo.

«Está bien, hermano, si te compadeces del animal, deja tu mercancía», dijeron los del pueblo.

Dejó su mercancía a cambio del perro. Cuando llegó con su madre ya no llevaba nada.

«Hola, hijo ¿cómo estás, regresaste bien?», dijo su madre.

«Regresé bien madre, nada más que no me pagaron la ropa. Hasta cuando voy otra vez me van a pagar», dijo.

«Ahora, ¿por qué no vas otra vez con el rey? A ver si nos presta otro poquito de capital, y cuando regrese vamos a ir a dejarle su dinero», le dijo a su madre.

«Ya no nos va a dar el dinero, hijo, mira que no le pagamos el de ahora», dijo.

«No, él puede darme otro poquito de capital. De todos modos, ve a hacer la lucha», dijo.

Y se fue su madre para preguntarle al rey. Se fue con mucho miedo, porque no llevaba el dinero que había prestado la primera vez.

«Señor rey, vengo a contarte otra necesidad mía, porque no vamos a poder darte ahora el dinero que nos prestaste. Por eso me mandó mi hijo a ver si nos puedes prestar más, porque él sólo dejó la mercancía fiada, y cuando va otra vez te va a pagar», dijo.

«Está bien, les voy a ayudar, pero que se preocupe él de traerme el dinero», dijo el rey.

La madre se llevó de nuevo el dinero.

«Aquí está el dinero. Haz un esfuerzo para juntar el dinero, para no quedarnos con mucha deuda», le dijo a su hijo.

«No te preocupes, madre, voy a traer el dinero», dijo el muchacho.

Tomó el dinero y se fue a vender otra vez. Esta vez era más grande su capital. Pasó a comprar la mercancía a donde había ido la primera vez, y se fue a vender de nuevo. Cuando llegó a otro pueblo estaban matando a un gato.

«¿Qué mal ha hecho este animal? ¿Por qué lo están matando?», les dijo a las personas paradas alrededor del gato.

«No, hermano, este gato sólo vive así. No hace nada, sólo se mantiene comiendo pollitos, para eso sí es listo», dijeron los señores.

«Ahora pues, suéltenlo, pobrecito. ¿Qué culpa tiene? Es su naturaleza», dijo.

«Está bien, hermano, déjanos lo que traes. No es malo lo que vas a hacer, si te compadeces mucho de él», dijeron los señores.

Dejó su mercancía otra vez y regresó a la casa. Cuando llegó con su madre, no traía nada de dinero consigo.

«¿Ya viniste hijo, cómo estás, vendiste bien la mercancía?»

«Estuvo bien madre, nada más que esta vez tampoco traje el dinero. Es porque no pasé por el pueblo donde dejé la ropa la primera vez. No alcanzó mi venta, y por eso no pasé por allí. Mañana voy a ir otra vez a donde fui a vender la primera vez. Nada más que tengo que llevar otro poquito de ropa para vender. Así puedo dejar otro poco con los señores donde dejé fiado la primera vez. Si no voy allá, no me van a pagar. Si vas a pedirle prestado otra vez al rey, podré llevarme más mercancía para vender. Ésta es la última vez que tienes que ir, y si no traigo el dinero, empezaré a trabajar con él para pagárselo», dijo él.

«No nos va a dar el dinero, hijo, mira, que ya son dos veces. No pagamos el dinero ni por segunda vez. El señor no nos va a dar», dijo la madre.

«En todo caso hay que ir a probar; tal vez él nos ayude», le dijo a su madre.

Se fue la señora otra vez con el rey. Ella se sentía avergonzada por lo que estaba haciendo. Era la tercera vez que iba a pedirle prestado al rey.

Cuando llegó con el rey, el señor estaba sentado descansando a la entrada de su casa.

«Señor rey, pido perdón porque vengo contigo otra vez con respecto al dinero que me has prestado. Fíjate que mi hijo está aprendiendo a salir a vender a los pueblos. Otra cosa, apenas ha empezado la venta; por eso no puede pagarle el dinero por ahora. No pienses que no te vaya a pagar. Sí, te va a pagar el dinero. Tal vez te compadeces de nosotros otra vez, y nos prestas más dinero», dijo la señora. El rey ya estaba preocupado porque era la tercera vez que le estaba pidiendo.

«Está bien, les voy a prestar, pero dile a tu hijo que tenga cuidado, que no invierta su dinero en algo que no valga la pena. Que se cuide en el camino, porque no sabe la situación en dónde va a vender» dijo el señor.

«Gracias señor, voy a aconsejarlo un poco, así se va a interesar a buscarte el dinero», dijo.

Regresó con el dinero, pero ella dudaba del hijo. No sabía si en realidad había dejado la mercancía fiada. Llegó con el dinero otra vez, y se lo dio al hijo.

«Hola madre, ¿te dio el dinero el rey?», dijo su hijo, aunque él sabía que no había dado nada fiado.

«Aquí esta el dinero, hijo. Sólo te recomiendo que te intereses por ganar dinero, y que no nos quedemos debiendo», dijo.

«No, mama, no te preocupes por el dinero. Voy a regresar con el dinero esta vez», dijo.

Habiendo dicho esto, se fue. Esta vez llevó más mercancía que las otras veces. Se llevó su mercancía y se fue.

Cuando llegó a un pueblo vio que había mucha gente reunida en el centro de la plaza. Se acercó para observar qué era lo que estaba haciendo esa gente.

«¿Qué está haciendo esta gente?», dijo dentro de sí.

Cuando llegó entre ellos, vio que estaban matando a una culebra grande.

«¿Por qué están matando a esta culebra? ¿Qué mal les ha hecho?», le preguntó a la gente. «Esta culebra es nuestra hermana».

«No ha hecho sólo un delito, sino que ha hecho muchas cosas malas. Ha mordido a la gente y a algunos de nuestros animales», dijeron las personas.

«Si quieren, hermanos, les dejo mi mercancía a cambio de ella si la sueltan. Seguramente ustedes la han molestado», dijo.

«Si dejas tu mercancía la podemos soltar», dijeron.

Les dejó la mercancía, y después empezaron a repartirla entre todos.

El hombre regresó a su casa. Cuando estaba en camino empezó a pensar cómo iba a pagar el dinero prestado. No hallaba qué hacer, y se sentó. Empezó a preocuparse por todo el dinero que debía, y empezó a llorar amargamente.

Después de un momento se dio cuenta de un movimiento de plantas cerca de donde estaba sentado. Sólo se oía arrastrarse una culebra que venía acercándose. Cuando se dio cuenta, la culebra ya estaba cerca de él. Luego se levantó por el miedo, olvidándose de su preocupación. Cuando escuchó, la culebra empezó a hablarle:

«Tú, hermano, no me tengas miedo, porque ahora ya te voy a ayudar en tu necesidad. Un día me salvaste de la muerte, ahora te voy a dar una bondad», dijo la culebra.

Encima de la cabeza de la culebra había una bolita que brillaba. El hombre se sentía muy asustado del animal.

«Esta bolita que tengo en la cabeza, es lo que vengo a dejarte. Puedes pedirle todo lo que quieras, dinero, casa, milpa, todo lo que quieras. Si me tienes mucho miedo, busca un palo y la empujas de mi cabeza», dijo la culebra.

El hombre buscó una varita y le quitó la bolita empujándola.

«Cuando llegas a tu casa no digas nada de cómo conseguiste la bolita. Además, cuando llegues guárdale en un lugar seguro. Así cuando vas a ver al día siguiente, ya tendrás el dinero con la bolita», así dijo la culebra.

El hombre se puso muy contento y regresó a su casa. Hizo todo tal como le había dicho la culebra. Cuando llegó a su casa, su madre le estaba esperando.

Luego que llegó fue a guardar la bolita.

Cuando fue a ver la bolita al día siguiente ya estaba lleno de dinero el lugar en donde la había dejado. Sólo lo vio y no le dijo nada a su madre.

Al amanecer le dio el dinero de la deuda a su madre. Cuando recibió su madre ese dinero, se puso muy contenta.

«Voy a dejar el dinero. El rey estará esperando que lleguemos con el dinero», dijo.

Fue a dejar el dinero prestado al rey. El rey se puso contento porque le devolvieron su dinero, así como ella había prometido.

«Si necesitan dinero, no se preocupen, vengan aquí», dijo el rey.

Ellos pasaron juntos unos días y un día el muchacho le dijo a su madre:

«Sabes una cosa, mamá; tal vez me case. Mira que ya soy joven», dijo.

«Piénsalo hijo, y si así piensas, empezaremos a buscarte una mujer», dijo.

«¿Por qué no vas con el rey? A ver si está de acuerdo en que me case con su hija mayor», dijo el muchacho.

«Pobre de ti, hijo. ¿Acaso el rey va a darnos su hija? Mira qué pobres somos», dijo ella.

«No, madre, en todo caso vete a preguntarle, a ver qué dice el rey».

Al escuchar ella todo esto le hizo caso y se fue con el rey. Así llegó con el rey, y entró a su casa.

«¿Qué mandado tienes?», preguntó el rey.

«Señor, ya ves que mi hijo ya es un joven, y me mandó contigo a ver si estás de acuerdo en darnos a tu hija mayor para que se case con mi hijo, porque él ha estado pensando en ella», dijo la madre del hombre.

«Les doy mi hija, si ponen dinero como una alfombra en el camino de ella, cuando ella va a casarse. Tiene que alcanzar el dinero desde la entrada de mi casa hasta la puerta de la iglesia», dijo el señor.

Cuando llegó con su hijo estaba muy triste.

«Hola madre. ¿Qué dijo el rey?», preguntó el hombre.

«Recuerda lo que te había dicho hijo. ¿Acaso piensas que el rey va a dar a su hija a cualquier persona? Sólo si tienes dinero para alfombrar el camino cuando ella vaya a casarse. Si comienza el dinero desde la puerta de su casa, y llega hasta la puerta de la iglesia, entonces ella se casará contigo».

«El señor exige mucho», contestó.

Cuando amaneció otro día se despertó la señora. Vio con sorpresa la casa en donde había dormido. Durante esa noche su hijo le había pedido una casa a la bolita.

Y cuando se levantó el señor rey, salió al patio de su casa. Ya no pudo ver por el reflejo del dinero que brillaba en el camino. Sólo vio el señor eso y se metió en la casa y empezó a llorar amargamente.

«Fíjate, mujer, ya se fue mi hija. Mira que el hombre ya alfombró el camino con dinero, igualmente su casa, que sólo se mira con reflejos», le dijo a su esposa.

Así fue como se casó el hombre con la hija del rey. Cuando se casaron, hubo una gran fiesta.

Su madre estaba muy contenta. Cuando terminó de casarse su hijo con la hija del rey, vivió muy feliz.

Pasaron unos meses, pero no le había contado nada a su esposa de cómo había conseguido el dinero o en dónde lo pedía. Llegó un día pues, y le dijo a la mujer como conseguía el dinero.

«Oye mujer, te voy a decir algo. Cuando nos casamos no te dije nada, ahora pues te voy a decir esto. Cuando todavía no nos casábamos, salía a vender cuando iba nuestra madre a pedirle prestado dinero a nuestro padre. Desde ese entonces, es cuando obtuve una fortuna», le dijo el hombre a su esposa.

«Ésta es la fortuna que había conseguido, es ésta», dijo, y le enseñó la bolita a la mujer.

Cuando miró la bolita, se quedó extrañada.

«Quien me regaló esta bolita fue una culebra», dijo el hombre.

«Esta culebra me regaló la bolita, porque una vez la gente estaba matando a la culebra en un pueblo cuando llegué con mi mercancía. Cuando vi eso la defendí, y regalé mi mercancía para salvarla. Cuando regresé a mi casa, ya no tenía dinero en la bolsa, y me puse triste», dijo.

«Cuando estaba llorando en el camino llegó la culebra cerca de mí después empezó a platicar conmigo».

«"Ahora hermano, te agradezco por haberme salvado de la muerte en un tiempo ya pasado. Ahora pues, te voy a dejar una bondad. La bolita que está sobre mi cabeza es tuya, pero si me tienes miedo, busca una varita y con eso vas a poder empujar la bolita y así me la quitas", así me dijo la culebra», dijo el hombre.

«Así conseguí esta bondad. Ahora pues, mira que ya estamos juntos. Tú vas a guardarla. Como siempre estoy saliendo, vas a tener que guardarla».

«A esta bolita podemos pedirle cualquier bondad que queremos», le dijo el hombre a su compañera.

Nada más que la compañera de este hombre tal vez no lo quería. Tal vez sólo se había casado con él por el dinero.

Al principio se llevaban muy bien. Pero una vez pasó esto. Otro hombre se metió con ella. Su esposo no estaba, porque estaba haciendo mandados fuera de la casa, así decían. Y cuando él llegó a su casa ella ya no estaba. Cuando el hombre se dio cuenta de esto, fue inmediatamente a avisarle a su suegro.

«Ahora, papá, te vengo a avisar que tu hija ha desaparecido de mi casa. No sé a dónde se haya ido. La había dejado cuidando nuestra casa y cuando regresé ya no estaba», dijo el hombre a su suegro.

«No sé, hermano, mi hija estaba bien cuando te la di. No sé, sólo quiero a mi hija», le dijo su suegro.

Se enojó su suegro con él y lo encerró en la cárcel.

Ni bien entró él a la cárcel y el señor prendió un gran fuego.

«Si mi hija no regresa mañana al amanecer, tendrás que pagar tu delito», dijo el señor. «Cuando te la di, estaba muy viva. Pero ahora quién sabe a dónde la hayas ido a dejar».

El hombre comenzó a sentir mucho miedo. Después empezó a ponerse triste a solas, así decían. Una vez cuando estaba muy triste, oyó chillar un perro y un gato. Cuando oyó el ruido de los dos animales se puso muy contento.

«Hermanos, abran para que entren esos mis animales, porque ellos están muy hallados conmigo. Por eso me vienen a buscar», les dijo a los guardias.

Los señores dejaron entrar al perro y al gato. Cuando llegaron junto a él, y se pusieron contentos los dos animales.

«Hermano, hemos venido a visitarte, porque supimos que hay un mal sobre tu persona», dijeron los animales.

«Gracias a ustedes hermanos, que han venido a verme», dijo el hombre.

«Lo que te decimos ahora, es que te venimos a corresponder, porque nos salvaste de la muerte una vez en el pasado. Así como nos salvaste, así nosotros te vamos a salvar ahora», le dijeron el gato y el perro al hombre. «Pero dinos cómo te podemos ayudar en tu necesidad», dijeron los animales.

«Gracias a ustedes, hermanos, porque se compadecen de mí me ayudan. Mi esposa y otro hombre robaron mi bondad. Esa bondad es una bolita que me regaló nuestra hermana, la culebra. Por favor, vayan a buscármela y traérmela. La voy a usar para que regresen mi esposa y ese hombre que se la llevó», dijo.

«Te la vamos a traer siempre, no te preocupes», dijeron los animales.

Los dos animales se fueron. Ese pueblo estaba situado a orillas del mar. El perro sabía nadar en el agua y el gato estaba pegado al lomo del perro. Cuando llegaron al otro lado del mar, había otro pueblo que quedaba cerca del pueblo del hombre. El gato se fue a reunir a todos los ratones que había en todas las casas de ese pueblo.

«Si no van conmigo a buscar una bolita, ustedes van a morir», les dijo el gato a los ratones.

«Sí, hermano, te vamos a ayudar a buscarla. Se lo vamos a decir a los otros compañeros, y van a buscar la bolita con nosotros», dijeron todos los ratones al gato.

Se reunieron todos los ratones, y se fueron a buscar la bolita por todas las casas. Cuando llegaron a buscar la bolita, ya era la medianoche. Toda la gente estaba dormida cuando llegaron los ratones. Todos cosquillaron las narices de la gente, y así llegaron con la esposa del hombre. Ni bien cosquillaron la nariz de la mujer, y estornudó. Cuando se dieron cuenta, bajó la bolita. Los ratones recogieron la bolita y se la llevaron para enseñársela al gato.

«¿Será ésta la bolita, hermano?», dijeron.

«Sí, ésta es, hermanos, ahora ustedes se van a quedar contentos, porque trajeron la bolita», dijo el gato.

Todos los ratones se quedaron muy contentos, así decían. El perro regresó con el gato.

«Ahora, tienes que llevar la bolita, porque yo voy a guiar nuestro camino. Lleva la bolita en la boca», le dijo el perro al gato.

«Está bien; tendremos que apurarnos para irnos; nos estará esperando con la bolita», dijo el gato.

Cuando estaban pasando por el agua, casi se cayó el gato. Abrió la boca y se le cayó la bolita. El gato no le dijo al perro que había perdido la bolita. Cuando llegaron al otro lado le contó al perro que se había quedado tirada la bolita en medio del agua.

«Ahora hermano, ¿qué me vas a hacer? La bolita se me cayó de la boca. Estábamos pasando por encima del agua, y me iba a caer, pero abrí la boca y se me cayó» dijo el gato.

«Busca cómo sacarla pues. ¿No ves que queremos ayudar a nuestro hermano? ¿Por qué dejaste caer la bolita?», preguntó el perro.

Entonces el perro empezó a tomar toda el agua. Se fijó que venían muchos peces junto a él.

«¿Por qué estas tomando toda nuestra agua? ¿Acaso no ves que aquí vivimos?», dijeron.

«Ahora hermanos, los vamos a dejar vivos si buscan una bolita que se quedó en medio del agua», dijo el perro.

Después de un tiempo llegó uno de ellos con la bolita:

«¿No será ésta la bolita?», dijo.

«Es la bolita, hermano», dijeron el gato y el perro.

«Gracias a ustedes, se van a quedar tranquilos», dijeron.

Cuando sacaron la bolita ya estaba amaneciendo. Por eso rápido vinieron con la bolita, así decían.

Después llegaron a donde estaba encarcelado el hombre. Estaba temblando de miedo. Cuando oyó que regresaban el perro y el gato le dio fuerza. Había pensado que tal vez lo iban a engañar los dos animales.

«Abran para que entren mis animales, hermanos», les dijo a los guardias en la cárcel.

Los señores oyeron y dejaron entrar al gato y al perro.

«Hola, hermano, ¿estás bien?», le dijeron los dos animales al hombre.

El hombre que se hizo rico

«Estoy bien, hermanos, gracias a ustedes. ¿Tuvieron éxito, no les pasó nada malo?», les preguntó.

«Nos tocó suerte, hermano, aquí está la bolita», dijeron.

«Gracias a ustedes, hermanos», dijo el hombre.

«No te preocupes hermano, porque somos muchos. Nos ayudamos de cualquier mal que surja», así dijeron el gato y el perro.

El hombre se puso muy contento porque encontraron la bolita. Fue solamente porque primero él había defendido al gato y al perro. Por eso ahora los animales lo salvaron de su pena.

Cuando amaneció llegó el rey de casualidad a la cárcel. Allí vio a su hija acostada con el otro hombre, y se avergonzó. Después dejaron libre al yerno del señor.

«Señor, aquí está tu hija. A ver qué vas a hacer con ella. No vayas a decir que yo la haya abusado. Ahora tú mismo puedes ver qué camino ha tomado ella», le dijo el hombre a su suegro.

«Sí, yerno mío, estoy viendo que eres muy hombre. Yo decía que tú eras él que la abusaba, pero fue mi hija que te engañaba a ti», dijo el señor.

Y la esposa del hombre estaba llorando mucho por lo que había hecho, pues su papá la encontró haciendo mal.

«Padre mío, esposo mío, perdónenme por el mal que les hice. Yo no les obedecí, aunque ustedes fueron muy buenos conmigo, pero me han descubierto ahora», dijo la mujer.

«Ahora te vas a casar con otra de mis hijas, porque no eres el culpable. Yo voy a pagar toda la fiesta que vamos a hacer cuando te cases», dijo el rey.

Así se acabó el sufrimiento del hombre pobre y su madre.

SEVEN COLORS

This story was told in 1930 by Mr. Ambrosio Dzib to Dr. Manuel J. Andrade in Chichén Itzá, Yucatán. It comes from Cuentos mayas yucatecos *(*Yucatecan Mayan Stories*), compiled by Dr. Andrade and Hilaria Máas Collí. It talks about trustworthiness and reliability.*

*O*nce there was a man who had three children, all boys. One day, he made a field in a fertile depression where he planted only cacao. As the plants grew, so also did his sons grow. The first harvest was very good, and the sons now were young men.

Later, the cacao gave a second harvest that also was very good. There was nothing that had damaged the crop. By the next year's harvest, something started to destroy it. So the father said to the oldest son,

"Son, I hope that you will agree to go to take care of the cacao, because it is our only income."

"Yes, dad, I will go," he answered.

"Very well, son. What do you need me to buy for you?"

"I only want a machete, a rifle, my shoes, my hat, a bag, and a sickle."

Then the father bought everything for him. At dusk he left. When he passed by the casino he heard that they were talking to him,

"Come play."

"Have you gone crazy? I have something to do," he answered them.

"Come on, man!"

"You're all liars; you don't have anything to do." He turned around and left.

As he left, a very beautiful woman came out and called him,

"Come so we can play, young man. Why be such a dummy that you don't want to come?"

Then he realized that it was the woman who was talking to him and he went back.

"What is it that you're playing?" he asked.

"We're playing cards. Come in to play with us."

"Very well," he said, "but I do not have much money,"

"That doesn't matter, maybe that little bit will increase."

Then they started to play. His father had given him only ten pesos. He began making bets of one peso, later of three pesos, and he began to lose. After he lost all of his money, he realized that he did not have even one cent left and he said,

"Well, now, I'll play my hat, won't I?"

He bet his hat and after losing it, bet his rifle and lost that also. After, he took off his clothing and bet that also. Finally, he took off his shoes and bet them. Now he had nothing left. Meanwhile, night had fallen and he went back to his house to sleep.

When dawn arrived, his father asked him if the cacao had not been eaten and he answered no. But later the poor old man went to see the plants. When he arrived at the field, he saw that many of the plants were damaged. On the way back to his house he scolded his son, and he said to the middle son,

"I hope you can see [to] my cacao field; as you will be able to see, your brother did not go to see it. He who has enough interest to care for my fields, to him I will give all my properties." So the son answered him,

"I will go, dad."

"Very well, son. What do you need?" he asked him.

"I need my rifle, my clothes, my shoes, my hat, my machete, and at least ten pesos, then I will leave."

"Very well."

Then he bought what the son asked for. At dawn the son left. He left and when he passed by the casino they started to call him. He responded,

"You have nothing to do. You are lazy because you do not work. I have a job to do: I am going to see my fields." He turned around and left.

He had already moved on quite a ways when the woman came out and talked to him. He saw that she was very beautiful, and as he was now a big boy, he liked her and had to go back to the casino. When he arrived, the woman said to him,

"Boy, let's play."

"Let's," he answered, and he began to play.

"But they did not give me much money," said the young man.

"That does not matter, that little bit might increase," the woman answered him.

They started to play, and play, and play. Morning was about to come, and by then he had lost everything he had. He bet his hat, his shoes, his rifle, his clothing; he had only his underwear on when he went back home to sleep. The next day his father asked him,

"The cacao was not eaten, right, son?"

"No, dad," he answered.

Later, the father went to see how the cacao was. When he arrived he saw that the cacao was very damaged. He returned and started to scold his son. Then he said this,

"Youngest son, I hope that you have the patience to care for the cacao field, because your brothers don't know what the devil to do. Surely they go gamble, they bet everything they have and then come back. I hope you have more patience."

"Well, dad, tomorrow I will go to see what can be done," said the youngest son.

"What do you need, son?"

"I don't need many things. Only my rifle, my machete, my shoes, about 25 pounds of wax, and a stool."

"Very well, son," answered his father.

At dusk, his father had already bought everything and gave it to him. He took his things and left. When he passed by the place where the gamblers were, they began to call him, but he answered them,

"I will not return. You don't have anything to do, whereas I have a job. I am going to care for my fields." He turned around and left.

He had already gotten away when the beautiful woman went out and started to call him,

"Come, so that we can play," she said to him.

"I will not play! I am going to care for my fields," he said, and he continued on his way and did not return.

When he arrived at the field, he sat down on the stool and started to make a doll with the wax he had brought. He gave it the shape of a man. Afterwards, he set it on the stool and tied it in the high part of a cacao tree. Then he climbed down and sat down. He stayed seated until about midnight, when he heard that a strong wind was coming and making a lot of noise. Suddenly, he heard that something stopped in the middle of the plants, and he heard that it was saying,

"Let me eat. Get off the branch of that tree. If you do not let me eat, I will bite you," it said.

But how was the man going to hear it if the man was made of wax? The thing got tired of talking to him and how he did not answer; the thing got down and gave the doll a slap in the face, getting his hand stuck, and he exclaimed,

"Let go of my hand! If you don't let it go I have another!"

The thing got tired of talking without receiving any reply, and gave the doll another slap in the face with the other hand, which also became stuck. When the thing felt that its other hand had gotten stuck, it said,

"Let go of my hand or I'll give you a kick. Let me loose, because if I get to kicking you, you'll see where you are going to fall."

The thing was annoyed at not receiving any answer; it kicked him with the other foot, and so became stuck by feet and hands.

"Let go of my feet, because if you do not, I am going to give you a push with my belly and you are going to see how far away you are going to fall," said that animal.

Because the doll paid him no mind, it gave him a shove with its belly, and it also became stuck.

"Let go of me! If you don't let me go, I will give you a bite on the head and then you will see how I will mess you up for once and for all."

But it was useless. The thing got tired of talking and the doll not answering him, then it bit the doll and became stuck by the mouth. When the youngest son realized that the animal now had its hands, feet, and mouth stuck to the doll, he climbed up and with a chop of the machete cut the rope with which the stool was tied, and it all went crashing down to the ground.

"Ea!" said the animal difficultly, "free me so that I can save you, because if you kill me, misfortune will befall you. I want you to know that I am Seven Colors.

When the boy heard this, he unstuck Seven Colors' mouth and Seven Colors began to say,

"Boy, you had courage to trap me, but now you know that if you kill me, a great misfortune will befall you."

"I will kill you, because already you have done so much damage to my property; you have made me lose much money."

"If you let me go, boy, listen well to what I am going to say to you: I will serve you obediently, but you will have to let me loose," said the animal.

"And what do I do to you to let you loose?"

"One way would be cutting my hand and staining yourself with my blood, and the same with your machete; then you will say that you killed me and threw me into the *cenote* [on the limestone plain of the Yucatán peninsula, a *cenote* is a collapsed sinkhole, usually with water at the bottom]. Also you will spray around here with blood. Then whatever thing happens to you, boy, I will help you, you will just say, 'Where are you, Seven Colors?' and there I will be to serve you in any problem you encounter," he said to the youngest son.

When the boy heard this, he let him loose and the animal left. Later he went back to his house. The next morning his father asked him,

"Could you see what it is that is ruining the plants?"

"I saw it and I killed it."

"You killed it, son?"

"I killed it."

"If you really managed to do it, we will go to see it."

When they arrived, the father saw a lot of blood sprayed on the ground, where supposedly the son had macheted the animal.

"I threw it in the *cenote*."

After verifying it his father returned to his house. The brothers, who were in the kitchen, felt ashamed when they heard what the youngest son was saying to their father and they said,

"Since we did not do what our father asked us, our little brother will inherit all of his property and make us his servants, so we are not going to be his dummies staying here to serve him."

When the little brother saw that his brothers had already left, he went out after them, running and shouting to them.

"Brothers, wait for me, wait for me!" shouted the young man, following them.

Annoyed because the youngest brother was going after them, they said,

"What the devil does he come to do behind us? We will not be the servants of a dummy; better that we go far from him. We are going to wait for him to kill him. We will tie him to the trunk of that tree so that he dies. There he will die of hunger," said the brothers.

They stayed to wait for him and began to gather vines to tie him with. When the younger brother got to them they said to him,

"Why do you follow us, don't you know that you are going to be rich? We are not about to serve any dummy. But since you have caught up to us, help us get down vines to tie our house," the brothers said to him.

This they said just to fool the poor boy. Well, he started to help them get vines together. When they finished, they grabbed the boy and tied him to the trunk of a tree, covering him from foot to head with the vines. After, they took off from the place. The poor boy began to cry. Suddenly he started to hear the voice of Seven Colors, who asked him,

"Boy, didn't I tell you that when you had any problem to call me, saying 'Where are you, Seven Colors?' and right away I would be with you. But you didn't call me, and now I have come to help you; you can see that I do what I promise," said Seven Colors, and he cut the vines by biting them.

"Now continue with your brothers. Whatever thing they do to you I will go to save you, but don't forget me," he said to the boy.

Then he followed his brothers.

"Wait for me, brothers, wait for me!"

The brothers heard the shouts and realized that the boy was coming behind them again.

"But this boy, how the devil could he get loose? Is he a demon? How could he get himself loose and come back again?" they said and continued walking.

"The final thing we will do to him so that he does not survive will be to throw him into the *cenote*."

They stayed next to the *cenote* and began to take out water. They were doing this when he caught up to them and said to them,

"Good heavens, you sure insist on doing bad things to me! I come following you and you treat me badly, but men, remember this: I do not want to do anything bad to you, I only want to go where you go."

Then his brothers answered him,

"Good, get water from the *cenote* so we can drink."

The poor boy, since he did not know what they were planning to do to him, approached the edge of the *cenote* and they pushed him, making him fall in. However, when he fell, he held on to a poplar tree and remained hanging there.

Seven Colors came upon that and got him out. His brothers had already left.

"Go. If they kill you, I will return you to life. Follow them."

Then the boy went following them.

"Wait for me, brothers, wait for me!"

"But this boy, surely we saw him fall into the *cenote*. I think he is the devil."

"Why did he not die?" they said among themselves.

"Finally, we are going to burn him. We will burn him; that way we will see if he doesn't die," said the middle brother.

They started to cut sticks and lit them on fire. Later they talked to the boy and said to him,

"Climb up to see if the fire has started in the middle by now."

He left climbing, hanging himself from the branches of a tree, but his brothers cut the tree on him and he went falling directly into the middle of the fire and the poor boy burned up. His brothers continued their trip. When Seven Colors came, he found the poor boy turned into ashes. He gathered them up and stuffed them into a little reed, blew on it, and revived the boy.

"What did they do to you?"

"You saw it, Seven Colors," he said, "they killed me."

"Eh, they are not doing anything to you. Go after them, don't be a dummy," he said to the boy.

Suddenly his brothers heard that he was shouting behind them, even though they knew that they had already burned him up.

"Wait for me, brothers, wait for me!"

"But this boy, what is he? Maybe he is the devil? Now we have burned him, tied him up, killed him. I think he is the devil," they said.

They stopped to wait for him, because they were annoyed that he was following them and shouting.

"Well, what we will do is work together with him in the city. We will dress him with woman's clothing so that we can say he is our wife," they said.

And so one of them left and bought an old *huipil* [a blouse worn by Maya women], a skirt, and a black shawl, then they made the little brother dress himself with them. After, they made him walk in front of them. When they arrived at the great city, they said that they were looking for work. They arrived at the house of an old woman who said to them,

"Hey, there is a competition that the king of this village is making: he who is able to retrieve the ring of his daughter will marry her."

"Eh, well we will participate," said the oldest brother.

And so they started to get money to buy a horse. After they earned a bit of money, they bought an old mule and they said to their little brother,

"Hey, stupid old woman! You have to make our food. And if you don't hurry we will whip you, because today we will attend that great party to see if we win the bet that the king is making. Maybe we will be able to win the girl."

When they finished eating, the oldest brother climbed on top of the old mule and the other pulled her forward. They dragged her along. They were annoyed that she did not go; they paid another person to hit her from behind so she would go more rapidly. When they crossed the plaza, the big party was about to end. The brothers had scarcely left when the little brother said,

"Where are you, Seven Colors?"

"Here I am. What do you want?"

"What I want now is a beautiful white horse with golden horseshoes and golden decorations on my hat and shoes."

He only pronounced those words and, when he turned to see, he realized that there was everything that he had asked for and he went to the plaza. When he arrived, all the princes that were at the big party of that city were left with their mouths wide open, seeing the new prince who had arrived.

When the party ended, the brothers left; and they said to their little brother,

"Hey, old woman! If you hurry with your work maybe you can go to the festivities. A neat prince arrived at the party and almost got the girl's ring, tomorrow maybe he will; but you, don't hurry with your chores so you can see it."

After all, it was the same youngest brother who had gone out with the beautiful horse and who[m] they had not recognized.

"Tomorrow there will be a better party. If you hurry with your work, old woman, maybe we will be able to take you," they said to him.

"So if I don't hurry, I will not be able to go," answered the little brother.

The next day, they left very early again to the party that the king was having. His brothers had scarcely left when the little brother said to the old woman,

"Make food for my brothers, I will pay you for it. I am going now."

When he left, the little boy said,

"Where are you, Seven Colors?"

"Here I am. What do you want?"

"Again I want a beautiful horse so I can get the ring."

"Very well," he said.

When he turned around, the boy saw that on one side was the fine horse. He mounted it, then went out running with him to the plaza. When the horse jumped, he only was able to grab the handkerchief of the princess. When he came back again, he got the ring. Then he got down from the horse and entered the balcony where he met the father of the girl, and he said to him,

"Sir king, here is your daughter's ring. What do you say about her?"

"Very well, yes, you did it, you will marry her."

Meanwhile, the boy's brothers were still going along whipping the mule. But, to win that prize, they were paying a person to whip her from behind. One was mounted on her and the other was pulling her.

They left the prince in the king's house. Immediately all the people were invited to be present at the young man's wedding.

When his brothers arrived, the boy was not there and they left him like that.

The next day all the people gathered. They killed pigs, cattle, turkeys to make the food for the great wedding. After the wedding, the boy ordered that the two men who went around pulling their mule be looked for, so that he could talk with them.

"Very well," the people said to him, and they went to look for the brothers.

They found the two men and they brought them, making them walk in front of the king's police. Now, it was the youngest brother who had become king of that place. After marrying, he was crowned by his father-in-law. He ordered his brothers to be called, but he did not say who they were. When they arrived, he said to them,

"Gentlemen, you treated me with great cruelty; but because you are my brothers, I cannot have the audacity to do you harm, because if I wanted to it would be very easy, right now I could have your burned.

"You," he said to his brother, "you will just be the stable man and the only thing you will do will be to sweep my horse's manure." "You, you will only sweep inside the house," he said to his other brother.

"Very well, I think we will have to stay, what else?" the brothers replied.

So it was that the bad that they had planned to do to the little brother resulted in a good thing, because they themselves took him to the city so that he could be made king. They lived very happily with their little brother.

EL SIETE COLORES

Este cuento fue narrado en 1930 por el Sr. Ambrosio Dzib al Dr. Manuel J. Andrade en Chichén Itzá, Yucatán. Viene del libro Cuentos mayas yucatecos, *recopilado por el Dr. Andrade e Hilaria Máas Collí. Trata de la confianza y la fiabilidad.*

*H*ubo una vez un hombre que tenia tres hijos, todos varones. Cierto día, hizo una milpa en una rejollada en donde solamente sembró cacao. Mientras la plantación de cacao crecía, los niños también crecían. La primera cosecha fue muy buena y los muchachos ya eran unos jóvenes.

Después, el cacao tuvo una segunda cosecha que también fue muy buena. No hubo nada que lo dañara. Para la cosecha del año siguiente, algo la empezó a destruir. Entonces dijo el padre al hijo mayor:

«Hijo, ojalá aceptarás ir a cuidar el cacao, pues es nuestro único ingreso».

«Sí, papá, iré», le contestó.

«Bien, hijo, ¿qué necesitas para que yo te lo compre?»

«Solamente quiero un machete, un rifle, mis zapatos, mi sombrero, un sabucán y una corva».

Entonces el padre le compró todo. Al anochecer se fue. Al pasar frente a la casa de juegos de azar, oyó que le hablaban:

«Ven a jugar».

«¿Se han vuelto locos ustedes? Yo tengo algo que hacer», les contestó.

«¡Vente, hombre!»

«Ustedes son unos mentirosos, no tienen nada qué hacer». Dio media vuelta y se fue.

Mientras se iba, salió una mujer muy hermosa y lo llamó:

«Ven para que juguemos, joven. ¿Por qué serás tan pendejo que no quieres venir?»

Entonces se dio cuenta que era la muchacha quien le hablaba y regresó.

«¿Qué es lo que juegan?», preguntó.

«Estamos jugando barajas. Entra para que juegues con nosotros».

«Está bien», dijo, «sólo que yo no tengo mucho dinero».

«No importa, tal vez ese poquito aumente».

Entonces empezaron a jugar. Su papá le había dado solamente diez pesos. Empezó haciendo apuestas de a peso; luego de a tres pesos y comenzó a perder. Después que perdió todo su dinero, se dio cuenta que ya no le quedaba ni un centavo y dijo:

«Pues ahora, ¡qué va! jugaré mi sombrero».

Apostó su sombrero y después de perderlo, apostó su rifle y lo perdió también. Después se quitó la ropa y la jugó también. Finalmente, se quito los zapatos y los apostó. Ya no le quedaba nada. Mientras tanto ya había anochecido y regresó a su casa a dormir.

Cuando amaneció, su padre le preguntó si no se habían comido el cacao y él contestó que no. Pero más tarde fue el pobre viejo a ver los sembrados. Cuando llegó a la plantación, vio que eran muchos los sembrados dañados. De regreso a su casa regañó a su hijo, y le dijo a su hijo mediano:

«Ojalá tú pudieras ver mi plantío de cacao; como podrás darte cuenta, tu hermano no fue a verlo. El que tenga el suficiente interés por cuidarme los sembradíos, a él le daré todas mis propiedades». Entonces le contestó.

«Yo iré, papá».

«Bueno, hijo, ¿qué necesitas?», le pregunto.

«Necesito mi rifle, mi ropa, mis zapatos, mi sombrero, mi machete y aunque sea diez pesos, luego me iré».

«Está bien».

Entonces le compraron la que pidió. Al amanecer partió. Se fue y cuando pasó frente a la casa de juegos lo empezaron a llamar. El respondió:

«Ustedes no tienen qué hacer. Son unos flojos porque no trabajan. Yo tengo un trabajo que hacer: voy a ver mis sembrados», dio media vuelta y se fue.

Ya había avanzado bastante cuando salió una muchacha y le habló. Él vio que era muy hermosa y como ya era un muchacho grande le gustó y tuvo que regresar a la casa de juegos. Al llegar la muchacha le dijo:

«Muchacho, vamos a jugar».

«Vamos», contestó él y empezó a jugar.

«Pero a mí no me dieron mucho dinero», dijo el joven.

«No importa, ese poco podría aumentar», le respondió la mujer.

Empezaron a jugar, a jugar, a jugar. Estaba por amanecer y ya había perdido todo lo que tenía. Jugó su sombrero, sus zapatos, su rifle, su ropa, sólo le quedaron los calzoncillos puestos cuando regresó a dormir. Al día siguiente su papá le preguntó:

«¿No se comieron el cacao, hijo?»

«No, papá», contestó.

Más tarde el papá fue a ver cómo estaba el cacao. Cuando llegó vio que el cacao estaba muy dañado. Volvió y empezó a regañar a su hijo. Entonces dijo así:

«Hijo menor, ojalá tuvieras paciencia para cuidar el plantío de cacao, ya que tus hermanos no sé qué diablos hacen. Seguramente van a los juegos, apuestan todo lo que tienen y después regresan. Ojalá tú tengas más paciencia».

«Bien, papá, mañana iré a ver qué se puede hacer», dijo el hijo menor.

«¿Qué necesitas, hijo?»

«No necesito muchas cosas. Solamente mi rifle, mi machete, mis zapatos, una arroba de cera y un banquillo».

«Muy bien, hijo», le contestó su padre.

Al anochecer, su padre ya había comprado todo y se lo entregó. Cargó con sus cosas y se fue. Cuando pasó por el lugar donde se encontraban los jugadores, lo empezaron a llamar, pero él les contestó:

«Yo no regreso. Ustedes no tienen qué hacer. Yo en cambio tengo una tarea. Voy a cuidar mis sembrados», dio media vuelta y se fue.

Ya se había alejado, cuando la bella mujer salió y lo empezó a llamar:

«Ven para que juguemos», le dijo.

«¡Yo no jugaré! Voy a cuidar mis sembrados», dijo, siguió su camino y no regresó.

Cuando llegó a la plantación, se sentó en el banquillo y empezó a hacer un muñeco con la cera que había llevado. Le dio forma de hombre. Después lo sentó en el banquillo y lo amarró en la parte alta de un árbol de cacao. Luego bajó y se sentó. Permaneció sentado hasta cerca de la medianoche, cuando oyó que venía un fuerte viento haciendo mucho ruido. De pronto escuchó que en medio de las plantaciones algo se detuvo y oyó que decía:

«Deja que yo coma. Quítate de la rama de ese árbol. Si no me permites comer, te muerdo», le dijo.

¿Pero cómo le iban a escuchar si el hombre era de cera? Se cansó de hablarle y como no le contestaba, se bajó y le dio una bofetada al muñeco de cera, quedándose una mano pegada, y exclamó:

«¡Suelta mi mano! ¡Si no la sueltas, tengo otra!»

Se cansó de hablar sin tener respuesta. Le dio otra bofetada con la otra mano, la cual también se quedó pegada. Cuando sintió que se le había pegado la otra mano, dijo:

«Suelta mi mano o te doy una patada. Suéltame, porque si te llego a patear, verás donde te irás a caer».

Se fastidió de no recibir contestación alguna, y lo pateó con el otro pie, quedando así pegado de pies y manos.

«Suelta mis pies, porque si no, te voy a dar un aventón con mi barriga y vas a ver hasta dónde vas a caer», dijo ese animal.

Como el muñeco no le hacia caso, le dio un empujón con la barriga y también quedó pegada.

«¡Suéltame! Si no me sueltas te doy una mordida en la cabeza y ya veras cómo te desbarato de una buena vez».

Pero fue inútil. Se canso de hablar y no le contestaba el muñeco, entonces le dio un mordisco, quedándose pegado también de la boca. Cuando el hijo menor se dio cuenta que el animal ya tenía las manos, los pies y la boca pegados en el muñeco, se subió y de un machetazo cortó la soga con que tenía atado el banquillo cayéndose estruendosamente al suelo.

«¡Ea!», dijo el animal con dificultad «líbrame para que yo pueda salvarte, porque si me matas, te sucederá una desgracia. Quiero que sepas que yo soy El Siete Colores».

Al escuchar esto el muchachito, le despegó la boca al Siete Colores y empezó a decir:

«Muchacho, tuviste valor al atraparme, pero ya sabes que si me matas, te sucederá una gran desgracia».

«Te mataré, porque ya has hecho bastante daño a mi propiedad, me has hecho perder mucho dinero».

«Si me dejas ir, muchacho, escucha bien lo que te voy a decir: te serviré dócilmente, pero deberás soltarme», dijo el animal.

«¿Y cómo le hago para soltarte?»

«Una forma sería cortando mi mano y manchándote con mi sangre, al igual que tu machete; entonces dirás que me mataste y que me arrojaste al cenote. También rociaré lo de aquí con sangre. Entonces cualquier cosa que te suceda, muchacho, yo te ayudaré, solamente pronunciarás: "¿dónde estás Siete Colores?", y allí estaré para servirte en cualquier problema que te encuentres», le dijo al hijo menor.

Cuando oyó esto el muchacho, lo soltó y el animal se fue. Luego él regresó a su casa. A la mañana siguiente su papá le preguntó:

«¿Pudiste ver qué es lo que está arruinando los sembrados?»

«Lo vi y lo maté».

«¿Lo mataste, hijo?»

«Lo maté».

«Si en realidad lo lograste, iremos a verlo».

Cuando llegaron, el padre vio mucha sangre regada en el suelo, donde supuestamente había macheteado al animal.

«Lo arrojé al cenote».

Después de comprobarlo su padre regresó a su casa. Sus hermanos, que estaban en la cocina, se sintieron avergonzados cuando oyeron lo que decía el hijo menor a su padre y dijeron:

«Como nosotros no hicimos lo que nuestro padre nos pidió, nuestro hermanito heredará todos sus bienes y nos hará sus sirvientes, así que no vamos a ser sus pendejos quedándonos aquí para servirle».

Cuando vio el hermanito que ya se habían ido sus hermanos, salió tras ellos corriendo y gritándoles:

«Hermanos, espérenme, espérenme», gritaba el muchacho, siguiéndolos.

Fastidiados porque el hermano menor iba tras ellos, dijeron:

«¿Qué diablos vienes a hacer detrás de nosotros? No seremos los sirvientes de un pendejo: mejor nos vamos lejos de él. Vamos a esperarlo para matarlo. Lo amarraremos en el tronco de aquel árbol para que se muera. Allí se morirá de hambre», dijeron los hermanos.

Se quedaron a esperarlo y empezaron a juntar bejucos para amarrarlo. Cuando llegó el hermano menor junto a ellos les dijo:

«¿Para qué nos sigues, no sabes que vas a ser rico? Nosotros no estamos para servir a ningún pendejo. Pero así como ya nos alcanzaste, ayúdanos a bajar bejucos para amarrar nuestra casa», le dijeron los hermanos.

Pero esto lo dijeron sólo para engañar al pobre muchacho. Pues empezó a ayudarlos a juntar bejucos. Al terminar, agarraron al muchacho y lo amarraron en el tronco de un árbol, cubriéndolo de pies a cabeza con los bejucos. Después se retiraron del lugar. El pobre muchacho empezó a llorar. De pronto comenzó a oír la voz de El Siete Colores y le preguntó:

«Muchacho, ¿no te dije que cuando tuvieras algún problema me llamaras? diciendo: "¿dónde estás, Siete Colores?" y enseguida estaría contigo. Pero tú no me llamaste; ahora he venido a verte. Puedes comprobar que yo cumplo lo que prometo», dijo el Siete Colores y cortó los bejucos a mordidas.

«Ahora continúa con tus hermanos. Cualquier cosa que te hagan yo te iré a salvar, pero no me olvides», le dijo al muchacho.

Entonces él siguió a sus hermanos.

«¡Espérenme, hermanos, espérenme!"

Los hermanos escucharon los gritos y se dieron cuenta que el muchacho venía detrás de ellos otra vez.

«Pero este muchacho, ¿cómo diablos pudo soltarse? ¿Será un demonio? ¿Cómo pudo soltarse y volver otra vez?», dijeron y siguieron caminando.

«Lo último que le haremos para que no sobreviva será arrojarlo al cenote».

Se quedaron junto al cenote y empezaron a sacar agua. Esto hacían cuando los alcanzó y les dijo:

«Caray, ¡sí que se empeñan en hacerme maldades! Vengo siguiéndoles, y ustedes me tratan mal, pero hombres, lo recordarán: yo no deseo hacerles ningún mal, sólo quiero ir donde ustedes van».

Entonces sus hermanos le contestaron:

«Bueno, saca agua del cenote para que bebamos».

El pobre muchacho, como no sabía lo que planeaban hacerle, se acercó al borde del cenote y lo empujaron, yendo a caer dentro. Sin embargo, al caer, se sujetó de un álamo quedando colgado allí.

En eso vino el Siete Colores y lo sacó. Sus hermanos ya se habían ido.

«Anda, si te matan, yo te devuelvo la vida. Síguelos».

Entonces el muchacho los fue siguiendo.

«¡Espérenme, hermanos, espérenme!»

«¡Pero este muchacho! Sí, lo vimos caer al cenote. Creo que es el demonio. ¿Por qué no se moriría», decían entre ellos.

«Por último, vamos a quemarlo. Lo quemaremos; así veremos si no se muere», dijo el mediano.

Empezaron a cortar palos y les prendieron fuego. Luego hablaron al muchacho y le dijeron:

«Súbete a ver si ya prendió el fuego en media».

El se fue subiendo, colgándose de las ramas de un árbol, pero sus hermanos le cortaron el árbol y fue a caer directamente en media del fuego y el pobre muchacho se quemó. Sus hermanos continuaron su camino. Cuando vino el Siete Colores, encontró al pobre muchacho convertido en cenizas. Las recogió y rellenó un pequeño cañuto, lo sopló y resucitó al muchacho.

«¿Qué te hicieron?»

«Ya lo viste, Siete Colores», le dijo, «me mataron».

«Eh, no te hacen nada. Anda detrás de ellos, no seas pendejo», le dijo.

De repente oyeron sus hermanos que gritaban detrás de ellos. Aunque vieron que ya se había quemado.

«¡Espérenme, hermanos, espérenme, hermanos!»

«Pero este muchacho, ¿qué será? ¿Acaso es el demonio? Ya lo hemos quemado, amarrado, matado. Creo que es el demonio», decían ellos.

Se detuvieron a esperarlo, porque se fastidiaron de que los estaba siguiendo y gritando.

«Pues lo que haremos será trabajar juntamente con él en la ciudad. Lo vestiremos con ropas de mujer para que digamos que es nuestra esposa», dijeron.

Entonces se fue uno de ellos y compró un viejo huipil, un fustán y un rebozo negro, luego obligaron al hermanito a vestirse con ello. Después lo hicieron caminar delante de ellos. Cuando llegaron a la gran ciudad, dijeron que andaban buscando trabajo. Llegaron a casa de una anciana que les dijo:

«Eh, hay una competencia que hace el señor rey de este pueblo: el que logre recuperar el anillo de su hija se casará con ella».

«Eh, pues participaremos», dijo el hermano mayor.

Entonces empezaron a conseguir dinero para comprar un caballo. Después que ganaron un poco de dinero compraron una vieja mula y le dijeron a su hermanito:

«¡Ea, chingada vieja!, tienes que hacer nuestra comida. Y si no te apuras, te azotaremos porque hoy asistiremos a esa gran fiesta para ver si nos ganemos la apuesta que hace el señor rey, tal vez logremos ganar a la muchacha».

Cuando terminaron de comer se subió el hermano mayor encima de la vieja mula y el otro la jalaba por delante. La llevaban arrastrada. Se fastidiaron que no avanzara. Le pagaron a una persona para que le pegara por atrás para que fuera más rápido. Cuando cruzaron la plaza, ya la gran fiesta estaba para terminar. Apenas salieron sus hermanos, el hermanito dijo:

«¿Dónde estás, Siete Colores?»

«Aquí estoy, ¿qué quieres?»

«Lo que quiero ahora es un hermoso caballo blanco con sus herraduras de oro, los adornos de mi sombrero y mis zapatos».

Solamente pronunció esas palabras y, al voltear a ver se dio cuenta que allí estaba todo lo que había pedido, y se fue a la plaza. Cuando llegó, todos los príncipes que estaban en la gran fiesta de aquella ciudad se quedaron con la boca abierta al ver al nuevo príncipe que había llegado.

Al terminar, se fueron los hermanos y le dijeron a su hermanito:

«¡Ea, vieja!, si te apuras con tu trabajo, tal vez puedas ir a ver el festejo. Un apuesto príncipe llegó a la fiesta y por poco coge el anillo de la muchacha, mañana quizá lo logre, pero tú, no te apuras con tus quehaceres para que puedas ir a verlo».

Después de todo era el mismo hermano menor quién había salido con el hermoso caballo y que no habían reconocido.

«Mañana se pondrá mejor la fiesta. Si te apuras con tu trabajo, vieja, tal vez podríamos llevarte», le decían.

«Así que no me apuro, no podré ir», les contestó el hermanito.

Al día siguiente, muy temprano salieron otra vez a la fiesta que hacía el señor rey. Apenas salieron sus hermanos, el hermanito le dijo a la viejita:

«Haga usted comida para mis hermanos, yo se la pagaré. Ya me voy».

Al salir el muchachito dijo:

«¿Dónde estás, Siete Colores?»

«Aquí estoy, ¿qué quieres?»

«Quiero otra vez un hermoso caballo para que yo obtenga el anillo».

«Está bien», dijo él.

Al voltearse el muchacho vio que a un lado estaba el lindo caballo. Lo montó, luego salió corriendo con él a la plaza. Cuando saltó el caballo, sólo logró agarrar el pañuelo de la princesa. Al regresar de nuevo, obtuvo el anillo. Entonces se bajó del caballo y entró en el balcón donde se encontraba el papá de la muchacha y le dijo:

«Señor rey, aquí está el anillo de su hija, ¿qué dice usted de ella?»

«Muy bien, sí lo lograste, con ella te casarás».

Mientras tanto, sus hermanos todavía iban azotando la mula. Pero, para ganar aquel premio, pagaban a una persona para azotarla por atrás. Uno la montaba y el otro la jalaba.

Al príncipe lo dejaron en la casa del rey. Inmediatamente se invitó a todo el pueblo para que acudiera a presenciar la boda del joven.

Cuando sus hermanos llegaron, no estaba el muchacho y lo dejaron así.

Al día siguiente se congregó todo el pueblo. Mataron cochinos, ganados, y pavos para hacer la comida de la gran boda. Después de la boda, el muchacho mandó buscar a los dos hombres que andaban arrastrando su mula, para que pudiera hablar con ellos.

«Está bien», le dijeron, y fueron a buscarlos.

Los encontraron y los llevaron obligándolos a caminar delante de los policías del rey. El hermano menor fue él que se había convertido en rey de aquel lugar. Después de casarse fue coronado por su suegro. Mandó llamar a sus hermanos, pero no dijo de quiénes se trataba. Cuando llegaron les dijo:

«Señores, ustedes se ensañaron mucho contra mí pero como son mis hermanos, no puedo tener el valor de hacerles daño, por que si yo quisiera, sería muy fácil, y ahora mismo podría hacer que los quemen. Tú», dijo a su hermano, «sólo serás cuidador de caballos y lo único que harás será barrer donde ponga mi caballo. Tú, sólo barrerás dentro de la casa», dijo a su otro hermano.

«Está bien, creo que tendremos que quedarnos. ¿Qué más?».

El mal que habían planeado hacer al hermanito resultó un bien, porque ellos mismos lo llevaron a la ciudad para que fuera electo rey. Vivieron muy felices con su hermanito.

BIBLIOGRAPHY

General Information on Maya History, Culture, and Area

Asturias de Barrios, Linda. *Mayan Clothing of Guatemala* (video). Guatemala City: Museo Ixchel del Traje Indígena, 1994.

Brennan, Martin. *The Hidden Maya*. Santa Fe, NM: Bear & Company, 1998.

Chang-Rodríguez, Eugenio. *Latinoamérica: su civilización y su cultura*. 3d ed. Boston: Heinle & Heinle, 2000.

Coe, Michael D. *The Maya*. 6th ed. New York: Thames & Hudson, 1999.

Coe, Michael D., and Mark Van Stone. *Reading the Maya Glyphs*. London: Thames & Hudson, 2001.

Dienhart, John M. *The Mayan Languages—A Comparative Vocabulary*. Odense University, 1997. Available at http://maya.hum.sdu.dk/mayainfo.html (accessed May 12, 2007).

Ford, Robert E. *Greater Salt Lake Ecoregion Virtual Tour and Learning Module*. Rev. ed. Loma Linda University, Department of Earth and Biological Sciences, 2005. Available at http://resweb.llu.edu/rford/docs/VGD/GSLVT/index.html (accessed May 18, 2007).

Gordon, Raymond G., Jr., ed. *Ethnologue: Languages of the World, Fifteenth edition*. Dallas, Tex.: SIL International, 2005. Available at version: http://www.ethnologue.com/ (accessed May 12, 2007).

Gorry, Connor, Lucas Vidgen, and Danny Palmerlee. *Guatemala, Belize & Yucatán: La Ruta Maya*. 5th ed. Hawthorn, Victoria, Australia: Lonely Planet Publications, 2004.

Grandin, Greg. *The Blood of Guatemala: A History of Race and Nation*. London: Duke University Press, 2000.

Janson, Thor. *Guatemala*. Guatemala City: Editorial Artemis Edinter, 2001.

———. *Maya Nature: An Introduction to the Ecosystems, Plants and Animals of the Mayan World*. Guatemala City: Vista Publications, 2001.

Loucky, James, and Marilyn M. Moors, eds. *The Maya Diaspora: Guatemalan Roots, New American Lives*. Philadelphia: Temple University Press, 2000.

Morley, Sylvanus G. *La Civilización Maya*. [Mexico City]: Fondo de Cultura Económica, 1983.

O'Kane, Trish. *Guatemala in Focus: A Guide to the People, Politics and Culture*. Brooklyn: Interlink Books, 2000.

Peñalosa, Fernando. *El Cuento Popular Maya, Una Introducción*. Rancho Palos Verdes, CA: Yax Te' Foundation, 2001.

Peyton, James W. *A (Relatively) Short History of Mexican Cooking*. 2000.Available at http://lomexicano.com/history_mexican_f4ood_cooking.htm (accessed May 12, 2007).

Shea, Maureen E. *Culture and Customs of Guatemala*. Westport, CT: Greenwood Press, 2001.

Simon, Jean-Marie. *Guatemala: Eternal Spring, Eternal Tyranny*. New York: W.W. Norton, 1987.

Solá, Michéle. *Angela Weaves a Dream: The Story of a Young Maya Artist*. New York: Hyperion Press, 1997.

United Nations Children's Emergency Fund (UNICEF). *At a Glance: Guatemala—Statistics*. 2007. Available at http://www.unicef.org/infobycountry/guatemala_statistics.html (accessed May 12, 2007).

———. *Situación de la Niñez y la Mujer*. 2007. Available at http://www.unicef.org/guatemala/unicef_gt_situacion.htm (accessed May 12, 2007).

Young, Peter A. *Secrets of the Maya*. From the Editors of *Archaeology Magazine,* with a preface by Peter A Young. Long Island City, NY: Hatherleigh Press, 2003.

Books and Collections of Mayan Tales

Abreu Gómez, Emilio. *Leyendas y consejas del viejo Yucatán*. [Mexico City]: Fondo de Cultura Económica, 1985.

Alvarez, Francisco. *Cuentos de Sna Jtz'ibajom/Sk''op ya'yeej Sna Jtz'ibajom*. [Mexico City]: Instituto Nacional Indigenista, 1998.

Andrade, Manuel J., and Hilaria Máas Collí, comps. *Cuentos mayas yucatecos. U tzikbalilo' ob mayab (Uuchben tsikbalo' ob)*. Mérida: Universidad Autónoma de Yucatán, Centro de Investigaciones Regionales, 1990.

Baer, Mary E. "The Rabbit and the Mountain Lion; a Lacondon Myth." *Tlalocan* 6 (1970): 268–75.

Búcaro Moraga, Jaime Ismael. *Leyendas, Cuentos, Mitos y Fabulas Indígenas*. Guatemala City: Instituto Indigenista Nacional, 1959.

Burns, Allan F. *An Epoch of Miracles: Oral Literature of the Yucatec Maya.* Austin: University of Texas Press, 1983.

El muchacho en la cueva y otros cuentos. Illustrated by Adolfo Mexiac. San Cristóbal de las Casas, Chiapas: Instituto Nacional Indigenista (México), 1960.

Gómez, Emelio Abreu, and Joseph S. Flores. *Leyendas Mexicanas, Mayas, Quichés, Zapotecas, Toltecas.* New York: American Book, 1951.

Juan, José. *Cuentos Antiguos de Animales y Gente/Yik'ti'al No' Noq' Yetoj Anima Yet Payxa.* Rancho Palos Verdes, CA: Ediciones Yax Te', 1996.

La casa de los tigres, y otros cuentos. San Cristóbal de las Casas, Chiapas: Instituto Nacional Indigenista (México), 1960.

Maxwell, Judith M. *Textos Chujes de San Mateo Ixtatán.* Rancho Palos Verdes, CA: Yax Te' Foundation, 2001.

Montejo, Ruperto, comp. *Cuentos de San Pedro Soloma/Ik'ti' Yet Tz'uluma'.* Rancho Palos Verdes, CA: Ediciones Yax Te', 1996.

Montejo, Victor D. *The Bird Who Cleans the World and Other Mayan Fables.* Willimantic, CT: Curbstone Press, 1991.

———. *El pájaro que limpia el mundo y otras fábulas mayas/No'ch'ik xtx'ahtx'en sat yib'anh q'inal.* Rancho Palos Verdes, CA: Yax Te' Foundation, 2000.

Petrich, Renée, and Margarita Molina. "Mitos y creencias mayas en Quintana Roo." *Cultura sur* 1, no. 2 (1989): 29–31.

Rubel, Arthur J. "Two Tzotil Tales from San Bartolomé de los Llanos (Venustiano Carranza), Chiapas." *América Indígena* 24 (1964): 49–57.

Sánchez Gómez, Armando. *Creencias de nuestros padres en la siembra del maíz/Ch'ul awal ts'un ixim yu'um jme'tatik.* México, D.F.: Instituto Nacional Indigenista, 1998.

———. *Voces de la naturaleza/Sk'op, lum k'inal.* México, D.F.: Instituto Nacional Indigenista, 1998.

Say, Pedro Miguel. *Cuentos migueleños. Ik'ti' yu naj Pel Mekel Ana.* 2d ed. Rancho Palos Verdes, CA: Ediciones Yax Te', 1996.

———. *Ik'ti' yu naj Pel Mekel Ana. Cuentos de don Pedro Miguel Say.* Edición trilingüe. Los Angeles: Ediciones IXIM, 1992. (in Q'anjob'al, Español, and English)

Sexton, James D., trans. and ed. *Mayan Folktales: Folklore from Lake Atitlán, Guatemala.* Albuquerque: University of New Mexico Press, 1999.

Books with Mayan Tales for Children

Bierhorst, John. *The Deekatoo.* New York: William Morrow, 1998.

Briceño Chel, Fidencio. *Voces de Colores/Na'at le ba'ala' paalen, Adivino Iluminado, Colorín color mayas.* México, D.F.: Instituto Nacional Indigenista, 2000.

Delal, Anita. *Myths of Pre-Colombian America*. Austin, TX: Steck-Vaughn, 2001.

Gerson, Mary-Joan. *Fiesta Femenina*. Cambridge, MA: Barefoot Books, 2001.

McCaughren, Geraldine. *The Bronze Cauldron*. New York: Margaret McElderry Books, 1997.

Mora, Pat. *The Race of Toad and Deer*. Toronto: Groundwood Books/Douglas & McIntyre, 2001.

THE STORYTELLERS

Felipa b'ix
The Moon (La luna)

Felipa b'ix was born in the department of Sololá, Guatemala, and has lived there all her life. She learned many stories that had been handed down in her family. Felipa appreciates this story because it demonstrates that many of her ancestors' beliefs were based on facts. She enjoys playing with her five children in Sololá.

One activity enjoyed by many people in Sololá is the game of the flying pole, or *palo volador*. More of a performance than a game, it is usually put on during festivals. A very tall pole is stood up in an open area, often the town center or a large field where the festival is being held. To the top of the pole are tied a number of ropes long enough to almost reach the ground. The performers tie the rope to their ankles, and while they are suspended on the ropes they then "fly" in circles around the pole, flying higher as they go faster and flying lower as they go slower.

Felipa b'ix nació en Sololá y allá ha vivido toda su vida. Felipa aprecia este cuento porque demuestra cómo muchas de las creencias de sus antepasados están basadas en hechos. A ella le gusta jugar con sus cinco hijos en Sololá.

Una de las cosas que disfruta mucho la gente en Sololá es el juego del palo volador. Más una actuación que un juego, se hace generalmente durante los festivales. Un poste o sea un tronco muy alto se levanta en un área abierta, a menudo el parque central del pueblo o un campo grande donde está el festival. A la copa del poste se atan un número de cuerdas que se extienden casi hasta el suelo. Los intérpretes atan la cuerda a sus tobillos, se les suspenden en las cuerdas y entonces «vuelan» en círculos alrededor del palo, volando más alto mientras que van más rápidamente y más bajo mientras que van más despacio.

María Caley

The Screamer of the Night (El gritón de la noche)

The Simanagua (La Simanagua)

Storyteller María Caley has eight children and has lived in Chichicastenango, Quiché, all her life. The tales she tells have been handed down to her by her ancestors. She selected these stories to tell because "The Screamer of the Night" illustrates the need to respect nature even when it is not well understood, and "The Simanagua" relates to her appreciation for family customs and her understanding of the need to respect them.

María and her family observe religious traditions and enjoy attending the January Corn Celebration in their town. Their favorite recipe is cochinita pibil, marinated pork.

La cuentista María Caley tiene ocho hijos y ha vivido en Chichicastenango, Quiché, toda su vida. Los cuentos que ella cuenta llegaron a ella por sus antepasados. Seleccionó estos cuentos debido a que el primero, «El gritón de la noche», trata de la necesidad de respetar a la naturaleza aun cuando no sea bien entendido, y el segundo, «La Simanagua», se relaciona con las costumbres familiares y su entendimiento de la necesidad de respetarlas.

A María y a su familia les gustan las tradiciones religiosas y asistir a la fiesta del maíz en su pueblo en enero. Su receta favorita es la cochinita pibil, cerdo adobado.

Victorino Canek

The Song of the Owl and the Howl of the Coyote (El canto del tecolote y el aullido del coyote)

Victorino Canek has lived in Uaxactún, Petén, all his life, and lives there now with his wife and six children. He likes the Mayan ball game, which is the game of his town, as well as soccer. This story is a legend that his family has passed down through the generations. Victorino considers it special because of the respect the tale shows for predictions and nature. Victorino's family also enjoys eating the foods made in harmony within the family, and they enjoy living together in community.

Victorino Canek ha vivido toda su vida en Uaxactún, Petén, Guatemala, donde también viven su esposa y sus seis hijos. A él le gusta el juego de pelota maya, lo cual es el juego de su pueblo, y el fútbol. Este cuento es una leyenda que ha pasado a través de las generaciones en su familia. Victorino lo considera especial por el respeto que da el cuento a las predicciones y a la naturaleza. A la familia de Victorino le gusta comer las comidas preparadas por la familia en armonía, y les gusta vivir juntos en comunidad.

Macario Chigüil

The Dwarf (El enanito)

Macario Chigüil has lived for the last twenty years in La Guitarra hamlet, Retalhuleu. He shares "The Dwarf" with his four sons. The story is special to him because it is based on his own experience and emphasizes coexistence with animals.

Many families in La Guitarra hamlet enjoy riding horses. Macario's family finds pleasure in getting together on Sundays and chatting about the crops and animals. The community celebrates the Patron Saint's festival December 2–13, which is the same as that of the department of Retalhuleu. His family's favorite food is chicken soup.

Marcario Chigüil tiene 20 años en el caserío la Guitarra, Retalhuleu. Comparte su cuento «El enanito» con sus cuatro hijos. A él este cuento le importa mucho porque se basa en su propia experiencia y hace énfasis en la coexistencia con los animales.

Muchas de las familias en la Guitarra disfrutan de montar a caballo. A la familia de Macario le gusta asistir a las reuniones dominicales y platicar de los animales y la cosecha. La comunidad disfruta de la feria titular del 2 al 13 de diciembre, la cual es la misma que la del departamento de Retalhuleu. La comida favorita de la familia de don Macario es el caldo de gallina.

Ambrosio Dzib

The Ant, the Flea, the Puma, and the Fox (La hormiga, el piojo, el puma, y la zorra)
Seven Colors (El siete colores)

We unfortunately have no historical notes about Ambrosio Dzib other than that some of his stories were recorded by Dr. Manuel J. Andrade at Chichén Itzá, Yucatán, in 1930. Dr. Andrade recorded these stories and others in many parts of the Americas while conducting linguistics research for the Carnegie Institute during the 1930s.

Desgraciadamente, no tenemos ningún comentario acerca de Ambrosio Dzib aparte de saber que algunos de sus cuentos fueron grabados por el Dr. Manuel J. Andrade en Chichón Itzá, Yucatán, en 1930. El Dr. Andrade grabó estos cuentos y otros en muchas partes de América mientras realizaba investigaciones lingüísticas por el Instituto Carnegie (Carnegie Institute) durante los 1930.

Ruperto Montejo Esteban

The Two Orphans (Los dos huérfanos)

The Spirit of the Water (El espítiru del agua)

The Man Who Became Rich (El hombre que se hizo rico)

Ruperto Montejo Esteban, who compiled these and other stories in *Cuentos de San Pedro Soloma* (*Stories of San Pedro Soloma*), was born in the village of Najab', San Pedro Soloma, Huehuetenango, Guatemala. He studied linguistics in the Proyecto Lingüístico Francisco Marroquín and at Rafael Landívar University and has taught classes in urban primary education and for the Programa para el Desarrollo Integral de la Población Maya (Maya Population Comprehensive Development Program). He has worked as a linguistics researcher, wrote the *Manual of Q'anjob'al Writing* and papers and articles on the grammar of the Q'anjob'al language, and served as coordinator of the Linguistics Studies Program of the Academy of Mayan Languages of Guatemala.

Ruperto Montejo Esteban, quien recopiló estos cuentos y otros en Cuentos *Cuentos de San Pedro Soloma*, nació en la Aldea Najab', San Pedro Soloma, Huehuetenango, Guatemala. Estudió lingüísticos en el Proyecto Lingüístico Francisco Marroquín y en la Universidad de Rafael Landívar y ha impartido clases en la educación primaria urbana y para el Programa para el Desarrollo Integral de la Población Maya. Ha trabajado como investigador de lingüísticos, escribió el *Manual de Redacción Q'anjob'al*, ensayos, y trabajos académicos sobre la gramática del idioma Q'anjob'al, y fue Coordinador del Programa de Estudios Lingüísticos de ka Academia de las Lenguas Mayas de Guatemala.

José Juan

The Stingy Old Woman (La anciana miserable)

The Lying King (El rey mentiroso)

The Rabbit and the Crab (El conejo y el cangrejo)

José Juan was born in San Miguel Acatán in 1953. He compiled these and other stories from the older men of the village while he was working on the language, culture, and oral literature of the Q'anjob'al Maya in San Miguel as part of the Proyecto Lingüístico Francisco Marroquín between 1974 and 1980. He is also one of the authors of the *Diccionario Akateco-Español,* published by Yax Te' Press.

José Juan nació en San Miguel Acatán en 1953. Recopiló estos cuentos y otros de los ancianos del pueblo mientras que trabajaba en el idioma, la cultura y la literatura oral de los maya q'anjob'al en San Migues como parte del Proyecto Lingüístico Francisco Marroquín entre 1974 y 1980. También es uno de los autores del *Diccionario Akateco-Español* publicado por Yax Te' Press.

Margarita López

The Giant Nimalej' mo's (El gigante Nimalej'mós)

Margarita López was born in San Antonio Aguas Calientes, Sacatepequez, and lives there near her six children and many grandchildren. She learned this story from her ancestors and remembers spending many evenings, before electricity came to San Antonio, enthralled by listening to her father and other relatives tell stories like these. She has passed on this tradition to her children, and they are doing the same with their children.

Margarita López nació en San Antonio Aguas Calientes, Sacatepéquez, y vive allá al lado de sus seis hijos y sus muchos nietos. Aprendió este cuento de sus antepasados y recuerda muchas noches que pasó, en los años antes de que hubiera luz eléctrica, cautivada al escuchar a su padre y a otros familiares contar cuentos tales como estos. Ella les ha pasado esta costumbre a sus hijos también, y ellos a los suyos.

Porfirio López

Uncle Rabbit, Uncle Coyote (Tío conejo, tío coyote)
The Cadejo (El cadejo)

Porfirio López was born in San Antonio Aguas Calientes, Sacatepequez, many years ago. He learned these and other stories from his family. Porfirio enjoys being with his family, particularly on holidays. He likes to eat traditional chicken soup.

Porfirio López nació en San Antonio Aguas Calientes, Sacatepéquez, hace muchos años. Aprendió estos cuentos y otros de su familia. Le gusta pasar el tiempo con su familia, especialmente en los días feriados. El caldo de gallina tradicional es su comida favorita.

Lidia Amanda López de López

The Weeping Woman (La Llorona)

Lidia Amanda López de López has lived in San Antonio Aguas Calientes, Sacatepequez, all her life. She learned this story from her family when she was a child, and Lidia especially values the tale because it came from her ancestors. She has shared this story with her own sons.

Lidia's favorite family traditions are the get-togethers where family members share different experiences with one another. Her family, as well as many others in the town, enjoy typical Mayan dishes such as chiles rellenos at such gatherings. Her town holds a Patron Saint fair on June 13, which her family enjoys going to. The townspeople also enjoy watching the popular game soccer.

Lidia Amanda López de López es de San Antonio Aguas Calientes, Sacatepéquez, y allí ha vivido toda su vida. Aprendió este cuento de su familia cuando era niña, y lo valora porque le llegó de sus antepasados. Ella ha compartido este cuento con sus hijos.

Sus tradiciones familiares favoritas son las reuniones familiares en las que los miembros de la familia comparten sus diferentes experiencias entre sí. La familia de Lidia, como muchas otras del pueblo, disfruta de platos típicos mayas como chiles rellenos en estas reuniones. A la familia López le gusta asistir a la feria titular que su pueblo celebra el 13 de junio. En San Antonio Aguas Calientes, también les gusta ver el juego más popular, el fútbol.

Víctor Dionisio Montejo

How the Serpent Was Born (De como nació la víbora)

The Man and the Buzzard (El hombre y el zopilote)

The Little Boy Who Talked with Birds (El niño que hablaba con los pájaros)

The Disobedient Child (El niño desobediente)

Sometime Right Is Repaid with Wrong (A veces el bien con el mal se paga)

The Buzzard and the Dove (La paloma y el zopilote)

Victor Dionisio Montejo is from Jacaltenango, Huehuetenango, Guatemala, and is an anthropologist and professor of Native American Studies at the University of California at Davis. While he was growing up in Jacaltenango, his mother told him the stories reproduced here. They were first published with a collection of other stories in English in *The Bird Who Cleans the World and Other Fables* and later in Spanish and their original Mayan language, Popb'al Ti' (Jakaltek), in *El pájaro que limpia el mundo y otras fábulas mayas*. Dr. Montejo is the author of numerous other books, essays, and academic papers. He served as the director of the Secretariat of Peace (Secretaría de la Paz) of Guatemala from 2004 to 2005.

Víctor Dionisio Montejo es de Jacaltenango, Huehuetenango, Guatemala y es antropólogo y catedrático del Departamento de Estudios Nativos Americanos de la Universidad de California en Davis. Mientras se criaba en Jacaltenango, su madre le contó los cuentos reproducidos aquí. Fueron publicados primero con una colección de otros cuentos en inglés en su libro *The Bird Who Cleans the World and Other Fables* y más tarde en su idioma materna maya popb'al ti' (jakalteko) en *El pájaro que limpia el mundo y otras fábulas mayas*. El Dr. Montejo es autor de numerosos otros libros, ensayos, y trabajos académicos. Fue el director de la Secretaría de la Paz de Guatemala de 2004 a 2005.

Santiago Morales

The Master of the Canyons (El dueño de los barrancos)

The Goblin (El duende)

Santiago Morales is from San José Media Cuesta, Santa Rosa, where "The Master of the Canyons" originated. Mr. Morales enjoys going to the feast of the village's patron saint on October 24. Through the years the family has treasured their family gatherings. On special occasions he likes to cook his favorite recipe, iguana in pepita (iguana in pumpkin seed sauce)

Santiago Morales es de San José Media Cuesta, Santa Rosa, donde se originó el cuento «El dueño de los barrancos.» Al señor Morales le gusta asistir a la fiesta titular del 24 de octubre. A través de los años, su familia ha recibido mucho placer de las reuniones familiares. Durante las ocasiones especiales, a él le gusta cocina su receta favorita, iguana en pepita.

Eulogio Shutuc

Mirandía Hill (El cerro Mirandía)

Eulogio Shutuc is from Aguacatán, Huehuetenango. The story "Mirandía Hill" originated at the San Diego Escuintla plantation in southern Guatemala, where there is a well-known hill with that name. Eulogio and his family go there to harvest coffee. They like this story because it addresses the idea of respect and living only with what is necessary. The family's favorite dish is pepián (see recipe on p. xxxvi). They deeply value the time they spend together. Many families in Aguacatán enjoy horse racing and attending the Patron Saint's fair July 12 through 18.

Eulogio Shutuc es de Aguacatán, Huehuetenango. El cuento del cerro Mirandía tiene su orígen en la finca San Diego Escuintla en el sur de Guatemala, donde hay un cerro bien conocido que se llama Mirandía. Eulogio y su familia van allá para trabajar en la cosecha

---

del café. A Eulogio y a su familia les gusta este cuento porque habla de la idea del respeto y de vivir con lo necesario. Su receta favorita es el pepián (la receta se encuentra en la página xxxvi). La familia aprecia mucho el tiempo que pasan juntos. A muchas familias en Aguacatán les gusta la carrera de caballos y asistir a la feria titular que es del 12 al 18 de julio.

INDEX

ABOUT THE AUTHORS

Susan Thompson is a professor of education at the University of Northern Colorado. She has worked extensively with children as an elementary school teacher, parent, and university professor. Susan has authored numerous articles, seven books for teachers and two multicultural books for children. She has received several university awards for teaching excellence and outstanding research and scholarship. Over the last 12 years, she traveled frequently to Guatemala, and her experiences during the trips have changed her life in significant and rich ways. Susan and her husband, Keith, have four daughters, two of who are Mayan and from Guatemala. All four children appreciate the Maya culture and love the stories.

Keith Thompson is a hydrogeologist in Greeley, Colorado. His work with water has taken him to Guatemala, El Salvador and Peru and throughout the United States. Keith is fluent in Spanish and thoroughly enjoys his work in Latin America. He co-authored a children's book about Lenten processions in Guatemala. He has illustrated five books with his photographs, and his photographs have won several awards. Keith lives with his wife, Susan, and their two young daughters. His many trips to Guatemala over the years have influenced his life in a variety of ways.

Lidia López de López lives in San Antonio Aguas Calientes, Guatemala with her two sons and husband and near her mother, siblings and twelve nieces and nephews. Lidia takes great pride in her weaving and feels strongly about keeping Mayan traditions alive. She travels to various places in the world to teach about weaving and Mayan culture. Lidia has taught weaving classes on the back-strap loom in the United States, Germany, and Japan. She is a very personable, kind woman who develops deep friendships in the places where she visits. Her journeys enrich the lives of others.

Recent Titles in the World Folklore Series

Additional titles in this series can be found at www.lu.com